Creating a Pathway to Your Dream Career

Creating a Pathway to Your Dream Career

Designing and Controlling a Career Around Your Life Goals

Tom Kucharvy

BEP BUSINESS EXPERT PRESS

First published in 2014 by
Business Expert Press, LLC
222 East 46th Street, New York, NY 10017
www.businessexpertpress.com

ISBN-13: 978-1-60649-898-9 (paperback)
ISBN-13: 978-1-60649-899-6 (e-book)

Business Expert Press Human Resource Management and Organizational Behavior Collection

Collection ISSN: 1946-5637 (print)
Collection ISSN: 1946-5645 (electronic)

Cover and interior design by Exeter Premedia Services Private Ltd., Chennai, India

First edition: 2014

10 9 8 7 6 5 4 3 2 1

Printed in the United States of America.

To

My parents for encouraging me to identify and pursue my own dreams

My wife, Joyce, for being my partner in fulfilling my dreams and the dreams we created together

My former managers and clients for shaping and enabling my previous career dreams

Jim Spohrer for providing the spark that helped me crystalize and begin on the path to my next dream—helping students create their own career destinies

Abstract

What do you want your life to be like when you're 25? 35? 55? Do you want a job that will feed you and your family or do you want a career that will be an integral part of your life—a career that will feed your passions, enable the lifestyle you choose, and be a continual source of engagement and pride?

But do you really have the luxury of even considering your dream job in an era in which more than 40 percent of college graduates can't even get jobs that require college degrees, much less jobs in their field? Or can you even afford to go to college at all?

Not only should you think about your dream job—you owe it to yourself to do so. First, if done properly, the very process of deciding upon and preparing for your dream job can dramatically improve your employability, expand your employment options, and increase the value you can provide your employer or your clients. Better yet, you can apply this same process through your entire career, as your interests and life goals continually evolve.

Preparing for your dream job, however, requires much more than dreaming about the type of job that will make you happy. It also requires an objective evaluation of your strengths and limitations, a careful evaluation of the type of post-high school education that is best suited to you, and your specific career objectives and proactive management of your education to ensure that you develop the skills and personality traits you will need not just for your first job, but for your future careers and your life. And speaking of jobs, it requires a full understanding of the employment prospects and requirements for jobs in your field and intense focus on developing the skills that will be required to give you an advantage in getting that job. It also needs a contingency plan, including selection of and preparation for a safety career.

A lot of work? Sure it is. And if all you want is a job—any job—you don't have to worry about it. But if you want a career (or multiple careers) that will engage your passions and put you in control of your life, you need a plan. And you need one now.

This book will help you develop that plan. It begins by examining how the careers of the future will differ from those of the past, where these jobs and careers will and won't be, and the range of skills (many of which are not taught in schools) they will require. With this context, it then lays out a three-stage, 20-step plan that will help you:

- identify and prioritize your interests and passions;
- objectively assess and develop your skills and align them with your passions;
- assess the career opportunities that will best utilize your skills in pursuit of your passion;
- expand your career options and hedge your bets by identifying complementary safety careers;
- evaluate your post-high school education options and create an education plan that is best suited to you and your career choice; and
- prioritize the factors you should consider in targeting your critical first career-track job and use that job to expand your long-term career options.

Most importantly, it will show you how to take responsibility for defining your own dream; for identifying your own career objectives; for ensuring that you develop the skills and get the education required to achieve these objectives; and for managing your own career.

This is as it should be. After all, if you don't take responsibility for your dream, your career, and your life, who will?

Keywords

career planning, college planning, education planning, job prospects, jobs of the future, skills requirements, three-stage plan, 20-step plan

Contents

Introduction

A pessimist sees the difficulty in every opportunity; an optimist sees the opportunity in every difficulty.

—Winston Churchill

Key Points

- No surprise: Although the job market for college graduates is improving, it remains spotty, with hiring and salaries still below 1999 levels.
- Although jobs will remain tight, some occupations have grown through the recession and will continue to grow for the foreseeable future.
- Those with the aptitude, skills, and the persistence to anticipate, embrace, and exploit change for their own benefit will have unprecedented new opportunities to chart their own courses.
- Success in this new world requires particularly diligent career planning.

What do you want your life to be like when you're 25? 35? 55? What are you looking for in a career? Do you want any type of job that will pay the bills and fund your eventual retirement; or are you looking for a career that will be an integral part of your life—one that will allow you to feed your passions, as well as your family and provide enjoyment and self-satisfaction in and of itself? Do you want a high-powered, high-commitment career that entails 60-hour workweeks and continuous business travel, or a lifestyle career that will give you the time and flexibility to spend time with your family or pursue your own outside interests?

Just as importantly, what do you want your life's work to be? Do you want to be a carpenter, an artist, a teacher, a doctor, or a marketing executive? Even if you get a job in your chosen field, what are the odds that you will love your job 10, 20, or even 30 years in the future? Or the odds that that job or that field will even exist in 30 years?

Given all the gloom and doom surrounding yesterday's and today's employment prospects, it may be hard to believe that you may have the power to make such decisions for yourself, rather than accept whatever position a potential employer may choose to bestow upon you. After all, even though the economy is improving, progress is excruciatingly slow and good jobs will remain scarce for years to come.

This being said, some professions are struggling to find and hire employees with the right skills. More importantly, many of the forces that are destroying the jobs of today are simultaneously creating the jobs of the future. But exactly what are these jobs and how can you prepare for them? Better yet, what is your dream job and how can you find or create a position that will allow you to not only achieve your dreams but also control your own career and life in the process?

The good news is that if you're still in school, you still have time to prepare for this future. But you had better hurry. Although the planning process doesn't take that long, developing the skills and building the types of accomplishments that employers look for takes time, focus, and commitment. In order to prepare for the jobs of the future, you must understand how the job market is changing, the type of occupations that offer the best long-term career prospects, and how to position your own unique interests and skills in a way that will best appeal to prospective employers. You must understand and develop the skills that will not only be required to get a job when you graduate, but that will provide you with the capabilities and the personality traits you will need throughout your entire career. Or more likely, through the many different careers you are likely to have.

Just as importantly, you must understand yourself: your skills, your real interests and passions, the ways in which you learn, and the options that are open to you. You must understand how to most effectively apply your unique skills to your passions as a means of preparing for your dream job—and how to identify and prepare for a complementary safety career that will allow you to get another good job in your dream field, even if you don't achieve your ideal objective, such as becoming a neurosurgeon or playing in the NBA.

You then need a plan. The sooner you develop and begin executing a comprehensive career plan—and an education plan that will enable it—the better your chance of not only getting a good job out of school but also of building your long-term dream career and of controlling your own career destiny. The longer you wait, the more opportunities that will be foreclosed to you.

Not Your Father's Job Market

It used to be that you could take your time to answer these questions. Go to college and study any field in which you had an interest; take a job that sounded interesting and let your life play out. After all, a college degree had all but guaranteed a comfortable (if not necessarily psychically fulfilling) job and a salary that would ensure a reasonably comfortable lifestyle and a secure retirement. That is ancient history. To the extent these good-old days ever existed, they certainly don't exist now. Nor will they return in the foreseeable future.

During the depths of the recent recession, half of all college graduates were either unable to get any job at all or if they were lucky enough to land a job, it did not make use of their education and did not offer a professional career path. Even many of those with two of the most marketable graduate degrees—MBAs and JDs—couldn't get jobs in their fields.

Although the job market is slowly improving, most university graduates, not to speak of community college and high school graduates, still face a very rough and uncertain road to the American Dream. After all, there are still far fewer mid-skill/mid-income jobs than there are people applying for them. And to make matters worse, the number of employers willing to hire and train new graduates on the basis of their "potential" is rapidly declining. They want people who are immediately capable of performing the job they are looking to fill. And many are not convinced that college grads are capable. A McKinsey Center for Government study, for example, found that only 42 percent of surveyed companies thought that colleges and universities had prepared graduates for today's jobs (in contrast to the two-thirds of the schools, who thought their graduates were prepared).[1]

One result: as of mid-2013, only half of 2011/2012 college grads had jobs working full time in their field.[2]

Even when college grads do get jobs, the jobs are not always the type of positions that their school's career services office may have led them to expect. According to a 2014 Federal Reserve Bank of New York study on college graduate employment, the quality of young (age 22 to 27) college graduate jobs declined significantly during the 2001 recession and has not recovered.[3] As of the end of 2013, four and a half years after the official end of the Great Recession, underemployment (those working in jobs that typically don't require a college degree) rates have risen from their historical levels of about 33 percent to 40+ percent, where they have remained. Although the underemployment rate has certainly fallen from its 2009 to 2011 peak of 56 percent, in April 2013, it was still 44 percent.[4] Meanwhile, the share of recent grads consigned to part-time jobs has also risen and now hovers just under 20 percent.

Few of these jobs provide meaningful career paths or pay well. Consider that the average inflation-adjusted starting salaries for college grads remain below those starting salaries at the turn of the century. Lower starting salaries, combined with the need to pay off student loans (40 percent of recent grads have loans that average $29,400), dramatically limit these graduate's financial freedom and diminish their ability to take the risk of changing careers or starting their own companies.

And if things are still bad for the average college grad, they can be downright dismal for those with only a high-school degree (see Chapter 7). And, those without any degree at all face even a more challenging future.

It should be little surprise that a 2012 Center for Workforce Development survey found that only one-fifth of recent graduates thought their generation will have more success than the generation before them.[5] One in three believed that "hard work and determination are no guarantee of success" and a quarter of respondents believed that "success in life is pretty much determined by outside forces."

But even with all these horror stories, Accenture's survey of 2013 college graduates found that many aspiring graduates are significantly more optimistic about their prospects for getting jobs, getting jobs in their fields, earning good salaries, and finding employers that will train them than was the case for those who graduated the previous year.[6]

Welcome to the New Normal

We have now entered a new chapter in the country's economic history; a chapter that many call the New Normal. It is a period in which jobs that pay middle-class wages are scarce, competition for such jobs is steep, and inflation-adjusted wages remain below those of the late 1990s. In the New Normal, traditionally mid-skill factory jobs are disappearing and even increasingly sophisticated trade and professional jobs are being automated or moved offshore. Those jobs that remain are being continually redefined to require new skills.

In this era, high school graduates are not even considered for most jobs. Many college graduates are saddled with debt, are lucky to get a job at Starbucks, and are unable to move out of their parents' homes. In this period, employers are cutting full-time workers in favor of part-timers and freelancers who can be dismissed if times get tough and who have to pay their own insurance and fund their own retirements.

And career stability? That too is a vestige of the past. Even some companies that had reputations for never laying off employees were forced to reverse course during the recession. These and a host of related factors are taking another toll—on people's enjoyment of their jobs. According to a 2013 Gallup survey, 52 percent of workers claimed they were not engaged in their job, and another 18 percent said they were actively disengaged from their work.[7]

The changes that are charactering the New Normal, however, are not all being driven by employers. Employees are looking for different things from their employers. Gone are the days in which individuals are willing to provide undying loyalty to their first employer in return for a virtual guarantee of lifetime employment, raises that offset inflation, and lifetime pensions and insurance.

Employees now change jobs an average of every four years and many will totally change careers at least once during their working lives. Nor are workers willing to accept traditional, one-size-fit-all work rules, such as 9–5 workdays, Monday–Friday workweeks, all work in the office and two-weeks per year of vacation time. They are looking for more flexibility and an opportunity to tailor their work to the needs of their lives, rather than having to tailor their lives to their jobs.

But whatever the changes, and whoever is driving them, we are in for more of them. Generational expectations will certainly continue to change. More importantly, however, the four big catalysts forcing companies to change the way they look at their businesses and their hiring are continuing unabated. These catalysts are:

1. *Automation*, which is eliminating or transforming jobs traditionally performed by humans, is accelerating and expanding to cover not just factory and administrative jobs, but even some high-skill financial, legal, and even medical jobs. The Internet, meanwhile, is disintermediating or obsoleting entire industries, from newspapers to retail stores.

2. *Globalization*, which initially moved manufacturing jobs offshore, is now expanding to all types of professional jobs as increasingly educated and skilled emerging country citizens vie for jobs that had been the exclusive province of developed countries.

3. *Flexible hiring*, where companies attempt to reduce fixed costs by looking to part-time or contract "contingent workers" as alternatives to full-time employees, is rapidly becoming a standard business practice.

4. *Politico-economic volatility*, where political, economic, social, technology, and market forces are changing so suddenly and profoundly as to make it all but impossible to anticipate the future—thus prompting companies to reduce fixed costs and limit investments.

Remember the question I posed at the beginning of this chapter: What do you want your life to be like when you're 25? 35? 55? In reality, regardless of how you answered that question, your life and certainly your career are not likely to look anything like what you predict today. Technology, globalization, geopolitics, demographics, and hundreds of other factors are changing so rapidly (and combining in such unexpected ways) as to make it impossible to anticipate what the world will look like. It is even more difficult to anticipate the types of jobs that will be created or the ways in which these jobs will be done.

What does all this mean for your future? How can you plan for a career when you can't even know how a particular job, company, or industry will change in the future? Or whether it will even exist? How do you decide on and prepare for a career when all the rules are changing?

You don't have to throw in the towel. You just need to think differently.

Creating Your Own Rules

The New Normal will be a very, very uncomfortable place for many people of all ages. For others, however, it will be an era of unprecedented opportunity. It depends largely on your skills, your preparation, your personality attributes, and your perspective.

If you are looking for stability, predictability, and stasis in your life, the New Normal may look like a version of hell. Those who hope to maintain relevancy amidst continual change (not to speak of those who hope to command premium compensation) must, at the very least, continually upgrade their current skills and add complementary new capabilities. In some cases, they will have to go much further: they will have to totally reinvent themselves or risk becoming obsolete long before they plan to, or are able to retire. And they must always be prepared to rebound from the unforeseen—such as by being prepared to find another job or go out on their own, perhaps with little or no notice.

This same environment, however, can be a nirvana for those who view change as an opportunity and uncertainty as an adventure. Every day creates a new opportunity to find new ways of doing your job—or redefining it. New technology may allow you to automate or subcontract the parts of your job you don't enjoy, and provide you with more tools to expand or provide new levels of value to the parts that you love. Globalization requires people who can productively participate in and manage global teams and increasingly those you wish to travel to or get posted in exotic locations. Meanwhile, the rapid-fire creation of new industries and companies will provide you with totally new opportunities to change your job or redefine your career.

Need more education or hands-on training to keep up with these changes or prepare yourself for a new industry or career? Not a problem. You can now get an associate's or master's degree in virtually any field you can imagine. Don't want to commit the time or the money required to get another degree? How about a certificate in a new field from a community college or one of the hundreds of new one-to-three-month "boot camps" that are springing up to teach everything from programming to launching your own software-as-a-service (SaaS) company, to running your own bed and breakfast. Or you can just take some combination of the thousands of new Massive Open Online Courses (MOOCs) that allow you to learn a new programming language or bone up on advanced astrophysics, all from your home computer, and often for free.

And all of these new educational options come at a time when employers are increasingly willing to hire qualified people, regardless of how or where they learned their skills. Remember when a college education was thought to be the only way to get ahead on the world?

Think about the real world: a world in which master plumbers can earn well over $100,000 annually and where only half of all technology workers in New York City have college degrees—but still earn 45 percent more than the city's average hourly wage.[8] A world in which Google incents students to drop out of college so they can learn (not to speak of earn) more by working with them than by finishing school. Or where a Silicon Valley entrepreneur gives high school graduates $100,000 to skip college in favor of starting their own dream company.[9] And let's not forget college dropouts like Steve Jobs, Bill Gates, and Mark Zuckerberg.

It's certainly true that the higher your level of education, the better your chances of getting a good job, earning a good salary, getting promoted, and starting and succeeding in your own company. Having said this, why do many college grads struggle while some dropouts thrive? If not education, what will separate the winners from the losers in the New Normal? Who will maintain control of their careers and their futures and who will be perpetual victims of forces that always seem to be beyond their control?

Change as a Double-Edge Sword

The New Normal is, for better or worse (or typically better and worse), a world in which change is the only constant. Depending on your personality, preparation, and skills, a world with continual uncertainty will either provide you with continual frustration and challenge or will provide you with continual stimulation and opportunity.

Consider, for example, the four core sources of job market angst: automation, globalization, flexible hiring, and politico-economic instability. Are these trends, in today's political parlance, job destroyers or job creators? While these are discussed in more depth in this book, let's look at each at a higher level.

Automation may take the form of computers, robots, and other intelligent tools. On one hand, it has already destroyed many jobs and has totally redefined others. And with microprocessors, storage, and communication technology advancing (and getting cheaper) at geometric rates, this is just the beginning. Computers not only beat humans at chess and Jeopardy, they are even diagnosing some cancers more reliably than experienced oncologists and performing discovery more thoroughly than lawyers. And how many accountants and tax preparers have been replaced by a $24.95 software package?

On the other hand, these same technologies have created millions of high-paying jobs for people capable of designing, building, coding, and maintaining them. It has allowed millions of others to transform their jobs, such as by automating the routine parts of their work while simultaneously giving them power to do new things that were previously impossible, such as in running complex what-ifs and simulations, and finding obscure information in a Google-instant, rather than spending hours or days in a library.

Globalization has eliminated hundreds of thousands of low- and mid-skill jobs and is now taking aim at high-skill jobs. Indian lawyers now provide back-office services for hundreds of U.S. law firms and corporate legal departments. Vietnamese radiologists now read U.S. X-rays while U.S. doctors are sleeping, and Thai hospitals perform heart bypass and hip replacement surgery for thousands of Western "medical tourists" each year. All of the major technology companies have globalized their research and development efforts, hiring Chinese, Indian, and Russian PhDs to complement and supplement their United States, European, and Japanese research scientists. Now, universities in China and India (not to speak of Canada, England, and Australia) are cutting into U.S. universities' dominance in educating foreign students.

On the other hand, domestic and foreign companies operating in this country are training and hiring U.S. employees to participate in and manage global teams and sending U.S. experts to consult with or manage foreign subsidiaries. And this does not even begin to consider the benefits that U.S. farmers, artists, entertainers, movie studios, investment bankers, and one-person Internet-based businesses gain by being able to sell their services into global markets, rather than being confined to their local markets.

Flexible hiring also cuts both ways. On one hand, it incents companies to reduce the number of well-paid, full-benefit, full-time workers in favor of often lower-priced independent contractors who must pay for their own insurance, fund their own retirements, and can be terminated even more easily than today's employees. On the other hand, companies are more willing than ever to contract with third-party freelancers and consultants. This provides new opportunities for highly motivated people with unique skills to start their own companies and to be their own bosses. Even if their earnings and income security may be less than if they worked full-time for an employer, these new employment relationships can provide much more flexibility in building a career around your lifestyle and in giving you an opportunity to focus on projects you enjoy, rather than those that are forced upon you.

Meanwhile, it has never been less expensive for individuals to launch their own companies. For the cost of a personal computer (or even a notebook or smart phone) and an Internet connection, you can work, promote your company's offerings, and engage with clients all while sitting on your couch, in your pajamas. New technologies and cloud-based services enable individuals or small groups of people to launch sophisticated, even global companies on a veritable shoestring, with little fixed investment.

Politico-economic volatility, which creates huge risks, also creates vast new opportunities for political and economic researchers and consultants, as well as creating new, high-pay, high-profile jobs for professional risk managers. It, for example, dramatically increases the need for people who can connect disparate dots in innovative new ways that allow them to see around the corners of dramatic change—to turn volatility into business opportunity. And this doesn't even begin to account for all the high-frequency financial traders and hedge fund managers that exploit uncertainty and volatility for enormous profit.

But as important as these forces of change are, they do not even begin to account for the opportunities that are being created by trends in areas including demography (such as the need to treat and serve an aging population, or the need for people who can speak Spanish and Asian languages in addition to English), climate change, (alternative energy sources, energy efficiency, etc.), increased supply and reduced cost of domestic energy (through exports and lower-priced feedstocks), globalization (larger markets for U.S. products and services, need for languages, cross-cultural sensitivity), and many, many others.

The New Normal will certainly be disruptive. It will, however, also create far more and far better career opportunities than any time in the nation's history. More opportunities to build not just a secure and rewarding career, but the career of your dreams. A career that you will be able to shape and adapt to your own ever-evolving interests and circumstances as well as your own lifestyle priorities. A career over which you will be able to maintain control, rather than being at the mercy of people and forces beyond your control.

Creating Your Own Future

Some people fear and recoil from change. Others embrace and exploit it. Since the pace and magnitude of change will only accelerate, you are going to have to live with it. Only you can decide if you will be victim of perpetual change or whether you will exploit that change for your own benefit.

Of course, that is easier said than done! You certainly want to be the exploiter, rather than exploitee of change. The question is how? What type of career will give you the greatest opportunities for employment and growth, not to speak of earning potential and job satisfaction? What type of education should you get to not only prepare for your first job and career but also for your second, third, and fourth? What life skills will you need to anticipate and adapt to the inevitable curves that you will be thrown? What industry, type and size company should you choose to work for—or should you start your own?

How can you even hope to prepare yourself to control your own career (much less multiple careers) in a world in which the rules are continually changing?

These are all tough questions. But you have taken the first step to answering them by reading this book. And it helps if you are still in school or are young enough to return to school—or get some other type of education—without disrupting an established career or risking defaulting on your mortgage, or not being able to pay for your children's braces or education. You have taken the first steps to plan for your future and develop the skills, the traits, and the networks you will need to take control of your own career, whatever that career might be, or however it may evolve or transform in the future.

But you also need a plan. And you need one now. The sooner you develop and begin executing a comprehensive career plan—and an education plan that will enable it—the better your chance of not only getting a good job out of school but also of building your dream career and of controlling your own career destiny. The longer you wait, the more opportunities that will be foreclosed.

How This Book Will Help You

This book can provide the tools you will need to plan and prepare for a rewarding career that builds upon your strengths and your interests, engages your passions, and provides you with the flexibility to adapt your career to your continually changing lifestyle. It explains the forces and trends that are reshaping the job market and the nature of careers in the 21st century, and especially the types of skills that will be required to thrive in virtually all types of careers in a volatile, unpredictable world.

The book's 20-step process will take you all the way from identifying your unique combination of strengths, interests, and passions around which you can begin to identify the types of careers for which you are best suited, to what you should look for and how you can improve your chances of getting your first job. It provides a guide for simultaneously narrowing your focus to the types of "dream careers," which are most likely to feed your passions, and selectively expanding your focus to a synergistic set of "safety careers," which not only provide fallback options but can also improve your chances of working with and around the field you love (even if you don't get your dream job).

Once you have identified your career options, you will learn how to determine the types of skills and experiences that will not only maximize your chances of getting the job you want but also of preparing you for a 30-, 40-, or 50-year career in which you are likely to change jobs and fields multiple times. You'll gain insight into the various ways of developing these skills and gaining these experiences: the different types of colleges and universities and the much less formal (and less expensive) non-college options—from online courses through apprenticeships and Gap Year programs. The goal is to help you determine the types of majors, courses, and extracurricular activities that will best prepare you for your career and then, when you are ready to launch your career, what you should look for in a company, a manager, and in your specific job.

And, since the number of nontraditional career options is expanding so rapidly, the book also discusses the advantages, limitations, and requirements for success in start-up companies, in freelance businesses, and in starting your own company.

CHAPTER 1

Transformation of the U.S. Jobs Market

. . .the underemployment rate [among recent college graduates] rose somewhat sharply after both the 2001 and 2007–09 recessions, and in each case, only partially retreated, resulting in an increase to roughly 44 percent by 2012.

—Jaison R. Abel, Richard Deitz, and Yaqin Su
Federal Reserve Bank of New York

Key Points

- Higher levels of education directly correlate with higher employment rates and salaries.
- Employers increasingly require that new employees contribute immediately to the company, but are skeptical of whether many college graduates can do so.
- Underemployment is rampant, with an estimated 44 percent of recent graduates not getting jobs that require college degrees.
- Majors matter: science, technology, engineering, and mathematics; healthcare; and education graduates are much more likely to get jobs—especially jobs that require college degrees.
- Up to 95 percent of jobs lost during the recession and recovery were among the middle-income type jobs that typically go to recent college grads. Virtually all job gains are going to workers at the top and bottom of the wage scale.
- The big winners will be those with high levels of highly differentiated skills. Average performers will lose big in the New Normal.

The Great Recession marked the end of an era. A college degree, long viewed as the passport to a stable, rewarding career and comfortable life-style, will no longer guarantee you a job. It certainly won't ensure a job in the field for which you have prepared—much less a predictable and secure career that allows you to pursue your passions and live a life of your own choosing.

Although reading this fact may be painful, you have to understand the future if you hope to prepare for it. You have to understand the odds, if you hope to beat them.

Employment Realities

Hundreds of studies portray and attempt to explain the current job market. Although each study has a somewhat different focus and comes up with somewhat different results (due to different assumptions, meth-odologies, and sampling bases), all agree that U.S. workers have taken a beating during the recent Great Recession (the economic downturn that began in June 2007). For example, although the nation's Gross Domestic Product (GDP) has surpassed prerecession levels, and corporate profits and stock markets have hit record highs, employment and wages remain far below their prerecession levels. The U.S. economy still employs fewer people than before the Great Recession. Real wages (after adjusting for inflation), meanwhile, are still below those of 1999!

All of these studies also agree on a number of other facts. For example:

- Young adults, as is often the case in recessions, have fared worse than their older counterparts. They are among the first to be laid off and the last to be hired or rehired. Compared to older and more experienced workers, they have higher unem-ployment rates, their time out of work is longer, their wages fall more rapidly, and they experience far worse underemploy-ment (the ability to get a job that requires and makes use of their education). They are also less likely to get jobs that offer insurance, retirement contributions, and other benefits.
- Regardless of age, the higher one's level of education, the more likely they are to be employed, earn higher wages, enjoy

higher lifetime earnings, have longer life expectancies and lower divorce rates, and live in safer neighborhoods. Their children are also more likely to attend better schools and achieve higher levels of academic and economic success.

- Despite that U.S. educational attainment has reached record high levels (as of 2012, 33.5 percent of Americans aged 25 to 29 had at least a bachelor's degree), employers claim they face a continual shortage of workers with the skills they need and that even most college graduates are ill-prepared for today's jobs.

- Workers with degrees in high-demand fields, such as health-care, education, and one of the STEM fields (science, technology, engineering, and mathematics), are more likely to find employment that actually requires a college degree than are those with degrees in other fields.

Behind the Headlines

Let's look at a few findings from some of these reports and studies that illustrate the previous conclusions as well as provide a broad range of other insights important to those who hope to enter the workforce.

Consider, for example, unemployment rates. As shown in Figure 1.1, unemployment rates, as compiled in the Economic Policy Institute (EPI)

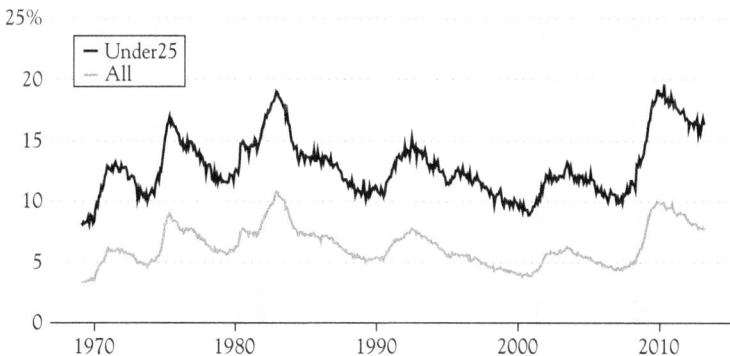

Figure 1.1 Unemployment rate of workers who are less than 25 years old and all workers, 1969–2013

Note: Shaded areas denote recessions.
Source: Shierholz et al. (2013), Figure A.

Unemployment rate in 2012%   Median weekly earnings in 2012 ($)

Unemployment rate		Median weekly earnings
2.5	Doctoral degree	1,624
2.1	Professional degree	1,735
3.5	Master's degree	1,300
4.5	Bachelor's degree	1,066
6.2	Associate's degree	785
7.7	Some college, no degree	727
8.3	High school diploma	652
12.4	Less than a high school diploma	471

All workers: 6.8%   All workers: $815

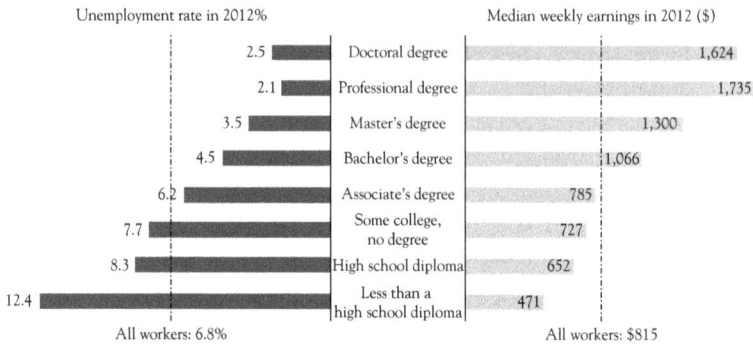

Figure 1.2 Earnings and unemployment rates by educational attainment

Note: Data are for persons aged 25 and over. Earnings are for full-time wage and salary workers.[1]
Source: Data Table from Bureau of Labor Statistics, Current Population Survey (2013)

Study "The Class of 2013," are consistently higher for those under the age of 25 than for older workers. This gap between older and younger workers has grown greater since the Great Recession than at any time since 1970.

Education also plays a critical role in determining your prospects for getting a job and how much you will earn (see Chapter 7 for more details on this point). The U.S. Bureau of Labor Statistics[2] neatly sums up the correlation between the level of education one achieves and their employment and earnings prospects (see Figure 1.2). This doesn't mean that college grads will necessarily get jobs that match or make use of their education. However, when employers have a choice (and experience is not a deciding issue), they are more likely to hire and pay more to a candidate with a higher level of education. This education premium, which has doubled over the last 30 years, from $17,411 in 1979 to $34,969 in 2012, will continue to grow.[3]

> Although unemployment rates are consistently higher for those under the age of 25 than for older workers, those with college degrees have significantly lower unemployment and higher wages than do those without.

Higher education certainly helps, but it does not guarantee a job. When comparing the linkage between education and employment across nine countries, for example, a McKinsey Center for Government study[4] found that 48 percent of U.S. companies contend that a lack of candidate skills is an important reason for their inability to fill empty positions.

Accenture's 2013 Skills and Employment Trends Survey: Perspectives on Training[5] confirmed these findings. Executives at 46 percent of surveyed large U.S. companies claimed concern that they won't have the skills their company will need in the next one to two years.[6] Thirty-eight percent said they would hire more people if they could find qualified candidates.[7] These skill gaps are twofold:

- Many applicants do not have the required hard skills (especially in IT, engineering, sciences, and sales).
- Even those that have these hard skills may lack soft skills such as leadership, written and oral communication, an entrepreneurial mindset, or the ability to drive change.

Recent graduates, in contrast, generally do believe their education has prepared them to get and succeed in jobs. According to Accenture's 2013 College Graduate Survey, 84 percent of surveyed 2012 graduates thought their investment in education was worthwhile and 70 percent of those who were employed thought it prepared them for their jobs.[8] To the extent they did find it difficult to find a job, 48 percent thought it was primarily due to their major.[9] Only 16 percent attributed it to deficiencies in their school. (In contrast, a 2012 McKinsey study found that 44 percent of U.S. students thought their college studies improved their employment opportunities.[10])

Although Accenture does see gaps in the educational system, it places a good portion of the blame on the companies themselves. So does McKinsey. In a 2013 report on talent and organization, it contends that automated resume keyword searches disqualify too many qualified candidates and that too many companies require that employees be able to step immediately into empty slots, rather than looking for candidates with a developable fit—those with good general skills and an ability to learn and respond to new opportunities.[11] No matter what the cause, the result is a slowdown and a much more selective process in hiring.

The Underemployment Crisis

Whatever the reason for the mismatch, 41 percent of those survey respondents who graduated from college in 2011 and 2012 and are working indicate that they are underemployed—working in jobs that do not require college degrees.[12] Forty-seven percent of respondents said their jobs did not match their fields of study.[13] A number of objective studies confirm these graduates' perceptions.

> 41 percent of those who graduated from college in 2011 and 2012 and are working indicate that they are underemployed—working in jobs that do not require college degree. Forty-seven percent said their jobs did not match their fields of study.

The U.S. Bureau of Labor Statistics, which uses its rather narrowly defined "U-6" measure of underemployment (total unemployed, plus all persons marginally attached to the labor force, plus total employed part time for economic reasons, as a percent of the civilian labor force plus all persons marginally attached to the labor force) calculated the figure at just a shade over 13 percent at the end of 2013.[14]

A number of research organizations, meanwhile, specifically study the intersection of education and employment. These include:

- Northeastern University's Center for Labor Market Studies;[15]
- Drexel University's Center for Labor Markets and Policy;[16]
- Georgetown University's Center on Education and the Workforce;[17]
- The College Employment Research Institute at Michigan State University;[18] and
- Rutgers University's John J. Heldrich Center for Workforce Development.[19]

These organizations define underemployment much more broadly, as jobs that do not require or make use of a worker's education. Their calculations typically place underemployment in the 35 to 45 percent range.

The 2014 Federal Reserve Bank of New York study, "Are Recent College Graduates Finding Good Jobs?" that defines underemployment similarly, took a particularly rigorous approach to measuring it (see the report for the description of its methodology).[20] It found 44 percent of recent college graduates to be underemployed. Its calculations also showed a huge variation in underemployment by major. It, for example, found that, as shown in Figure 1.3, those who majored in high-growth, high-skill fields such as math and computers, and especially in engineering, education, and health, had very low underemployment rates. Those in lower growth fields (such as agriculture) and low-wage fields (especially travel and hospitality) were much more likely to be underemployed.

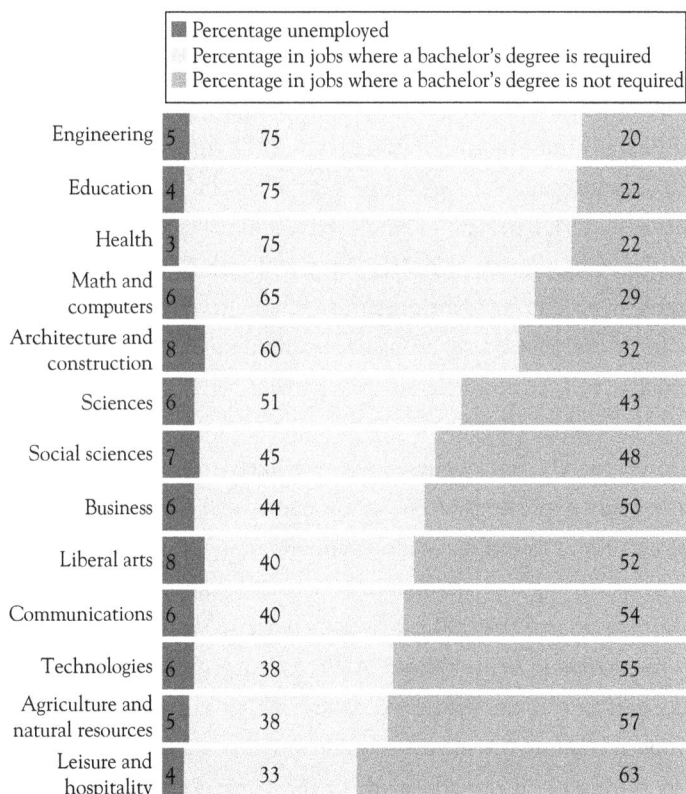

	Percentage unemployed	Percentage in jobs where a bachelor's degree is required	Percentage in jobs where a bachelor's degree is not required
Engineering	5	75	20
Education	4	75	22
Health	3	75	22
Math and computers	6	65	29
Architecture and construction	8	60	32
Sciences	6	51	43
Social sciences	7	45	48
Business	6	44	50
Liberal arts	8	40	52
Communications	6	40	54
Technologies	6	38	55
Agriculture and natural resources	5	38	57
Leisure and hospitality	4	33	63

Figure 1.3 Employment outcomes for recent college graduates

Source: Abel et al. (2014), Chart 7, p. 6.

Just as those with higher educations have higher rates of employment (albeit with a much greater risk of underemployment) than those with less education, they, as would be expected, also typically enjoy higher earnings. According to the EPI's study on The Class of 2013, young college graduates are likely to significantly out-earn those with just a high school degree: earning an average hourly wage of $16.60 per hour (the equivalent of $34,500 for a full-time worker) compared with $9.48 per hour ($19,700 for full-time).[21]

Wages of college graduates also fell less precipitously than those of high-school grads through the recession (7.6 percent compared with 11.7 percent between 2007 and 2012). These wage declines, however, began well before The Great Recession. By the time one adjusts for inflation, high school graduate wages have fallen by 12.7 percent since the year 2000. College grads fared marginally better, suffering a decline of only 8.5 percent.

And this does not even include big differences and recent reductions in employers' contributions to health insurance and retirement savings. The EPI study, for example, found that in 2011 (the most recent year for which data are available), just 7.1 percent of employed recent high school graduates and 31.1 percent of employed recent college graduates received health insurance through their job (compared with 12.4 and 51.4 percent, respectively, in 2007).[22] Nor does this include lower employer contributions for those who do cover insurance. Retirement fund contributions have fallen to even lower levels (5.9 percent for high school and 27.2 percent for college graduates).

Unfortunately, few of these losses are likely to be recouped anytime soon. A study of previous recessions by Yale School of Management economist Lisa Kahn found that those graduates unlucky enough to enter the job market during a recession, begin at—and continue to earn—lower wages (more than $100,000 less over the next 18 years) than people who enter the market in better times.[23] A 2013 Georgetown University Center on Education and the Workforce study, which modeled the impact of previous recessions on earnings, estimates that those who begin their careers during or in the aftermath of the Great Recession are likely to lose a minimum of 3 percent in earnings over their lifetimes.[24] Just as importantly, they also find it difficult to compete with younger, more recent graduates when normal hiring patterns resume and jobs for which they are qualified finally open up.

Then there is the debt load associated with the rapidly increasing costs of getting a college education. Roughly 40 percent of new college graduates have student loan debts that average $29,400. However, average loans often exceed $100,000 for those who go to graduate school. Such debt burdens, which cannot even be discharged by bankruptcy, are increasing, dictating career choices and confining about one in five graduates to living in their parents' homes. And now that outstanding student debt has surpassed $1 trillion (larger than any form of consumer debt except mortgages), it is also affecting the national economy, such as limiting consumer spending and the demand for new cars and houses.[25]

Not surprisingly, this is all taking a toll on student and graduate morale. According to the previously mentioned 2012 Heldrich Center for Workforce Development survey fewer than half (48 percent) of recent college graduates expect to achieve greater financial success than their parents.[26]

Prospects for Improvement

Although the employment prospects for college graduates are still pretty dismal, they have clearly improved since 2010. And, as discussed throughout this section, college graduates have much better employment prospects than those who have only graduated from (not to speak of those who dropped out of) high school.

Although these conditions are likely to continue improving over the next few years, the pace of post-recession employment and wage gains have slowed dramatically since the turn of the century. After past recessions, employment and wages tended to rebound at rates similar to that of GDP. But the pattern changed after the 2000 and 2007 recessions. First, as shown in a Federal Reserve Bank of Minneapolis study, recovery from each of these recessions has been slower than that from each of the nine recessions between World War II and 2000.[27]

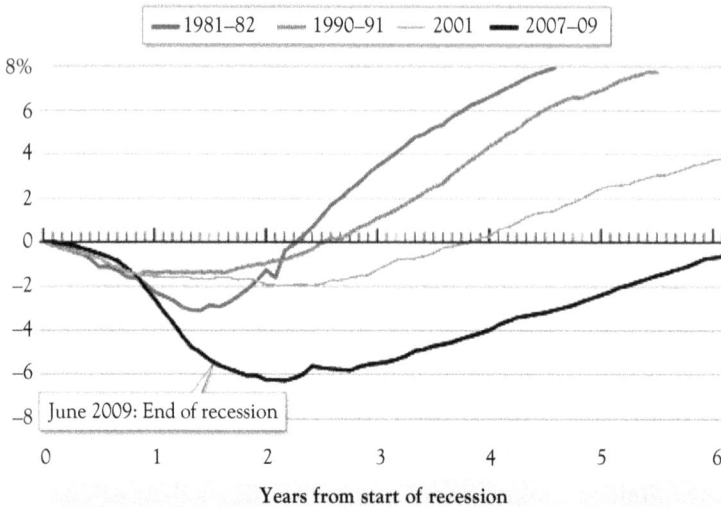

Figure 1.4 Percent change in nonfarm payroll employment since the start of recession

Source: CBPP calculation from Bureau of Labor Statistics data. "Percent Change in Nonfarm Payroll Employment" (2014), third chart.

Second, even though GDP growth has been slow, the growth in employment has, as shown in Figure 1.4, been even slower—much slower.

The Disappearance of Mid-Range Jobs

Where are the best prospects for good jobs likely to be? The National Employment Law Project study, as shown in Figure 1.5, calculated that the vast majority of jobs lost during the recession were those paying mid-level wages. The vast majority of jobs gained during the recovery have been those paying lower level wages. While high-wage jobs have also recovered a significant portion of their losses, the traditional sweet spot of the job market—especially manufacturing, construction, and mid-level office jobs—is being hollowed out.

> While high-skill, high-wage, and especially low-skill, low jobs are growing, the traditional mid-skill, mid-pay sweet spot of the job market is being hollowed out.

Jobs lost in the recession   Jobs gained in the recovery

Higher-wage
occupations

Mid-wage
occupations

Lower-wage
occupations

−4,000,000   −3,000,000   −2,000,000   −1,000,000   0   1,000,000   2,000,000
    −3,500,000   −2,500,000   −1,500,000   −500,000   500,000   1,500,000   2,500,000

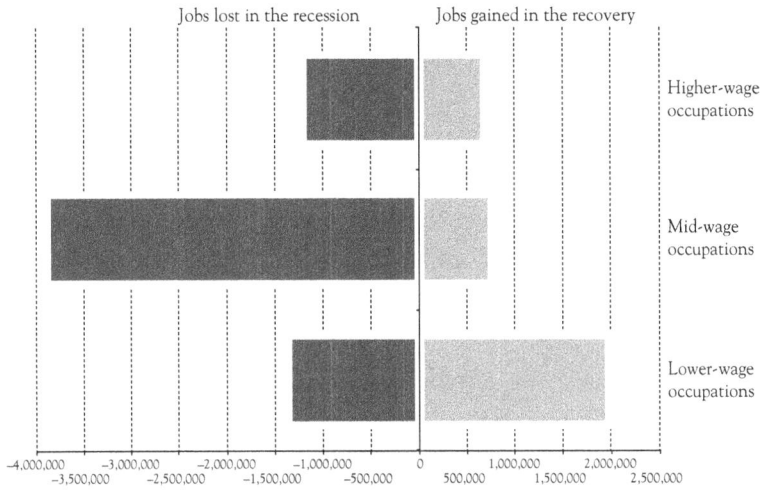

Figure 1.5 Net change in occupational employment, during and after the great recession

Source: "The Low Wage Recovery and Growing Inequality" (2012), Figure 1, p. 2.

A Brighter Future?

It may be comforting to think—to hope—that the employment situation will return to normal once the economy reaches traditional post-recession growth rates of around 3 percent. Unfortunately this isn't so much wishful thinking as it is self-delusion.

Although we can certainly hope for a change by the time you graduate, the U.S. Congressional Budget Office, one of the few economic research organizations that are cited and generally trusted by Republicans and Democrats alike has changed its expectations that the economy is about to see significant improvement. In February 2014, it released a report that acknowledged that a return to faster economic growth—and therefore job growth—is unlikely.[28] It now anticipates a prolonged period of economic growth of about 3.1 percent per year and the average number of newly created jobs between 2013 and 2024 to fall well below the 200,000 new jobs per month that are generally thought to be required to absorb new entrants into the labor force and to significantly reduce unemployment rates.

Does this mean your hopes for a career will be dashed? Not at all. It does, however, mean that you will have to choose your career options carefully, prepare for them rigorously, pursue them systematically, and always, always have a back-up plan!

> Does this mean your hopes for a career will be dashed? Not at all. It does, however, mean that you will have to choose your career options carefully, prepare for them rigorously, pursue them systematically, and always, always have a back-up plan!

Although the recession officially ended in June 2009, it took the economy until March 2014 to recover the private-sector jobs that were lost during the recession. It had not yet made up for the sharp reductions in the number of government jobs, much less created the additional jobs required to accommodate new entrants into the labor force. At that time, there were still almost two million fewer people employed than there were before the recession began. Just as importantly, as discussed later and shown in Figure 1.5, most of the jobs being created require lower skills and pay lower wages than did the jobs that were lost.

While some of the mid-skill, mid-pay jobs that were lost during the recession are certainly being recovered, most of these jobs are not coming back. They are gone forever.

One of the primary reasons for this loss of jobs is that the recession exposed a number of fundamental job market-altering trends that had been in place for more than a decade—trends that were largely masked by the financial and homebuilding bubbles. These trends, as mentioned in the Introduction, fall into four primary categories:

1. Automation, in which jobs—not just those of factory and administrative workers but increasingly of knowledge workers (as in routine accounting, programming, legal, and even some medical jobs)—are being automated. And, as argued in two recent books by two MIT professors, *Race Against the Machine*[29] and *The Second Machine Age*,[30] not only are these machines doing this work more cheaply than humans, they are also increasingly doing it better.

2. Globalization, which began in manufacturing, has rapidly expanded into knowledge jobs. Increasingly, educated engineers, financial analysts, doctors, lawyers, scientists, and other professionals from a

growing number of developing countries perform jobs for as little as one-tenth the cost of a comparably educated domestic white-collar worker.

3. Flexible hiring, with companies looking to reduce fixed costs by increasingly looking for part-time or contract workers as alternatives to full-time employees. In addition to wanting flexibility, many are trying to save money on employee health insurance and retirement benefits.

4. Politico-economic volatility, where political, economic, social, technology, and market forces are changing so suddenly and profoundly as to make it all but impossible to anticipate, much less prepare for major dislocations or their often unanticipated consequences.

The bad news is that those who are not prepared for these trends face a lifetime of uncertainty, disrupted career plans, and low earnings. Their careers, their financial security, and, to an extent, their lifestyles will be subject to the whims of the market and the good graces of others.

The good news is that those who understand and are prepared for the job market of the future—*and who plan and manage their careers effectively*—have the opportunity to not only minimize these risks but also turn them into opportunities. They will increasingly be able to define their jobs around their own interests and passions, and build careers that enable, rather than limit their lifestyles.

> Those who understand and are prepared for the job market of the future—*and who plan and manage their careers effectively*—have the opportunity to not only minimize career risks but also turn them into opportunities.

They will, for example, be able to capitalize on:

1. The growth of automation either by developing the next generation of intelligent tools or by understanding how to effectively use these tools to deliver business value in their own industries and jobs.

2. The growth of globalization by developing the type of skills required to contribute to (and increasingly to manage) global teams and to establish productive relationships with global partners and customers.

3. The trend toward flexible hiring by becoming their own bosses—giving themselves much more flexibility to tailor their careers to their lifestyles and potentially earn more money, enjoy greater job security (through client diversification), and even build companies that they can eventually sell or take public.

4. Politico-economic volatility by becoming a student of change—formally or informally helping your manager, your company, or your clients anticipate change, develop options for preparing for or responding to change, and helping them use it to their own advantage.

What does this mean for your career plan? You have three broad choices. You can focus on preparing for:

- The growing number of low-wage jobs, for which there will be many job openings, but low pay, few benefits, few opportunities for advancement, and little job security;
- The shrinking number of mid-range jobs, which will have extensive competition, require higher levels of education and skills, offer lower pay (due to increased demand and reduced supply), and offer less job security than in the past (due to continual competition from technology and offshoring); or
- The growing number of high-wage jobs, which will require high-level and increasingly well-differentiated skills, high-level cognitive and creative capabilities, strong communication and teamwork capabilities, strategic collaboration with computers, and high levels of drive and persistence.

Tough choice. Although few two-year, much less four-year college grads will want the millions of low-wage jobs that will be available, these may well be the only jobs available to those with lower level or undifferentiated skills. Mid-skill jobs will continue to be attractive, but will be limited and will face rapid erosion (see Chapter 2). Employers, therefore, will become increasingly demanding in who they hire, often mandating credentials that are not really required to do the job.

The big exception: mid-skill workers with technology skills. These skills, as discussed in Chapter 2, will be required in virtually every segment of the market. The Bureau of Labor Statistics, for example, expects technology-focused mid-skill jobs to grow by 17.5 percent through 2020—about the same rate as for high-skill jobs. And those with these skills will not only be in demand, they will also command handsome wage premiums. It is, for example, not uncommon for those with technology-based Associate degrees (and in some cases, even certificates) to outearn non-STEM Bachelor or even graduate degree holders. Then there are the high-wage jobs: the business executives, the doctors, the lawyers, the entrepreneurs, the professional athletes, and entertainers. But even ending up in one of these elite professions no longer guarantees a high salary, not to speak of job satisfaction, much less life satisfaction. Indeed, everybody will have their own criteria for determining success. It may be making a million dollars per year, it may be inventing a cure for cancer or creating an artistic masterpiece. It may be helping one other person improve their own life, or even of creating a loving, nurturing life for you and your family. Success is whatever you want it to be.

> Those with the right skills will not only be in demand, they will also command handsome wage premiums.

No, you don't have to be among the top One Percent to achieve success. Nor, at the other extreme, do you want to continually worry where your next meal or your next mortgage payment will come from. Money is certainly not everything. But as sad as it may be, money does have to be a factor in any career decision.

Bridging the Growing Wage Chasm

Although I absolutely do not want to overemphasize the role of money in a career decision, middle-class incomes and lifestyles are not what they used to be. As is discussed in detail in Chapter 2, the number of high-skill jobs—and the salaries they command—are growing. On the other hand traditional middle-skill, middle-class jobs are becoming— and will continue to become—increasingly scare. Just as importantly, the inflation-adjusted salaries that these jobs command are steadily declining. Worse still, the decline in mid-skill jobs means that those without high levels of differentiated skills will be increasingly relegated to low-skill, low-wage service jobs.

The sad fact is, that if you are not among the "winners"—the roughly 20 percent of workers with differentiated, in-demand skills—you will be a "loser" in an increasingly winner-takes-all economic sweepstakes.

It wasn't always like this. Back in the later part of the 20th century, the gap between high-wage and mid-wage jobs wasn't a huge problem. You didn't have to be among the economic elite to live well. Today, as mid-level jobs continue to hollow out, the difference between a com- fortable income and one in which you will have to continually scrimp is becoming a chasm.

Unfortunately, although many will want one of the high-wage, high- skill jobs, few will qualify for them. Do the math. As shown in Figure 1.6,

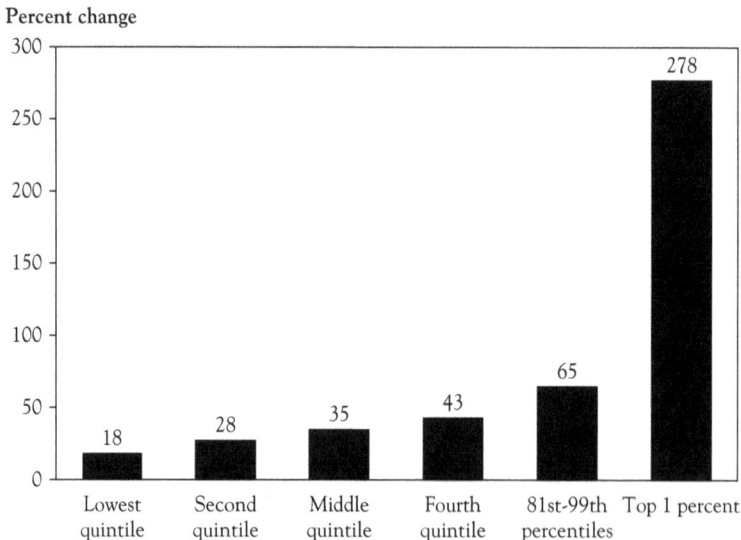

Percent change

Figure 1.6 Growth in real after-tax income, 1979–2007

Council of Economic Advisors' 2012 Annual Report to the President
Source: "Economic Report of the President" (2012), p. 179.

in this age of rapidly growing income disparity and superstar-driven winner-takes-all markets, the top 20 percent of U.S. households now account for more than 50 percent of the nation's total income (earning $92,000 and above, with a mean of $226,000) and 89 percent of the nation's net worth (a mean of more than $2 million). The division between the top 20 percent and the bottom 80 percent, however, barely hints at the widening chasm between this country's haves and its have-nots. When you drill more deeply into this top 20 percent, you find even deeper disparities. For example:

- The top 1 percent now accounts for 19 percent of national income ($350,000 and above, with a mean of $1.3 million) and 39.8 percent of the nation's net worth (a mean of $16.4 million)—more than the entire bottom 90 percent.
- The top 0.01 percent earn 6 percent of national income (starting at $11 million, with a mean of $31 million) and own 11.1 percent of the net worth (a mean of more than $24 million). In fact, these 16,000 households now own more assets than the bottom two-thirds of all American families!

These numbers fall off quickly as you move down through the quintiles. So do the rates at which the incomes of members of each quintile increase. A 2012 Congressional Budget Office study, for example, found that the real, after-tax income of the top 1 percent of American households grew by an incredible 278 percent between 1979 and 2007. The rest of the top quintile (81st through 99th percentile of households) experienced respectable gains of 65 percent. But the further the families fall down the income spectrum, the lower and lower the growth they have seen in their after-tax incomes. The second quintile (61st through 80th percentiles), for example, experienced a growth of 28 percent, while the lowest, only 18 percent.

In an era where the top 20 percent accounts for half of the nation's total income and a staggering 89 percent of the assets, those below are increasingly struggling. They are also the ones whose jobs are less secure and whose benefits are low; those for whom a layoff or a medical emergency could cost them their homes. Consider, for example, that as shown

Table 1.1 Income, net worth, and financial worth in the United States by percentile, in 2010 dollars

Wealth or income class	Mean household income	Mean household net worth	Mean household financial (nonhome) wealth
Top 1 percent	$1,318,200	$16,439,400	$15,171,600
Top 20 percent	$226,200	$2,061,600	$1,719,800
60th–80th percentile	$72,000	$216,900	$100,700
40th–60th percentile	$41,700	$61,000	$12,200
Bottom 40 percent	$17,300	–$10,600	–$14,800

From Wolff (2012); only mean figures are available, not medians.
Note that income and wealth are separate measures; so, for example, the top 1 percent of the income earners are not exactly the same group of people as the top 1 percent of wealth holders, although there is a considerable overlap.
Source: Domhoff (2013), Table 1.

in Table 1.1, even the second 20 percent (those between the 60th and 80th percentiles), who are doing pretty well in relation to the entire economy, had annual before-tax incomes that ranged from $61,736 to $100,065 and account for less than 20 percent of total national income. They are hardly wealthy in today's world. This is especially the case since the majority of households in the top two quartiles are two-income families.

No one, of course, should measure his or her success or life's worth by money. Everybody, however, wants to have income sufficient to buy a comfortable house, feed his or her family, afford the occasional vacations and luxuries, and afford to fund increasingly expensive educations and ever-longer retirements. Although few people (at least outside expensive cities such as New York, San Francisco, Boston, and Washington) need $226,000 in annual income (before taxes) to live comfortably, these percentiles are at least convenient surrogates for thinking about the winners, the stars, and the superstars in the national jobs sweepstakes.

As discussed in *The Second Machine Age*, this disparity is likely to grow even greater as three overlapping classes of economic winners further separate from the rest of the pack:[31]

1. Those who accumulate the right capital assets, either nonhuman capital (such as land, equipment, and money) or human capital (such as training, education, experience, and skills) versus those who do not;

2. Those who do nonroutine work (cognitive, creative, athletic, etc.) versus those who do routine work (routine and rules-based jobs such as manufacturing, bookkeeping, administrative, etc.); and

3. Superstars who have special talents and/or a lot of luck versus those with less and less differentiated talent and less luck.

You don't have to be a superstar to build a financially, not to speak of a psychically, rewarding career. In tomorrow's market, however, you will increasingly have to be a star—a high-value, well-differentiated provider of some type of service or product that others will value. As professor Tyler Cowen[32] and journalist Thomas Friedman[33] have been telling us, "Average is Over." Those with only average skills, average personal brands, and average determination will have no place in the world of the career stars, much less the superstars. Average workers—regardless of their education—will be increasingly relegated to average jobs, those that barely pay living wages and for which advancement opportunities are limited.

> You don't have to be a superstar to build a financially, not to speak of a psychically, rewarding career. In tomorrow's market, however, you will increasingly have to be a high-value, well-differentiated provider of some type of service or product that others will value.

After all, now that 38.7 percent of young adults are now graduating from some form of college, only about half of them can even realistically aspire to the top 20 percent, much less the top 1 percent. The good news is that the younger you are, the better your chances of putting yourself in a position to achieve your economic, as well as your career goals. But whatever your age, you need a plan—a plan to develop your own unique value proposition and to create a differentiated, high-value brand around yourself and your value proposition.

No, this book won't provide a detailed game plan to help you reach the top 1 percent or any other specific income strata. However, it will help you decide upon, prepare for, and find (or increasingly invent) a good job in whatever you select as your first career: Ideally a career that will build upon your interests and skills, feed your passions, and enable the lifestyle you choose for yourself. To the extent that money is part of this plan, it will suggest opportunities for shaping your career in a way that will improve your odds of getting a reasonably well paying job.

Notice also that the previous paragraph refers to your first career. Odds are extremely high that you will have two, three, or more different careers during your work life. This book, therefore, examines not only the skills, the personal attributes, and the resources you will need to find your first job, but also those that will equip you with the flexibility of changing your career, if you choose or need to do so.

But before getting into the steps you should take to prepare for the jobs of the future, it is important to understand exactly what the jobs of the future will (and will not) look like and the skills you will need not only to get these jobs but also to succeed in them.

CHAPTER 2

Why the Jobs of Tomorrow Won't Be Like Those of Today

If you are looking for a career where your services will be in high demand, you should find something where you provide a scarce, complementary service to something that is getting ubiquitous and cheap. So what's getting ubiquitous and cheap? Data.

—Hal Varian

Google Chief Economist

Key Points

- The U.S. economy has undergone a massive shift from producing products to producing services, with 86 percent of all U.S. workers now in the "service economy."
- While some service sectors are declining, others, like professional and business services, healthcare, education, finance, and information, have generally been big winners.
- The jobs market has bifurcated, with big gains among low-skill/low-pay and high-skill/high-pay jobs. Those in the middle will continue to decline.
- The good news is that high-skill workers will have many more opportunities to differentiate themselves and command premiums for their services.
- Some of the best long-term prospects are for those who partner with intelligent machines to do what neither people nor machines can do on their own.

Nobody can predict the future with any degree of certainty. One thing, however, is certain: The jobs of the future will not be the same as those of the past. To understand why, you have to first look back to the past—and then forward into the future.

Redefining U.S. Jobs

Like other countries, the U.S. economy is in a continual state of flux (see Figure 2.1). While the U.S. economy began as an almost exclusively agrarian economy, it began migrating to a manufacturing or product-based economy in the 1800s. This segment of the economy, however, peaked in about 1950, at which time services accounted for over half of all workers—a percentage that continues to surge.

Agriculture—the industry around which the country was built—now produces far more output than any time in its history, but employs just above one percent of all U.S. workers. Manufacturing

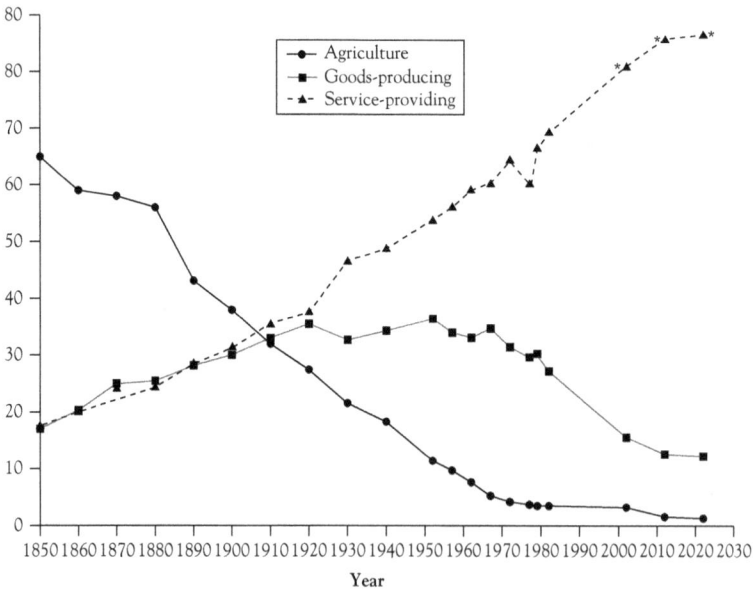

Figure 2.1 Distribution of employment by major sector, 1850–2007 (In percent)

*2002 and 2012 actuals and 2022 estimates from "Employment by Major Industry Sector" (2013).
Source: http://www.stats.bls.gov/opub/mlr/1984/04/art2full.pdf

employment, meanwhile, has been plummeting since its high point in the early 1950s. This sector, however, is beginning to pare some of its losses due to factors including international economic trends (exchange rates, wages, productivity, shipping costs, and so forth) and the emergence of advanced manufacturing.

Although both industries are subject to competition from imports, exports have helped shore up domestic agricultural employment by producing a trade surplus of more than $30 billion. Manufacturing hasn't fared as well. Virtually all low-value and much of mid-value manufacturing, and even some of the most sophisticated manufacturing processes have moved offshore, primarily to lower cost countries. This is attributable to a combination of factors such as wages that have been an order of magnitude below those in the United States, the rapid growth of foreign manufacturing powerhouses (like Toyota and Samsung), and huge contract manufacturing companies (such as Taiwan's 1.2-million employee Foxxconn, which assembles products for many of the world's largest electronics companies).

And what about the talk of a U.S. manufacturing renaissance? The country is likely to see some growth in manufacturing as offshore wages increase relative to U.S. wages, shipping costs increase and as products (such as nanotechnologies and biotech products) become more sophisticated, and new technologies (more functional robots, 3D printing, etc.) both limit the demand for and dramatically increase the skills required by newly hired workers.[1] And don't forget fracking technology, which is directly increasing the need for energy industry workers and indirectly making U.S. manufacturing more competitive (due to a combination of lower fuel prices, reduced fuel transportation requirements, and lower priced petrochemical feedstock).

On the positive side, both the U.S. agricultural and manufacturing sectors will almost certainly continue to grow in dollar revenues. Although the number of agricultural workers will continue to fall, the absolute number of U.S. manufacturing jobs will increase over the next several years. This increase, however, will be from the depths of the Great Recession. After falling during and never really recovering from the 2001 recession, U.S. manufacturing payrolls then fell by another two million employees (15 percent of its total workforce) during the last recession.[2]

Gains, however, will be relatively small, and both industries will account for smaller and smaller shares of the total U.S. workforce.

The skills required of these workers will also change dramatically from those required of traditional farming and factory floor workers, where jobs are being redefined by technology (equipment and, increasingly, software and online services in both sectors, plus chemicals in agriculture) and international competition (which is helping agriculture as a result of increased foreign demand, and hurting manufacturing through the offshoring of jobs).

While many of the physical requirements necessary for agricultural jobs have been greatly reduced, those who hope to do more than earn a very basic living from farming must now be as much scientists and financial managers as they are farmers. The fate and changing skills requirements in manufacturing, meanwhile, are generally summarized by the wry joke about modern textile mills: they now employ only two workers, a man and a dog.[3] The man is there to feed the dog, and the dog is there to keep the man away from the machines. Today's manufacturing workers also need very different skills. Requirements for strength, the willingness to follow simple orders and to endure hours of mind-numbing manual labor are out. Today's shop floor workers must be computer programmers, be able to anticipate, diagnose, and address diverse problems, and engage in dialogs with management as to ways to improve processes.

The U.S. as Service Economy

Regardless of what happens to agricultural and manufacturing employment, the U.S. economy is rapidly evolving into a service economy—86 percent of all U.S. workers are in this area and it is growing.

But what is a service economy? What's the meaning of a category that includes everybody from dishwashers to neurosurgeons? Everything from a taxi ride to buying a NetFlix subscription.

Since the term "services" is so inclusive, let's divide it into segments to help understand what service jobs are and what opportunities they provide for you.

The Bureau of Labor Statistics (BLS) divides this huge market into 13 industry-based sectors. Its most recent compilation shows that government and retail/wholesale workers account for the largest slice of this service pie, with each accounting for more than 20 million jobs and 20 percent of the total U.S. workforce.[4] These groups are followed by professional and business services, healthcare, leisure and hospitality (each of which employs more than 10 million people), and so forth.

More interesting than the numbers, however, are the trends among the various sectors. Just as the overall economy has undergone a long-term shift among different segments (among agriculture, manufacturing, and services), so has the service economy. In the early days of the country, the service industry consisted overwhelmingly of retail jobs. Segments such as government, finance, healthcare, and professional services were generally little more than rounding errors. Today, retail accounts for less than 13 percent. A 2012 article in The Atlantic looked specifically at the changes in employment in a number of segments over a recent 60-year period (1947 through 2008).[5] Although their numbers do not quite correspond with U.S. BLS figures, the trends are dramatic and telling (see Table 2.1). Some segments experienced phenomenal growth, while some services—especially retail/wholesale and transportation—experienced big declines in their roles in the overall U.S. economy. Clearly, the rising services tide has not raised all boats.

Although all segments, other than transportation and retail/wholesale, have increased their percentage of the overall economy, a lot has happened since the 2000 recession, and especially since the 2008 Great

Table 2.1 Key service sectors as a percentage of total U.S. employment

Sector	% in 1947	% in 2009	% Change
Professional/business services	3.3%	12.1%	Up 267%
Finance, insurance, real estate	10.5%	21.4%	Up 104%
Information	2.8%	4.4%	Up 57%
Construction	3.6%	4.1%	Up 14%
Hospitality and food services	2.6%	2.9%	Up 12%
Government	12.5%	13.8%	Up 11%
Retail/wholesale	15.9%	11.5%	Down 28%
Transportation	5.8%	2.8%	Down 52%

Source: Nicholson (2012).

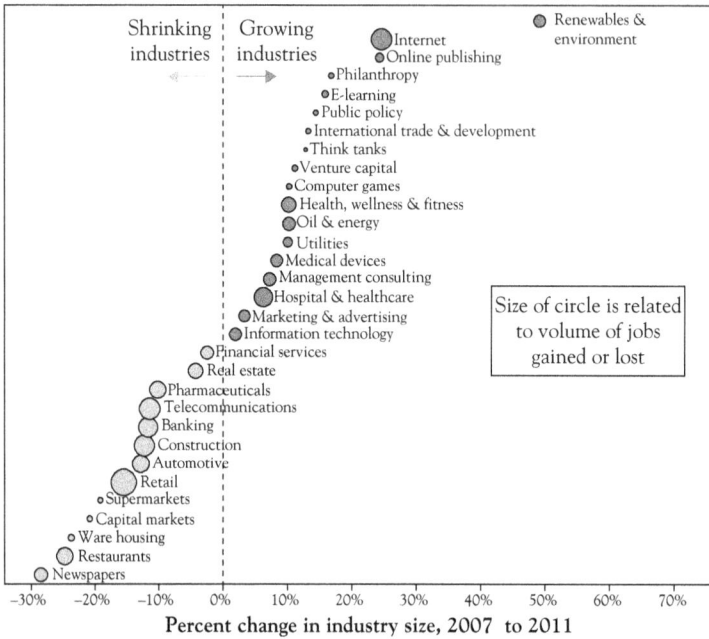

Figure 2.2 Industry winners and losers from the Great Recession

Source: Nicholson (2012).

Recession and its slow-motion recovery. Different service segments have fared very differently during this period. LinkedIn, for example, partnered with the U.S. Council of Economic Advisors to use its own data to assess the number of jobs gained and lost in a range of very diverse and highly specialized industry subsegments, ranging from newspapers to renewable energy. As shown in Figure 2.2, the two most recent recessions have produced some big winners and some big losers.[6]

The New York Times, meanwhile, examined the numbers of jobs gained and lost since the onset of the Great Recession, looking not only at the numbers by industry, but also by salary. The greatest percentage gains were concentrated in a number of expected fields (such as IT, healthcare, oil and gas exploration, consulting) along with some more surprising ones (pet grooming, sports promoters, and real estate property management). So too with the greatest percentage losers (construction, manufacturing, government, financial services, publishing sectors, architecture, and so forth).[7]

Some of these segments accounted for huge numbers (as well as percentages) of job gains (especially in healthcare, IT, and oil and gas) and losses (as in construction, manufacturing, government, and financial services) . The greatest absolute number of job gains, however, were in low-paying jobs, such as in home healthcare, temporary help and the largest of all, restaurants, and especially fast food restaurants. These are among the lowest paying of all U.S. jobs. The greatest number of losers, meanwhile, are, as will be specifically discussed below, concentrated in traditionally mid-skill, mid-pay occupations (especially construction and manufacturing). Many of these jobs are unlikely to ever be recovered.

As instructive as such analyses are, a true understanding of the dynamics of the jobs market requires deep analysis of smaller industries and subindustries. Consider manufacturing. Although most manufacturing segments have taken a beating during and after the recession, some segments have done quite well. While mining and other extractive industries took big initial hits, they have rebounded sharply, far surpassing their prerecession employment levels. Renewables and environment, meanwhile, produced a significant number of jobs and enjoyed, by far, the fastest percentage employment growth of any goods-producing sector.

The same types of disparities can be seen in services. Employment in some service industries, such as food service, leisure and hospitality, government, retail, construction, financial services, and government, has suffered the most during the recession. Some, such as food service and leisure, have rebounded nicely, surpassing their January 2008 levels. Others, like retail, financial services, construction, and government, have not come close to recovering their losses. Meanwhile, jobs in fields such as computer programming, nursing, business and environmental consulting not only did not decline but also have steadily increased employment during and after the most recent recession.

The Bureau of Labor Statistics, which pulls together the data from which all such historic analyses are based, also attempts to project employment trends into the future.[8] It breaks estimates down not just by industry, but down to specific job titles (currently 580 of them). It projects the number of new positions that are likely to be created (currently through 2022), the median pay of these jobs, and the education and experience that are required for these jobs.

Such industry and subindustry breakdowns are, as discussed in Chapter 5, particularly valuable to those planning their careers. Since they show you not only where the jobs are today, but where they are likely to be tomorrow. It is, after all, much easier to get a job and build a long-term career in an industry that is actively looking for people than in one that is contracting. Growing segments also provide greater opportunities for promotions and raises than do slow-growth or declining industries. Plus experience in a rapidly growing industry can significantly increase your potential for finding new jobs in other companies, not just those in that industry, but in those that contribute to, service, or use that industry's products or services.

This doesn't mean that you can't get a job in a declining industry. However, you must understand that your prospects of landing a position, your salary, and your future job prospects will probably be more limited than in a growing industry.

The Growing Skills and Pay Chasm

This type of industry-based view can certainly provide you with a valuable perspective on where the jobs of the future are likely—or unlikely—to be. Each industry, however, consists of hundreds of different jobs. A bank may have tellers, financial advisors, loan officers, investment bankers, financial analysts, IT specialists, janitors, and hundreds of other positions. Although you certainly want to know whether your specific target industry is likely to offer employment opportunities, you also have to understand which types of jobs in this industry offer the best employment prospects, growth potential, salary growth, job security, and so forth. This requires you to look at growth prospects of not just an industry but also of specific occupations. These prospects are changing in much more subtle, but in even more dramatic ways.

In the past, the job prospects, compensation, and job security offered by different occupations—from unskilled manual labor through ultra-high-skilled creative work and even corporate executives—fell on a rather steady continuum. This is no longer the case. The traditional distinctions, not to speak of the salaries, the benefits, and even the future existence of entire classes of jobs are growing into chasms.

Before getting into the prospects for individual jobs, it's important to understand the nature of this divide and why it is occurring. Consider, for example, the very high-level distinctions among three classes of jobs:

1. High-skill/high-pay jobs, the top of the labor pyramid is occupied primarily by university and graduate school-educated professionals with specialized knowledge-based skills, such as business managers, executives, engineers, doctors, and lawyers.
2. Middle-skill/middle-pay jobs, the foundation of the middle-class economy consists of traditionally relatively well-paying and secure blue-collar jobs (such as construction and manufacturing) and white-collar jobs (such as office administrators and mid-level office managers).
3. Low-skill/low-pay "commodity" jobs, such as fast-food clerks, hospital orderlies, and security guards, typically employ lesser educated workers, generally require little training, and provide low pay and limited job security.

Each of these segments was relatively large and rapidly growing from post-World War II through the 1980s. All was well, or so it seemed.

The U.S. job market, however, was at the cusp of a fundamental transformation. The broad, multitiered job market in which people of virtually every type and level of education, skill, and talent could find a job had begun to disappear.

A 2010 study by MIT economist David Autor and the National Bureau of Economic Research (The Polarization of Job Opportunities in the U.S. Market) examined the nature and implications of this change.[9] The authors divided the U.S. labor force into 326 occupations based on required skill and education levels. They then examined how the number of jobs in each occupation changed over a 40-year period. Although growth rates varied greatly year-by-year, the number of low-skill/low-pay jobs and high-skill/high-pay jobs both grew far more rapidly than that of mid-skill/mid-pay jobs (see Figure 2.3).

Then came the 2001 and 2007 recessions. These downturns, combined with the four key structural trends discussed in Chapter 1 (automation,

Percentage change in employment

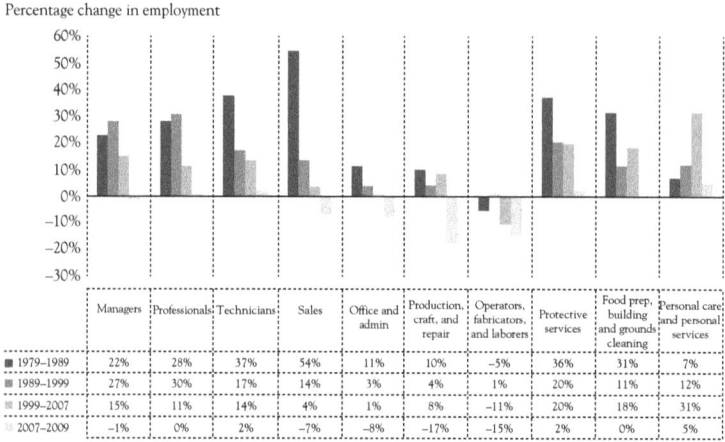

	Managers	Professionals	Technicians	Sales	Office and admin	Production, craft, and repair	Operators, fabricators, and laborers	Protective services	Food prep, building and grounds cleaning	Personal care and personal services
■ 1979–1989	22%	28%	37%	54%	11%	10%	–5%	36%	31%	7%
■ 1989–1999	27%	30%	17%	14%	3%	4%	1%	20%	11%	12%
▨ 1999–2007	15%	11%	14%	4%	1%	8%	–11%	20%	18%	31%
▨ 2007–2009	–1%	0%	2%	–7%	–8%	–17%	–15%	2%	0%	5%

Figure 2.3 Percentage change in U.S. employment by occupation, 1979–2009.

Source: Autor and Dorn (2013), Figure 3, p. 9; Autor (2010).

globalization, flexible hiring, and unpredictable volatility), exacerbated these employment trends. While the overall number of most low-skill jobs (with the particular exception of home and healthcare aides, both of which grew dramatically) and high-skill jobs remained relatively stable between 2008 and 2010, increasingly routinized mid-market jobs—both blue-collar and white-collar—plummeted 12 percent.

The differences among job categories are echoed in these broad trends. Skilled trade, management, professional, and technical jobs have either held their own or grown slightly through and after the recession. The lower skill service jobs on the right-hand side of the chart also held their own. Mid-skill sales, administrative, production, and laborer jobs, meanwhile, were decimated by the recession and have recovered little during the slow recovery.

> Skilled trade, management, professional, and technical jobs have either held their own or grown slightly through and after the recession. The lower skill service jobs also held their own. Mid-skill sales, administrative, production, and laborer jobs, meanwhile, were decimated by the recession and have recovered little during the slow recovery.

Wage growth between 1980 and 2005 (pre-Great Recession) showed a very different pattern. Average, inflation-adjusted hourly wages for high-skill/high-education/high-pay workers surged by almost one-third. Hourly wages for low-skill service workers grew at half that rate— 16 percent. Mid-skill categories again pulled up the rear, with machine operators and assemblers earning only six percent more. The wages for production and craft workers actually declined by four percent!

> Between 1980 and 2005, average, inflation-adjusted hourly wages for high-skill/high-education/high-pay workers surged by almost one-third. Hourly wages for low-skill service workers grew at half that rate—16 percent. Mid-skill categories pulled up the rear, with machine operators and assemblers earning only six percent more while wages for production and craft workers actually declined by four percent!

The recession hit the low- and mid-skill workers particularly hard as consumers cut back on discretionary personal service purchases (haircuts, restaurant meals, etc.) and as business investment slowed. Many laid-off mid-skill workers, not to speak of jobless college graduates, were forced into competition with lesser skilled workers for low-pay personal service jobs. The result: A sharp bifurcation of the U.S. labor market.

The Great Bifurcation

The Great Recession, especially when combined with the rapid growth in the automation and globalization of jobs, exacerbated the bifurcation process. Those who traditionally performed mid-skill jobs face the biggest and most jarring dislocations. Low-skill workers face the most pain.

The vast mid-market, in which millions of moderately skilled high school and college graduates had built rewarding life-time careers, is under siege. True, the number of such mid-market jobs will certainly grow as the cyclical recovery progresses. The problem is: the four big structural trends—automation, globalization, flexible hiring, and unpredictable volatility—promise to keep a tight lid on both the pace and the extent of the mid-tier jobs recovery. They will also keep a lid on the compensation and the security these jobs offer.

What will happen to those mid-skill/mid-income blue-collar and white-collar jobs that formed the foundation of great American middle class?

That future is already playing out. Even as the economy begins to recover, globalization (offshoring) and technology (i.e., automation) will simultaneously:

- Eliminate large numbers of routine, relatively low-discretion jobs; and
- Dramatically increase the skills required to perform the remaining available jobs, while dramatically reducing the number of workers needed to perform those jobs.

Think of how computer numerical control (CNC) machine tools eliminated the need for millions of assembly line workers and created new demands for computer-literate, numerically proficient operators. And, while some manufacturing jobs will return to the United States (although the vast majority will not return), the education and skills required for these jobs will be much greater than those for the jobs that had been lost. A 2014 Brookings Institution study, for example, found that while there only 0.2 job openings for every unemployed production worker, many companies still cannot find sufficient numbers of workers with required technical skills.[10] This need for STEM skills in manufacturing will only increase. Ford Motors, for example, claims that its most critical employment needs are in software and systems engineering. No surprise since cars are essentially becoming computers. The Chevy Volt, for example, currently runs on 10 million lines of code—2 million more than the F-35 fighter jet.[11]

Technology will, as discussed below, similarly eliminate, create and reshape jobs in hundreds of other mid-skill blue-collar occupations, from quality assurance inspectors to truck drivers over the next couple of decades.

The same forces are affecting mid-skill/mid-pay office workers. For example:

- Secretaries, bookkeepers, switchboard operators, and proof-readers have already lost their jobs to automation (as in the form of word processors, spreadsheets, and voice messaging systems); and
- Accountants, financial and marketing analysts, and even some lawyers have had to learn entirely new skills to deliver value atop that now provided by computers (such as tax preparation software, web-based analytics, and e-discovery software).

Meanwhile, millions of mid-level office jobs, such as accounts payable/receivable, account reconciliation, and computer programming, are increasingly being partially automated. Many of those that are not automated are being moved offshore to be performed by much lower cost, and in some cases, better educated workers. Just as importantly, some of those nonroutine jobs that cannot be effectively automated or offshored are being outsourced to specialized domestic companies (who use fewer, more-skilled people to perform tasks for multiple clients) or to freelancers who are retained and paid (usually with no benefits) by specific assignment, rather than by secure, long-term employment.

Even mid-level supervisory and middle management jobs are being slashed as companies restructure work and flatten their organizations. This reduces the number of management layers and, therefore, the number of necessary supervisors and mid-level managers. It also changes organizations from traditional hierarchical command and control structures to more flexible organisms based on self-managing and, in some cases, virtual (consisting of members from multiple locations) and continually redefined teams.

As if these private-sector job losses weren't bad enough, these displaced workers have been joined by millions of government employees and educators who fell victims to government spending cuts.

But not all mid-skill jobs will disappear. As David Autor and David Dorn explain in their August 25, 2013, New York Times article, *How Technology Wrecks the Middle Class*, we will always need a number of traditional mid-skill workers—building contractors, finish carpenters, electricians, plumbers, automotive technicians, customer service representatives, and so forth.[12] Many new mid-skill jobs, especially in healthcare (medical assistants, all levels of nurses, and therapists), education (teachers, tutors), and artisan professions (artists, jewelers, chocolate, and cheese makers), will be created.

Many of these jobs, however, will require new technical skills and continual learning to keep up with changes that will reshape these jobs much faster than in the past. They will also require workers who take more initiative, are more self-directed, have better communication skills, and are more collaborative and more accountable than ever before. They must also understand how different organizational functions work together and often must be able to perform a broader range of higher level functions. Harvard labor economist Lawrence Katz, in an effort to emphasize the difference between these mid-skill professionals and the mid-skill workers of the past, calls these people the "new artisans."[13]

In the end, large swaths of mid-skill, middle class jobs will disappear. These are primarily those based on routine mental and physical tasks in which the people stay in one place, such as at a desk or an assembly line station and with the advent of autonomous self-driving cars and trucks, even at a steering wheel. Those mid-skill jobs that require significant amounts of mobility, hand–eye coordination, empathetic human interaction, artistic expression, and discretionary decision making are less likely to be automated or outsourced.

This being said, opportunities will continue to exist, and will probably even grow, for many of the previously mentioned mid-skill craft workers and new artisans, for many types of teachers, virtually anyone in healthcare and for many business managers. This will be particularly true for those equipped with the self-management, communications and technology skills that will be increasingly required in all these jobs.

Most of these new jobs will require some form of postsecondary education. The Center of Education and the Workforce at Georgetown University estimates that two-thirds of all jobs that will be created in the U.S. will require some postsecondary education.[14] These jobs, according to the BLS's Occupational Handbook, will include 18 of the country's 25 fastest growing occupations (those expected to grow 30 percent or faster through 2022).[15]

> Two-thirds of all jobs that will be created in the U.S., including 18 of the country's 25 fastest growing occupations, will require some postsecondary education.

Three of these 18 high-growth occupations (information security analysts, interpreters, and event planners) typically require a minimum of a bachelor's degree and eight others (genetic counselors, industrial psychologists, audiologists, etc.) require graduate degrees. However, the other seven (especially nurses and other medical technicians and assistants) typically require only an Associate's degree or some other form of postsecondary credential. The majority of these high-growth fields will require far more technical or other highly specialized training, problem solving and complex communication skills, and much more individual initiative than was the case for traditional mid-skill jobs.

High-percentage job growth is one thing. The high growth in the actual number of jobs is another. A different cut at the same BLS databases shows 25 occupations that are expected to add a minimum of 50,000 new jobs (not to speak of the need to replace retiring baby boomers).[16] Most (15) of these are lower level, low-pay services jobs that require only high school degrees or less. This is as would be expected since the number of jobs in a particular occupation is typically inversely related to the job's level of pay. There all, for example, millions of retail sales clerks, but only a handful of cardiac surgeons.

This being said, six of the remaining high-growth occupations (especially different types of teachers, accountants, and business and IT managers) require bachelor degrees and the remainder (teacher assistants, hairdressers, and tractor–trailer drivers) require some level of college or postsecondary certificate.

A number of these degree-level (from Associate to Graduate) jobs, plus a number of others that require apprenticeships, not only offer strong employment opportunities but also provide psychic rewards, such as helping individuals, giving back to society, engaging and challenging work, and, in a few cases, very good pay. Nurses, for example, earn an average of almost $70,000 per year.

Then there are the types of high-skill advanced manufacturing jobs for which employers are finding it impossible to find sufficient numbers of qualified candidates. These positions include tool and die makers, precision welders, and industrial machine mechanics. And don't forget the most in-demand manufacturing job of all—CNC machine programmers and operators: an associate or trade school degree-level job that often starts at over $50,000 per year plus benefits. Nor are such jobs unique. BLS expects technology-focused mid-skill jobs to grow by 17.5 percent from 2010 to 2020—about the same rate as high-skill jobs.

The Plight of Low-Skill Workers

Although many high-growth high- and mid-skill jobs offer opportunities for fulfilling work, job security, and good pay and benefits, the same can't be said for the vast majority of low-skill jobs. True, the demand for many such workers is growing and there will be particularly strong demand in some large and high-growth areas such as retail, hospitality, office support, and, especially, all segments of healthcare. The vast majority of these jobs, however, will offer very low pay, few or no benefits, limited opportunities for advancement, and little job security.

Even worse, lesser educated entrants into the labor force will face growing competition from two new classes of higher skilled competitors who are forced to take lower skilled jobs. These include:

- Traditional mid-skill workers who lose their jobs, can't qualify for or find comparable positions, and are forced to take lower skill, lower pay positions; and of course
- College graduates who don't have the types of skills which employers seek to fill mid-skill positions.

On one hand, these people are becoming the new-generation of low-skill workers by default. As such, they will face many of the challenges of their less-skilled, less-educated counterparts. On the other hand, these people (especially young college grads) will have a big advantage over, and find far more opportunities than, their less-educated, less-experienced counterparts. As we have seen since the recession, they are often more favored in hiring, are given more responsibility more quickly, and are favored for entrance into store or branch management training programs.

In other words, many can potentially work into the type of mid-skill, mid-pay jobs from which they were precluded upon graduation or after being laid off from their previous jobs.

This will leave many unskilled high-school graduates in an even worse position than they were in before as they face greater competition in being hired and fewer opportunities for advancement.

High-Skill Professions: A World of Possibilities

There's no question: high-skill professions have the potential of providing you with some of the best employment prospects and greatest opportunities for both financial and psychic rewards. They will also provide you with some of the best opportunities for differentiating yourself on the basis of your talent or unique focus and will give you an opportunity to shape your own destiny and gain control of your own fate.

Sounds good, right? But what are these "high-skill" professions and what are their employment prospects?

Unfortunately, there is no single answer as the range of high-skill professions is huge. They run the gamut from data scientist to psychiatrist, and from fashion designer to professional athlete. Some may require a PhD; others a high-school degree, talent, and practice. Just as importantly for purposes of this book, their employment prospects, their salary ranges, and their long-term viability each range from wonderful to terrible. For example:

- Medical doctors, after eight years of postsecondary education (and probably hundreds of thousands of dollars in tuition, and usually debt), plus another four years of on-the-job training (internships and residency) will almost certainly find a job. Employment prospects, pay, and even job security, while generally good, vary greatly by specialty and location.
- Highly skilled software designers (especially those in high-demand fields such as mobile computing, wireless communications, and data analysis and visualization) will have their choice of well-paying jobs, or may even start and sell their own multimillion dollar company—even if they don't have stellar academic credentials.

- Artists and athletes may have the potential of earning huge amounts of money doing what they love. But if they aren't superstars (or at least stars), they may not even be able to get a make a living in their field.

True, not everybody can become a cardiac surgeon or a professional athlete. Yet it is possible to build a rewarding (both financially and psychically) career in virtually any high-skill field you can imagine. Who would have dreamed that you could create a global brand and lucrative career around the art of splashing paint on a canvas (abstract expressionist painter Jackson Pollock), by selling coffee at 10 times the price of other outlets (Starbuck's Howard Schultz), or by reconceiving how people interact with computers, play music, or perceive telephones (Apple's Steve Jobs)?

Virtually anybody with an idea, perseverance, and some basic combination of conceptual, creative, and interpersonal skills has the potential of building a rewarding career. No, you probably won't end up creating your own billion-dollar corporation. The vast majority of determined, high-skill individuals, however, can build solid, well-paying, and enjoyable careers (and possibly make a fortune to boot) with a combination of passion, planning, skills, and perseverance. You can build these careers around virtually any type of skill or any type of vision. You can build them within an established company, by operating as an independent contractor or consultant, or by creating your own company around your own unique value proposition.

But whichever course you choose, building a solid, high-skill 21st-century career won't be easy. It will require planning, preparation, and hard work—and the communication and interpersonal skills required to sell yourself and your value proposition; the resilience to bounce back from and the adaptability to learn from setbacks; and the perseverance to stick with it.

The bad news is that the vast majority of even college and graduate degree holders will face additional challenges. First, only a small percentage will begin their careers with the advantage of graduating from a top university or having a family with the type of connections to help get a high-potential position right out of school. And, as explained by professors Eric Brynjolfsson and Andrew McAfee in The Second Machine

Age,[17] the rewards of today's workplace are already heavily skewed in favor of three classes of people—and against three others:

- Those who provide capital have the advantage versus those who provide labor;
- Those with unique, high-value skills versus those with lower and more commoditized skills; and
- Superstars with incredible talent, luck or both, versus everyone else.

The good news is that some of the very technologies that are destroying or transforming today's jobs are creating new opportunities for re-leveling the playing field.

For example, it's true that few people have immediate access to the capital traditionally required to build a business (much less to live off the investment income). But, as mentioned in Chapter 1, new technologies and online services have slashed the amount of money required to launch a new business, globalization allows you to build a virtual company and tap a global market, and more flexible hiring practices make it easier for contractors to sell services to large corporations. And if you do need more funding, new tools, such as microlending and crowdfunding, provide access to capital. As discussed in Chapter 8, you can even find someone willing to finance your education in return for a portion of your future earnings. And as discussed in Chapter 9, at least one entrepreneur will even fund your decision to drop out of school to start your own company—without even taking a single share!

Meanwhile, people now have many new and lower cost options for developing the type of high-value skills that are required to succeed. You can certainly learn them in traditional colleges and universities or apprenticeship programs. But a growing number of new alternatives for learning new skills or enhancing or updating existing skills are popping up such as taking online courses (so-called MOOCs), enlisting in a wide range of specialized boot camps, and increasingly earning certifications that demonstrate your mastery of these skills.

But what about becoming a superstar? How many people have the combination of skills and luck that is required to become a LaBron

James, a Lady Gaga, a Mark Zuckerberg, or even a Barrack Obama? The good news is that you don't have to be a superstar to build the career of your dreams. Virtually any skilled and determined professional with the required combination of imagination, perseverance, and resilience has the potential of building a stable and rewarding career around his or her dream.

As will be discussed throughout this book, specialization will be one of the keys to success in this new era. This, however, isn't necessarily the type of hyper-specialization that we have seen over the last several decades, where an individual focuses on narrower and narrower niches within a sub-discipline. After all, most of today's most vexing problems (world hunger, climate change, income inequality, and so forth), and their solutions, span multiple domains. The most promising form of specialization may well be interdisciplinary—the integration of two or more types of complementary disciplines (think, for example, of economics and psychology or power plant engineering and environmental science), such as where content, principles, and methodologies from traditionally distinct disciplines are combined and applied in new ways. Think of it as a kind of macrospecialization, versus the type of microspecialization that has become so common.

Virtually everybody now has the potential to develop some type of unique, specialized skill that will provide value to someone who is willing to pay for it. The trick is to identify and fully develop your particular skills, align them around a specific market need (either an existing need or one that you create), and establish yourself as the preferred and widely recognized provider of that type of unique value. And, perhaps, you can even figure out a way of aligning all of this around your own particular passion.

Sounds like a lot of work? It is. But as they say, if it were easy, everyone would do it.

The Offshoring of High-Skill Jobs

Chapter 1 identified globalization (which includes, but is not limited to offshoring) as one of four fundamental trends reshaping the U.S. jobs market. While the current and previous chapter focused primarily on the trend's impact on low-skill and mid-skill jobs, they only tangentially mentioned some of the ways in which they will affect the jobs of high-skill professionals.

This is absolutely not to suggest that offshoring will play a limited role in this segment of the market. On the contrary, globalization has already begun, and will continue to transform some of the world's highest-skill jobs. It will eliminate some jobs, create others, and transform many.

Offshoring and the associated trend of globalizing corporate operations (decentralizing and spreading corporate functions out among different counties in which the company operates) are already sending a number of mid- and higher level jobs to lower wage countries. For example, as I discussed in a series of my 2010 blogs, offshoring has long since evolved from jobs that consist of standardized, repeatable processes to the offshoring of entire business processes—not to speak of the responsibility for re-engineering these business processes to facilitate their being offshored.[18]

In addition, many large companies have been establishing foreign operations, and partnering or contracting with specialized third parties, to move a number of high-skill functions to offshore professionals. While this began with computer programming, it has since expanded to include functions including law (as in the drafting of contracts or briefs, and discovery processes), radiology, accounting, financial, market and Big Data analysis, architecture, and the design and operation of clinical trials for new drugs. Meanwhile, many technology-intensive companies (IT, pharmaceutical, and so forth) are establishing global R&D networks in which offshore PhD-level scientists and engineers are taking responsibility not only for supporting U.S. research operations and for designing products for local markets but also for leading some global, corporate-wide research initiatives. Networking leader Cisco, for one, not only does this, but has also created a corporate co-headquarters in India.[19]

The offshoring and global decentralization of mid- and higher skill functions will continue. This will simultaneously reduce the number of these jobs for U.S. workers and create new opportunities for those capable of working within and managing global operations. This being said, foreign companies who are expanding their U.S. operations will help to mitigate these losses by hiring U.S. professionals to work for their companies.

But as important as globalization is, in the end, technology is likely to play a much more transformative role in reshaping high-skill jobs. As MIT's Andrew McAfee and Eric Brynjolfsson argue in their 2014 book, *The Second Machine Age*, offshoring prompts the re-engineering of business processes into smaller, more discrete tasks and thereby, makes it easier to create rules around these tasks—rules which can be programmed into computers.[20] Outsourcing, they claim, "is just a way-station on the road to automation."

Automation: The Elephant in the Middle of the Jobs Room

The entire question of technology's role in redefining high-skill jobs, and especially in the need it is creating for high-skilled workers, is still subject to some debate. Most economists agree that the growing role of computers increased the need for high-skill cognitive workers (especially college graduates) over the last couple of decades. But, as suggested in a 2013 paper, *The Great Reversal in the Demand for Skill and Cognitive Tasks*, a few economists contend that these days are over.[21] As they see it, computers are now ubiquitous and integrated into virtually all job functions, and the people who can program and work with them are already in place. The need for these cognitive skills, therefore, is declining. They claim that this is creating a "de-skilling process" in which the demand for college graduates is declining and forcing many into mid-skill jobs that do not make use of their skills.

It's hard to dispute that de-skilling has occurred. It is, however, a bridge too far to link this to a reduced need for cognitive skills. After all:

- Just because a person has a college degree does not mean that they have the skills for which employers are looking; and
- The capabilities of computers, and the roles they can play in all types of job functions, are increasing so rapidly that employers will continually demand workers who are capable of capitalizing on these capabilities.

Traditional automation initiatives have largely been limited to repetitive, relatively low-value manufacturing tasks and to those administrative and low-discretion jobs that were based on the application of defined rules and processes to facts, such as the authorization of payments to suppliers and the processing of receivables. Automation of these and other low-skill tasks has come in the form of robots, ATMs, voice messaging systems, personal computers, and, increasingly, advanced technologies such as voice recognition and pattern recognition software. This, however, is just the beginning.

Automation, like offshoring, is moving way beyond these modest beginnings into a number of nonroutine (both manual and cognitive) tasks. Computers perform some tasks not only more cheaply than humans, but for some tasks, better and more reliably. They, for example, are already used to write basic newspaper sports and financial stories, perform some types of legal discovery, and have even been shown to be more effective than some experienced oncologists in detecting and diagnosing some forms of cancer.[22] In some cases, they can even be more effective than humans, such as when compared to some teachers in determining exactly where a student is having problems and tailoring the lesson to that specific need.

The capabilities of these technologies, however, are expanding at an exponential rate. For example:

- Apple's Siri is making great progress in understanding natural speech and in inferring one's needs from previous patterns. It and other intelligent programs are already changing how we interact with banks, insurance companies, stores, and health-care providers.
- Google's autonomous car (which are likely to be generally available in the 2020s) can navigate traffic, avoid obstacles, and has compiled a better driving record than virtually any human on the planet. Even though it is still in trial, it has driven hundreds of thousands of miles without a single ticket. Although, these cars have been in two accidents, one was when it was being driven by a human and the other when it was rear-ended by another human driver.[23] Daimler and

other companies, meanwhile, have already begun testing autonomous trucks on Germany's autobahns.[24]

- Rethink Robotics' low-cost robot, affectionately named Baxter, can be "programmed" simply by moving its hand in the way that is desired. Household robots, meanwhile, can vacuum rooms while avoiding walls, furniture, and pets.

- Some new energy management[25] and home security[26] systems learn your habits so they anticipate your home heating needs and don't set off false alarms. The energy system, for example, will learn and adjust temperature based on factors including your sleep patterns and room occupancy. The security system learns that you have a pet and what a pet does, or that you get up in the middle of the night to go to the bathroom.

- The Dalu Robot restaurant, in Jinan Shandong China, is developing a robotic system to cook meals and then deliver the food to the customer's table. Momentum Machines of California is working on a "smart restaurants" robotic system that not only takes the order but then can create 360 gourmet burgers an hour.[27]

- The most impressive application of cognitive computing, meanwhile, has already made its television debut. IBM's Watson—the computer system that handily beat the reigning Jeopardy champions, demonstrated its ability to not only recognize natural language but also interpret idioms, parse puns, sift through enormous volumes of data to identify clues, and then to evaluate all options to identify the most likely answer (or in the case of Jeopardy, the most likely question). And it did all of this in fractions of a second.

Watson is now moving on to more commercial endeavors. As discussed in my February 2011 blog, Elementary, My Dear Watson?, one of its first commercial implementations is likely to be as a tool to help doctors in diagnosing and in recommending individualized, best-practices treatments for illnesses—especially cancer.[28] IBM is partnering with Memorial Sloan-Kettering to use Watson as a tool to help doctors research obscure combinations of symptoms, prioritize diagnostic options and present doctors with state-of-the-art best practices-based treatment options that are tailored to the individual patient.[29]

It is working with WellPoint to use Watson to help nurses make pre-approval and utilization management decisions and with a number of financial services companies to use Watson to help financial service professionals determine which financial services are best suited to the needs of specific customers.[30]

In each of these cases, IBM is positioning Watson as a tool to help professionals rather than displace them. Displacement, however, is probably just a matter of time. Processing power, after all, continues to follow the course of Moore's Law, with performance doubling about every 18 months.[31] Today's smart phones already have more power than last decade's room-sized supercomputers. Meanwhile, the cost of memory and communication is falling even more rapidly.

Given the rapidly growing performance, not to speak of the rapidly falling prices of technology, software will become increasingly sophisticated. More importantly, the types of artificial intelligence (increasingly called "Cognitive Computing") capabilities that are enabling Watson, Siri, autonomous cars, and intelligent robots are still in their infancy. Now that their capabilities are being proven in the market, companies and universities are pouring more money and focusing more resources into enhancing current and developing new capabilities. In January 2014, for example, IBM announced plans to invest $1 billion in its Watson program.[32]

Not only are computers gaining more "intelligence," they also have access to and are capable of analyzing the implications of far more data than humans. These "Big Data" capabilities will dramatically improve their ability to perform functions including analyzing biopsies, prioritizing investments, developing web-based marketing programs, developing and tracking budgets, and identifying tax strategies.

Opportunities and Risks for High-Skill Workers

How far are computers capable of going in performing high-skill tasks? Which jobs are the most and least susceptible to being performed by computers? Two Oxford University professors examined exactly this question in a 2012 study, The Future of Employment: How Susceptible Are Jobs to

Computerization?[33] They calculated the prospects of automation for more than 700 occupations and have labeled roughly 47 percent of total U.S. jobs (the vast majority of which are low- and mid-skill) as "at risk"—or having the potential of being automated over the next decade or two.

McKinsey Global Institute anticipates similar scale disruptions. Its May 2013 report, Disruptive Technologies: Advances that will transform life, business, and the global economy, anticipates that by 2025 robots may replace 40 to 75 million industrial workers and that the automation of knowledge work could displace an additional 110 to 140 million jobs worldwide.[34]

> By 2025 robots may replace 40 to 75 million industrial workers and that the automation of knowledge work could displace an additional 110 to 140 million jobs worldwide.

Marc Andresson, creator of the graphical web browser and now venture capitalist, looks beyond the automation of individual jobs to the automation of entire industries. In an ominously named 2011 essay, *Why Software Is Eating The World*, he contends that software, especially in the context of Internet services, will continue to disrupt more and more industries and overturn more established industry structures.[35]

What does all this mean for high-skill jobs? Computers will absolutely displace some people in traditional high-skill professions—particularly those at the low end of the professional ladder. In some circumstances, these machines already analyze financial statements and web-based marketing campaigns, prepare tax returns, handle legal discovery processes, pick stocks, write basic newspaper articles, and even diagnose some illnesses faster and more accurately than humans. This is just the beginning. They will, for example:

- Play bigger and bigger roles and gradually displace professionals in all types of lower level research, analytical, and even some original writing jobs;
- Transform existing industries, as in the way that Professor Tyler Cowen explains how they are transforming some

academic disciplines (such as economics, psychology, and marketing) from being theory-driven to being data-driven;[36]

- Change how people work with computers, such as by relying on computers for tasks such as analysis, for recommending options, and to make tactical decisions, while allowing humans to focus on strategy; and
- Create entirely new types of jobs.

In other words, professionals will have to "up their games" and change how they work with computers if they hope to remain viable in this new age. As suggested in books including *Average is Over*[37] and *The Second Machine Age*[38], high-skill cognitive workers will have to learn to partner with computers, rather than use them as mere tools.

Both books, for example, use an example of chess. Although even some home computer chess programs are now capable of beating the world's top Grand Master champions, the combination of computers and mere mid-upper level human players combine in "freestyle chess" matches to routinely beat the best programs and Grand Master chess champions playing individually.

This partnering can take any number of forms. As discussed in more depth in subsequent chapters, two forms of partnering in particular will create huge numbers of well-paying job opportunities; those for people who:

- Create the technology-based solutions that businesses and consumers will use; and
- Understand how to use technology to provide higher levels of business value for their employers, clients, and customers. The most important and the fastest growth opportunities will be for those who can analyze and derive actionable intelligence from the vast quantities of data and information that are being created.

Although computers will certainly eliminate some and transform many other high-skill jobs, they will create yet others. This will certainly include jobs for people who design, produce, program, operate, and support the hardware and software. More importantly, people who can put these data to use by understanding what information is required and how to apply it to the needs of the business will find huge new job opportunities.

For example, a 2011 McKinsey Global Institute study on Big Data claims that the explosive growth of Big Data alone will lead to shortages of 140,000 to 190,000 data scientists plus an additional 1.5 million executives and analysts who are able to use these data in their businesses by 2018.[39] A 2012 Harvard Business Review article agrees, calling data science "the sexiest job of the 21st century."[40] Not only will people with these skills be in demand, they will also command high salaries (often $90,000 or more for those with some experience) and play increasingly high-profile roles within their companies. McKinsey estimates that the demand for such people will outstrip supply by two to one.

The same will be the case who can use computers to design and facilitate the manufacturing of "products" including gene therapies, nanotechnologies, and all types of new technology-based offerings. The demand for people who can program and use computers to deliver business value is already evident. Those who have and apply such skills are already in great demand, and can command premium salaries.

As discussed in Chapter 8, students who graduate with STEM degrees get more job offers, earn higher salaries, are less likely to be unemployed, and are much more likely to get jobs that require a degree and are in their field than graduates in other fields. A 2014 Brookings Institution study, Still Searching: Job Vacancies and STEM Skills, found that employers pay those with STEM backgrounds an average of 21 percent more than workers without these backgrounds. And this demand crosses all types of STEM disciplines. For example, in an era when jobs—much less college-level jobs—are tight, the study finds that there five job openings for every unemployed computer worker, 3.3 for every unemployed healthcare worker, 1.7 for every unemployed architect/engineer and 1.1 for every unemployed scientist. Those with mathematics skills, ranging from actuarial science though finance and supply-chain management are also great demand.

Demand for STEM skills also extends into many non-STEM professions. Although there are only 0.7 jobs for every unemployed lawyer, lawyers with a specialty in intellectual property (for evaluating patents and so forth) continue to be in high demand. So too are office workers with quantitative analysis skills and social scientists skilled in programing and analytics.

Examples of jobs that will be created by computers go well beyond the private sector and academia. As discussed in *Average is Over*, the U.S. Air Force claims that it takes 168 people to keep a predator drone in operation for 24 hours and about 300 people for a larger drone.[41] These numbers compare with the 100 or so people required for an F-16 fighter.

This, however, is only the beginning. We have already seen how traditional supercomputer-like capabilities have migrated from room-size to desktop, to laptop, and to pocket-size—and the capabilities they have enabled over a couple of decades. We are now seeing similar functionality beginning to emerge in smart eyeglasses. Soon, new generations of chips will be integrated into clothes, bridges, and even inside humans.

But as rapidly as computers are evolving to new form factors and functionality, the functionality and usage of the Internet is expanding even more rapidly. In the 20 years since the graphical web browser was invented, the Internet has evolved from a platform for delivering content to one for processing data (in the form of transactions), to enabling social connections, to the creation of the "Internet of things" through which, by 2020, an estimated 25 billion smart devices, each with its own unique IP address, will communicate with each other. Just as the emergence of the content web created Google, and the social web created Facebook, the Internet of things—not to speak of whatever comes next—will create new categories of companies and new categories of high-skill jobs.

Mapping Your Own Path to a High-Skill Career

In other words, computers and the Internet will create some high-skill jobs, transform most, and obsolete others. The future lies not in competing with or fighting these tools, but in complementing and partnering with them.

As explained by MIT labor economist David Autor

This ongoing process of machine substitution for routine human labor complements educated workers who excel in abstract tasks that harness problem-solving ability, intuition, creativity, and persuasion—tasks that are at present difficult to automate but essential to perform. Simultaneously, it devalues the skills of workers, typically those without postsecondary education, who compete most directly with machinery in performing routine-intensive activities.[42]

Google Chief Economist, Hal Varian's career advise focuses on the output of these computers. As he puts it, "If you are looking for a career where your services will be in high demand, you should find something where you provide a scarce, complementary service to something that is getting ubiquitous and cheap. … Data."[43]

> Computers and the Internet will create some high-skill jobs, transform most, and obsolete others. The future lies not in competing with or fighting these tools, but in complementing and partnering with them.

But how can you best complement and partner with computers? What skills should you focus on to ensure that you will be one of those who will benefit from these increasingly powerful tools? I see three broad options. You can:

1. Design, produce, program, operate, and support these products.
2. Understand and develop the skills required to partner with them, such as the previously mentioned data scientists, analysts, and chess strategists; or you can
3. Build your own career around skills in which computers are not likely to master over the next decade or two. As I discuss in Chapter 3, these include, but are certainly not limited to, creativity, critical thinking, complex communications, empathy, sensorimotor skills, and management skills.

You will also have to recognize that as the capabilities and roles played by computers evolve (and as business needs and all types of technology, social, political, and economic, continually change), you will have to evolve and, in some cases, totally reinvent your own skills and your own brand. You can either proactively anticipate these changes and evolve yourself to take advantage of them, react and try to adapt to them, or become obsolete.

Keeping up with, much less keeping ahead of change, however, is becoming more and more of a challenge. After all, as McAfee and Brynjolfsson explain in *The Second Machine Age*, the steam engines that powered the first machine age replaced human muscle power and forced people to adapt by developing basic knowledge-based skills.[44] And since steam engines doubled in performance every 50 to 70 years, they gave humans time to adapt—to learn new skills that allowed them to differentiate themselves from or to complement these increasingly powerful machines. Computers are moving well beyond becoming repositories of information to becoming sources of cognitive reasoning. Moreover, computing capabilities are growing at an exponential rate—doubling in performance every 18 to 24 months! This requires humans to develop ever higher level skills (and to continually evolve their unique professional brand around these new skills) at an exponential pace.

If you hope to stay ahead of, maintain your differentiation from, or continue to be an indispensable partner to computers, you will have to continually upgrade and adapt your skills, or even be prepared to totally change fields. And you will be far better positioned if you anticipate the changes and build the required skills slightly before they are actually needed. This type of proactive analysis requires additional skills.

But which skills are best-suited to delivering the highest level of value? What are the employment and career prospects around these skills? Which are likely to command the greatest premiums? And most importantly, what type of skills you will need not just to land and succeed in your first job, but over your entire working life, no matter which and how many different careers you eventually have?

While this chapter examined how the jobs of the future will differ from those of past, the next chapter assesses how the skills that will be required to succeed in 21st century careers will differ from those required in the past.

CHAPTER 3

The Skills You Will Need for Tomorrow's High-Skill Careers

The world no longer cares how much you know; the world cares about what you can do with what you know. "To succeed in the 21st-century economy, students must learn to analyze and solve problems, collaborate, persevere, take calculated risks, and learn from failure."

—Tony Wagner
Harvard University Innovation Lab, Expert in Residence

Key Points

- New jobs require new skills—not as an alternative to, but in addition to the skills of the past.
- High-level information, media, IT, statistical, and entrepreneurial skills will be required in virtually all high- and mid-skill jobs.
- You can gain the greatest differentiation and rewards from critical thinking, complex problem solving, creativity, innovation, and complex communication skills.
- Even more important than skills are key personality traits including initiative, self-direction, flexibility, adaptability, a passion for continuous learning, self-restraint, and especially "grit."
- Most important is your ability to apply these skills and traits to real-world needs.
- One big problem; today's schools aren't really teaching many of these skills. You have to develop them on your own.

As the U.S. economy progressed through three very different eras (beginning as an agricultural economy, transforming into an industrial economy and then into an information or knowledge economy), employers looked for employees with different sets of skills and different types and levels of education.

- The agricultural economy, which calls for hard work in fields, primarily required physical strength, persistence, and adaptability to the whims of nature.
- The industrial economy, which basically required the ability to repeatedly follow defined rules, needed the "Three Rs" (reading, writing, and rithmatic), which helped spawn the move toward compulsory primary and secondary education.
- The information economy, which required the discretionary application of domain knowledge, was enabled by the growth of colleges and the post-WWII GI Bill, which helped millions of veterans get a college education.

The current economy is racing into a new era which some call the Creative Economy. It requires a change from the ability to manipulate information to the ability to manipulate abstract concepts and to create new types of knowledge.

As with the previous transformations, this one too will be very difficult: it will eliminate many jobs, transform many others, and create a number of totally new ones. The transition to this new economy will challenge those workers who are not prepared. It will, however, also richly reward those who understand how to deliver high levels of value. This value will come primarily in the form of identifying and finding innovative ways to address new needs; solving (or ideally, anticipating and preventing) difficult problems; and from effectively communicating and persuading others of the value of new ideas.

But just as the skills required for success in the information economy were built upon a foundation of reading, writing, speaking, and computational skills, success in the new creative economy will require and build upon a foundation that includes these plus solid domain knowledge skills. Success, however, will also require additional, and in many cases very different, skills than were required in the Information era. It will require an additional type of value add.

Those who anticipate and have developed the skills required for these new jobs will find themselves in great demand. Those who are not prepared will, as those who were left behind in previous shifts discovered, struggle to get and keep a job, much less build rewarding careers.

Herein lays one of your greatest challenges. The jobs created by this economy are emerging and changing much more rapidly than are the schools that are intended to educate people for these jobs. After all, most schools are still struggling to catch up with teaching the skills required for success in the information economy.

This, however, will not excuse you from the need to develop the skills. You will have to take responsibility for developing many of these skills yourself.

Skills of the Past Versus Skills of the Future

The future, as discussed in Chapter 2, will belong to those who can use high-end skills to create high levels of value. But what exactly are the high-value skills of the future? What separates them from the lower value skills that are still necessary, but are no longer sufficient foundations on which to build a high-value career?

MIT economists David Autor, Frank Levy, and Richard Murnane[1] approached this question by segmenting current jobs into five broad categories on the basis of the skills and education required to perform the primary tasks of each:

- **Routine cognitive**: Mental tasks that are well-defined by deductive or inductive rules. Examples include dealing with simple customer service questions, many kinds of administrative tasks, or formulaic tasks such as evaluating applications for mortgages.
- **Nonroutine cognitive or expert thinking**: Solving problems for which there are no rule-based solutions. Examples include the practice of law and medicine, scientific research, archi-

tecting software, managing complex organizations, as well as
some nonprofessional careers such as diagnosing tough auto
repair problems.

- **Routine manual**: Physical tasks that can be described
  through the use of deductive or inductive rules. Examples
  include traditional assembly line jobs or the counting and
  packaging of pills into containers.
- **Non-routine manual**: Physical tasks that cannot be well
  described by a predefined set of If-Then-Do rules or that
  require optical recognition and fine muscle control. Examples
  include driving a truck or taxi, cleaning a building, gardening,
  or serving as a healthcare aide.
- **Complex communication**: Interacting with humans to
  acquire information, to explain it, or to persuade others of its
  implications for action. Examples include a manager motivating the people whose work she supervises (or especially
  an individual who brings a team of peers to consensus and
  action), a designer gauging a client's taste and recommending
  furniture and furnishing that expresses that taste, a teacher
  explaining high-school-level concepts to a third-grade student,
  or an engineer describing why a new design for a micropro-
  cessor is an advance over previous designs.

Autor and Acemoglu, along with a number of their MIT and Harvard
colleagues (including Frank Levy, Richard Murnane, Erik Brynjolfsson,
and Andrew McAfee) have examined the future of jobs based on these
tasks from a number of different perspectives. They looked particularly
at the ways in which technology (and to a lesser extent offshoring) will
transform these jobs. Some of the most instructive of these authors' pub-
lications include:

- Autor, Levy, and Murnane's 2003 *The Skill Content of Recent
  Technological Change*;[2]
- Levy and Murnane's 2005/2006 *How Computerized Work and
  Globalization Shape Human Skill Demands*;[3]

- Autor's 2010 *The Polarization of Job Opportunities in the U.S. Labor Market.*[4]
- Erik Brynjolfsson and Andrew McAfee's book, *The Second Machine Age.*[5]

Although I have discussed much of this research in a series of blog posts that I wrote in October 2011[6] and November 2011,[7] and mention it through this chapter, many of their findings provide context for a number of changes we are already seeing in the labor force and the types of skills that will be required to get and excel at a job in the future. For example:

- Routine manual and cognitive tasks will be the primary victims of automation and globalization. Routine cognitive tasks (which can be accomplished by applying defined rules) and routine manual tasks (that can be defined in terms of a specific set of movements) are most subject to outsourcing and computerization. Jobs based on these tasks will increasingly disappear, first in the United States and other high-wage countries, and increasingly in lower wage countries. Many of those that remain will provide little job security and will be subject to intense price pressures. Many of these will be transformed into nonroutine manual or cognitive jobs.
- Nonroutine manual tasks are less subject to these trends. And since most of these services are site-specific, they cannot be readily outsourced. Most of these jobs, however, can be performed by people with relatively modest degrees of education and training and do not require particularly high levels of strength, stamina, or hand–eye coordination. They, like those for routine tasks, will be subject to much competition and will provide lower salaries and, often, less job security than in the past. This being said, some of these nonroutine tasks do require special training and skills, and produce particularly high-value results—think, for example, of particularly innovative gem cutters, artists, professional performers, or athletes. The relative handful of people who qualify for such jobs will

continue to enjoy high levels of differentiation and will often
be able to command high salaries. Indeed, globalization and
the rapid growth of middle class consumers in developing
countries has the potential of increasing the demand and
compensation for such services and, in some cases, of creating
globally branded superstars.

- Nonroutine cognitive tasks and complex communication,
  meanwhile, are less subject to (albeit, as discussed later, not
  fully protected from) offshoring and automation. However,
  as discussed in Chapter 2, technology will absolutely affect
  and increasingly transform these tasks. Those workers who
  best understand how to use technology to enhance the value
  they can deliver to their employers, clients, and customers will
  be among the biggest winners in this new era. So too will be
  those who use nonroutine cognitive and complex communication skills to create and promote this technology.

High-order cognitive or expert thinking skills will be instrumental in
jobs that require people to address problems for which "the rules are not yet
known." These problems, according to MIT's Irving Wladawsky-Berger,[8]
are of two broad types: Those for which

- The information is hard to represent in a form that computers
  can use, such as feelings or impressions derived from viewing
  body language; and
- Rules are difficult to articulate. This can include "complex
  processes" (such as those required to learn to ride a two-wheel
  bicycle), "pattern recognition" (the solving of problems that
  cannot be expressed in deductive or inductive rules), "diver-
  gent thinking" (as in starting from existing knowledge to ask
  new questions and develop new concepts), and the ability to
  exercise "good judgment" in the face of uncertainty.

Complex communication also includes a broad range of capabilities.
At the most basic, it entails the ability to describe (in speaking and/or
writing) complex phenomena and patterns in ways in which people can
understand, the ability to ask questions in ways that elicit enlightening

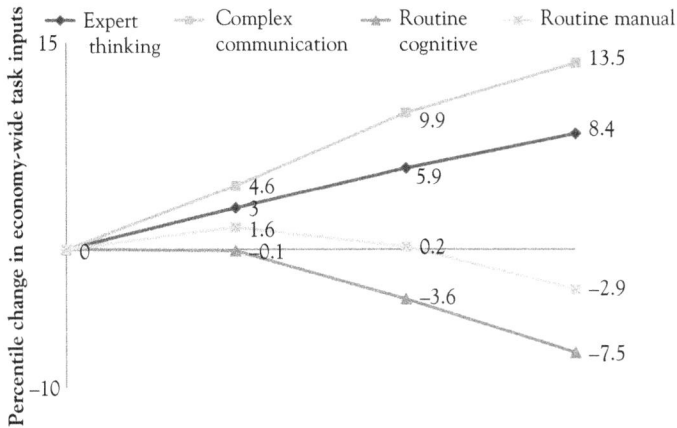

Figure 3.1 Skill demands changing across the economy (1969–1998)

Source: Murnane (2008, February 29); Murnane and Levy (2004).

answers and prompt people to think of issues in new ways, and the ability to listen to or read and comprehend concepts. At a higher level, it involves interaction (simultaneously communicating, receiving, and processing), empathy (as in understanding and addressing the feelings and motivations of others), and persuasion (especially in selling your ideas and motivating others to action).

MIT's Richard Murnane and Frank Levy summarize the changing demand for these skills in Figure 3.1.

Now that you have a high-level understanding of the types of jobs that will and will not be sustainable, and that will allow you to differentiate and command premium wages for your services in the future (especially those based on nonroutine cognitive tasks and complex communication), let's drill down into the broad range of knowledge and skills that you will need to prepare for these jobs.

New Skills for a New Era

The U.S. educational system generally recognizes the growing need for many of these higher level skills and is trying to determine how best to teach them (or more accurately, to help students "learn" skills that are inherently difficult to "teach"). A few organizations, meanwhile, have begun to delineate the types and levels of knowledge and skills that will be required for success in the Creative Economy, identify the type of curricula that will be most effective in helping students learn them, and develop the standards by which they can be measured. Two of the most important organizations doing this work are the:

- The Partnership for 21st Century Skills' (P21) Framework for 21st Century Learning[9] specifies the types of skills and content knowledge that will be required in the 21st century and the support systems that a student needs to learn them; and
- Common Core Standards specifies the skills, skill levels, and concepts (initially for math and English) that students should be expected to attain at each grade level.[10]

The P21 Framework provides a good starting point for delineating five key categories of skills that will be required in this new economy:

1. **Core foundational subjects** (English, reading or language arts, world languages, arts, mathematics, economics, science, geography, history, government, and civics) that students should master.
2. **Interdisciplinary themes** (global awareness, finance/economics/business, civics, health, and environment) around which these subjects can be taught to create literacy around current issues.
3. **Information, media, and information technology skills**;
4. **Learning and innovation skills** (critical thinking, problem solving, creativity, innovation, communication, and collaboration skills).
5. **Life and career skills** (flexibility and adaptability, initiative and self-direction, social and cross-cultural skills, productivity and accountability, and leadership and responsibility).

Although the subjects, themes, and skills shown in the first two levels of the P21 Framework list are still necessary prerequisites for most high-skill careers, they are no longer sufficient, especially if you hope to excel in the type of jobs that will allow you to differentiate yourself and add high levels of value in the Creative Economy. Information, media, and IT skills, for example, are now required for almost all such careers. The learning, innovation, and life and career skills mentioned in the fourth and fifth categories, meanwhile, will be critical in distinguishing the winners from the also-rans in the new Creative Economy.

Although the P21 Framework and the Common Core both recognize the importance of these higher level skills, it will likely take years or even decades before they percolate through the secondary educational system—assuming they are even accepted and enacted.

What about colleges where one may normally expect to learn such higher level skills? Which are the best schools for learning critical thinking and creativity? Adaptability? Initiative and leadership? In which major will you gain the deepest understanding of these skills and best learn to apply them? What degrees will best demonstrate your level of mastery of these skills?

Sure, you will be able to gain some of these skills through all levels of your education, not to speak of through your extracurricular activities, your work, and your life. But since these skills can be even more critical to your long-term success than the actual domain knowledge you develop, you can't afford to leave them to chance. And since few schools or colleges explicitly focus on these skills, you must take charge of developing them yourself.

The first step is to understand what each of these skills actually entails and why they are so important in developing and succeeding in a career.

The Core Learning and Career Skills You Will Need to Succeed

The P21 list provides a great starting point. However, let me take some creative liberties in reorganizing and extending this list to suggest the very different roles each can play not only in preparing you for a job in the new economy but also in positioning you as one of the winners in this demanding new world. Let's begin with what I see as the core skills: effectively the ante that will be required to even get a seat at the table. These "core skills" begin with three of P21's sets of life and career skills (which are labeled as number five):

- *Productivity and accountability*: These include the ability to set and meet your own goals; plan, prioritize, and manage your work; and to be accountable for the results. The importance of these skills is, of course, a given.

- *Leadership and responsibility*: These skills are required whether you are the leader or are a member of a group since they include the ability to leverage the strengths of multiple people to achieve common goals and, when appropriate, lead others to your point of view and inspire action. They also entail the responsibility to advance the group's goals, even if they may be at odds with your own—and the ability to step back and yield to others in the group, when appropriate.

- *Social and cross-cultural skills*: As collaboration becomes increasingly critical, the species of worker that just wants to lock themselves in their offices and do their work is on the verge of extinction in today's business world. Even if you're an introvert, you have to be able to work effectively with others. You have to know when and how to listen, be open to the ideas of others, and be able to express your own thoughts effectively and with respect. And in an age of diversity and globalization, you must also respect, understand the cultural nuances, and work effectively with people with whom you have little in common as well as those whose life choices you may totally disagree.

Two other types of core skills are bit different. Like the three previously mentioned life and career skills, they are so universally important as to be critical to virtually every high-skills career. But unlike those skills, they are in such demand and can produce so much value that you can effectively build entire careers around them. These include communication and collaboration skills (included in category 4 of P21's list), as well as information, media, and information technology skills (category 3 of the list). My additions to this list are statistics and entrepreneurship. Why are these four skills so important in the jobs of tomorrow?

Communication and collaboration skills are not only core to success in all high-value (and many lower-value) careers, they can also provide foundations upon which you can build an entire career. Entertainers, journalists, novelists, and salespeople are effectively professional, full-time communicators. Although college professors play many roles, the growing importance of student reviews is placing a greater priority on their communication skills. Meanwhile, the growing popularity of Massive Open Online Courses (MOOCs, as discussed in Chapter 9) is already beginning to turn some professors, who are particularly gifted communicators, into new-age rock stars.

This being said, communication and collaboration skills also play somewhat more prosaic, but equally important roles in making or breaking many other careers:

- Communication is the ability to effectively use oral, written, and nonverbal communication and media to inform, instruct, motivate, and persuade others;
- Collaboration requires the flexibility and the ability to compromise and assume shared responsibility in diverse teams. These skills will be particularly important in an era of flexible, ad hoc, loosely bonded, and decentralized teams.

Both are instrumental in conveying information and concepts, working productively in teams, and persuading others of and in gaining support for your ideas and recommendations. They are also valuable in their own right, such as in your ability to sell yourself (or the products or the ideas you choose to represent) to employers, clients, and customers.

Two types of communications skills have the potential of being particularly important high-value differentiators:

- Complex communication, such as the ability to persuasively convey particularly complex ideas or relationships.
- Emotive communication, in which you can express subtle emotions with sensitivity and ideally empathy.

Although these skills are required in virtually any high-value career, particularly gifted communicators—especially those with high degrees of empathy and cultural awareness—will have huge advantages. Those with such skills are likely to have greater success in selling themselves and their ideas, in mobilizing people to action, and in being viewed and accepted as leaders.

> Particularly gifted communicators are likely to have greater success in selling themselves and their ideas, in mobilizing people to action, and in being viewed and accepted as leaders.

Information, media, and information technology skills, as mentioned, are becoming fundamental to all types of high-skill work. One must, however, distinguish IT competence from IT fluency. IT competence, which allows you to use these resources in your own field, is a core requirement in virtually any profession. You must be able to effectively access, use, and critically evaluate information; effectively analyze, use, and create all types of media; and use technology to research, organize, evaluate, and communicate information.

Such skills are also becoming increasingly critical in building your own career—such as in communicating your brand and your value proposition and in building the type of network that you will need to get a job and advance your career.

Then there's IT fluency. Those who are particularly skilled in these areas can have big advantages in the job market. Software engineers, information architects, and new-age media professionals can often command $50,000 to $100,000 salaries with a bachelor's degree. Those with particular talent don't even need degrees. Witness Bill Gates and Mark Zuckerberg. Some don't even have to graduate high school. As discussed in Chapter 7, a growing number of software companies are luring particularly gifted undergraduates—and in some cases even high school students—out of high schools and colleges with six-figure offers.

Beyond the monetary rewards, people with deep IT skills have the potential of playing increasingly central roles in all types of industries and job functions. Some will become architects of the rapidly expanding information age. Others will develop the hardware, software, and services that will increasingly define our careers and our lives. Still others will help companies to use IT to achieve competitive advantage in their own industries. Millions of others will leverage their skills into creating their own companies.

> People with deep IT skills have the potential of playing increasingly central roles in all types of industries and job functions.

Statistics is one of my own additions to this list. Although this is generally included in the core foundational skill of mathematics, statistical skills, like IT skills, are becoming so critical in day-to-day business (not to speak of in your personal life) as to require special focus.

But although everyone must have a working knowledge of basic statistics, deep statistical analysis skills will become particularly critical in the era of Big Data. This data will allow you to track and measure virtually anything. The real value comes from the ability to understand what the data is telling you and what it means for your job and your business. These deep statistical skills are becoming so important that graduates capable of analyzing and especially of identifying business opportunities from Big Data are, as discussed in Chapter 2, already becoming some of the most sought after and highly paid professionals.

Entrepreneurship is my other addition and already one of the biggest, most important trends in business, accounting for more than 14 million people (nine percent of the total U.S. workforce). Millions of people, whether they are looking to recover from a layoff, want to become their own boss, or have a burning desire to create the next billion-dollar company, are starting their companies. Sometimes this is by choice; often, especially during the recession, by necessity. While 25 to 30 percent of U.S. workers currently work as freelancers or contingent workers, an Intuit Corporation study estimates that this figure will exceed 40 percent by 2020.[11]

The need for entrepreneurial skills is not limited to those who have their own businesses. Companies are increasingly looking for internal entrepreneurs. They can range from those who are not only capable but also anxious to run their own projects, their own branches, or to establish and run an in-house skunkworks (an in-house, experimental, independent research organization) to pioneer the company's next billion-dollar business.

Author and New York Times columnist Thomas Freidman goes further. As he explains in his March 2013 column, Need a Job? Invent It, while your parents were able to "find" jobs, you increasingly have to "invent" your own.[12] This may mean going out on your own if you can't find a position in an established company. It also means inventing a position within another company. Having done just this in the two companies for which I worked (before starting my own company), I completely agree.

> While your parents were able to "find" jobs, you increasingly have to "invent" your own.

If you get a job in a company, you will inevitably find untapped opportunities: projects that were begun but not completed; or unexplored market opportunities—whether unidentified or identified. If you can demonstrate how your company can benefit from these—and that you are the person that can make it happen—you may get a chance to invent your own job around your own interests and your own skills. Once you have gained experience and credibility within your organization, you may be able to go further: selling your idea to launch a new line of business or operation (again, around your own interests and skills). If you can sell the idea within your company, then presto—you're an in-house entrepreneur. If not, you may choose to shop the idea (and of course yourself) to another company or start you own company around the idea.

Whatever the type of business, entrepreneurship requires skills: everything from understanding how to test ideas, raise money, market your product or service, manage your finances, build and promote your company's brand, and dozens of others. These skills, and some of the many ways of learning them, are discussed in Chapter 9.

High-Value Skills on Which to Build Your Own Brand

Four P21's skills, which are combined into two categories, are somewhat different. While they will be required for success in virtually all high-value careers, they also promise to provide some of the greatest opportunities for differentiation among those high-skill workers. Those with these skills are best positioned to be the winners, not to speak of the stars, of the Creative Economy. These skills are:

- Creativity and innovation and
- Critical thinking and complex problem solving

Although one would be hard-pressed to build a specific career around these skills (as you can with communication and IT skills), they are arguably even more important in determining your ultimate success in the new economy. Let's look at each category.

Creativity and innovation are becoming much more than "nice-to-have" skills. They are rapidly becoming hallmarks of success in a 21st-century economy. These include the ability to look at old things in new ways, to recognize ideas or possibilities that others don't, and to identify new ways of connecting dots that others see only as random or unrelated points.

> Creativity and innovation are becoming much more than "nice-to-have" skills. They are rapidly becoming hallmarks of success in a 21st-century economy.

Creativity, such as in the form of art, may certainly be spontaneous and freeform. However, some of the most valuable forms of creativity—those that provide workable solutions to pressing problems or that identify innovative new business opportunities—seldom come as flashes from out of the blue. They entail much more than spouting off dozens of new top-of-the-head ideas. Creativity is often, as Einstein said of genius, more like "one percent inspiration and ninety-nine percent perspiration." And, as Steve Jobs showed us by integrating right-brain artistic sensibilities into the left-brain world of computer and software development, some of the most creative solutions are likely to combine knowledge, principles, and methodologies across very different disciplines.

While creativity typically entails a lot of hard work, innovation requires even more. Innovation, which is often based on creative ideas, requires the actual implementation of these ideas. This may entail the overcoming of all types of real-world obstacles and organizational resistance. It can require persuading people to embrace something new and increasingly, in today's IT-based Internet era, disciplined system and software design. Not all innovations, however, require that you invent new products or create original works of art. Most of today's innovations come from combining previously developed innovations in new ways (as by combining telephones and computers into smartphones) or building new layers atop an existing offering (such as paint on a canvas). Some of the highest-value innovations don't require the creation of products at all. Companies including Federal Express and Amazon.com redefined entire industries by reconceiving established processes and creating new business models.

Creativity and innovation both often entail knowledge of—and the ability to create linkages among—multiple domains and the ability to assess issues based on methodologies from different disciplines. It also appears that people can be taught to apply creative thinking to intractable business problems.[13]

A growing number of schools, such as Stanford's Institute of Design, MIT's Media Lab, and the University of Toronto's Rotman School of Management, *already* offer programs intended to do just this. These so-called D-schools teach methodologies for looking at problems from new and different perspectives and for using different types of processes to come up with more creative solutions. A growing number of large, traditionally innovative companies, such as Procter & Gamble, Google, Nike, and Fidelity, are putting considerable stock in such efforts, hiring people from such programs, putting their own employees through them, and launching their own in-house design-thinking courses.

The opportunities for success of particularly creative and innovative people are patently obvious. Artists, musicians, and performers, often viewed as the embodiment of creativity, have the potential (although not necessarily the likelihood) of gaining huge rewards—not just in terms of money but also in fame and the ability to define and control their own careers.

Creativity and innovation, as discussed, however, go far beyond the arts. Think of Albert Einstein, Thomas Edison, Fred Smith (the founder of Federal Express), or Howard Schultz (Starbucks' founder). These people had the creativity to identify business opportunities that nobody had previously dreamed of (not to speak of the perseverance required to succeed), and built iconic companies in the process. And then, of course, there's Steve Jobs.

Not everybody has the creativity to create a new artistic movement or to identify a business opportunity that will change the world, or even redefine the culture of drinking coffee. Nor does creativity necessarily require huge, unprecedented leaps of imagination. Incremental innovation—the ability to identify small, useful changes to an existing idea, product, or process—can also create incredible value. It can also be incredibly rewarding.

It will also be an increasingly important requirement for success in the 21st-centrury economy. In fact, Richard Florida argues in his book, *The Rise of the Creative Class Revisited*, that creativity is becoming the defining characteristic of an entire class of professionals whose services will be in greatest demand and will command the largest wage premiums.[14]

Critical thinking and problem solving skills entail the ability to reason and make sound judgments within a broad, systems framework. In some sense, these are a superset of analytical skills. But while analytical skills used to be the foundation of many of the middle-income, white collar jobs of the past, many of these jobs can be done more efficiently, and sometimes even better, by lower-priced offshore professionals or increasingly by software.

Critical thinking and problem solving go much further. They require the ability to:

- Conceptualize a problem;
- Pull together and systematically examine a broad range of seemingly random data;
- Filter out the irrelevant or misleading;
- Use a combination of structured and unstructured inquiry to identify underlying patterns;

- Identify and systematically evaluate multiple hypotheses with an open mind; and to
- Apply these patterns to different situations and problems.

One of the most critical and valuable components is the ability to identify and ask the right questions—questions that other people do not see; questions that will prompt you and others to think about a familiar situation in different ways; questions that will lead to solutions. It isn't surprising that a number of companies view the ability to ask perceptive questions as being even more important than actually solving a problem. They increasingly recognize, as did Einstein, that "the formulation of a problem is often more essential than its solution."

> A number of companies view the ability to ask perceptive questions as being even more important than actually solving a problem.

These skills can be applied to and provide value in any discipline, regardless of how specialized or how broad. But, in this age of hyperspecialization, generalists with these skills can provide particular value by helping teams reimagine problems by looking at them in a new light and by helping to draw upon other domains for innovative solutions. In fact, some of the most effective teams are those that combine generalists with specialists from different fields.

Universal Personality Traits You Will Need

Whether you call them personality traits, attributes, attitudes, life skills, or virtually anything else , they may be the most important of all the skills discussed in this chapter. These traits, particularly when applied in conjunction with combinations of the previously mentioned skills, or with core subjects or disciplines, often spell the difference between success and failure. You must have both the skills to conceive value and the traits to actually deliver this value if you hope to succeed in this new world. P21 identifies these attributes or traits as:

- Initiative and self-direction; and
- Flexibility and adaptability.

I would add a few others:

- Insatiable curiosity and a passion for learning;
- Self-restraint, or the patience to wait for deferred gratification; and
- Entrepreneurship.

Let's look at each in turn.

Initiative and self-direction go by many names, including motivation, focus, self-discipline, persistence, and grit. They entail the ability to set ambitious, yet (ideally) achievable long-term goals, to develop plans, and to prioritize your actions for achieving these goals—and to do all this independently, without having been told to do so, and without the need for oversight or coaxing. It requires that you manage your own efforts by allocating time and resources among multiple priorities, meeting (or ideally beating) deadlines, and of course, surpassing everybody's (possibly even your own, much higher) expectations.

Taking initiative also means taking risks. Any time you stretch yourself beyond what you know, beyond your comfort zone, or beyond what you had previously imagined, you are taking a risk. Although you will certainly want to mitigate these risks (such as by applying to a safety school while planning for admission into Harvard), the taking of calculated risks is the only way of stretching yourself. Yes, you may fail. But as long as you have a plan for limiting or protecting yourself from disastrous consequences, failure is one of the best learning experiences. And, as long as you have the later-discussed flexibility and adaptability to learn from and recover from failure, you can often turn failure into an even greater success. Think, for example, of Silicon Valley, where failure in a previous attempt to launch a business is not just a badge of honor, it is also often an advantage in attempting to get funding for your next start-up. As leading-edge design firm IDEO tells its employees: "fail early and fail often." Failing early, as they claim, allows you to succeed sooner.

Initiative is certainly one of the primary requirements for successfully building your own business, not to speak of for building your own career. It is also becoming increasingly important in working for others.

As Thomas Friedman explained in his October 22, 2012 New York Times op-ed piece The New Untouchables, gone are the days when you could advance in an organization by being a good and loyal soldier—by doing what you are told and staying out of trouble.[15] As he explains, the people who received pink slips during the recent recession were "the average practitioners"—those people who perform routine tasks and those that wait for work to be handed to them. Friedman calls those people who are too valuable to layoff "the new untouchables": those with "the ability to imagine new services, new opportunities, and new ways to recruit work." These people have the "imagination….to invent smarter ways to do old jobs, energy-saving ways to provide new services, new ways to attract old customers, or new ways to combine existing technologies."

> Gone are the days when you could advance in an organization by being a good and loyal soldier—by doing what you are told and staying out of trouble.

Meanwhile, even if these new untouchables do get laid off (or more likely, if they voluntarily leave an unfulfilling or frustrating job), they are best positioned to get another job or to go out on their own or start a new company to realize their visions. This form of initiative ties directly into the "self-direction" part of the personality trait equation.

Self-direction is at least as important as initiative. It entails the ability to recognize the need for and areas in which you must extend your current skills and knowledge or develop new or complementary skills. And then, just as importantly, to take the initiative in ensuring that you develop them. It is also one of the most important components of a commitment to lifelong learning—one of the best forms of insurance you can have for preventing your own obsolescence.

Flexibility and adaptability: Adaptability, as defined by P21, entails the ability to work in a climate of ambiguity and changing priorities and to adapt to different roles and responsibilities and changes in schedule or context. The corollary skill of flexibility entails the ability to accept and effectively respond to feedback (positive and negative) and the willingness to balance diverse views. Not only are these skills among the most important in preparing for a career, they may, in an era where the only certainty is uncertainty, well be the most important.

> In an era where the only certainty is uncertainty, flexibility and adaptability may well be the most important personality traits.

After all, while initiative and persistence are certainly among the most critical skills required for success in your career and your life, they can also be among the most dangerous. There is certainly great merit in the old maxim, "if at first you don't succeed, try, try again." But there is also wisdom in Albert Einstein's definition of insanity: "doing the same thing over and over again and expecting different results." Trying again does not mean doing the same thing over and over. It means, or at least it should mean, a continual process of adaptation: examining the source and reasons for a particular result, evaluating alternative approaches to solving the problem, and adjusting and readjusting your approach until either you succeed or you are forced to change your goal.

This adaptability is critical not only in broad objectives, such as in finding the job of your dreams or starting your own job. It is required in every aspect of your career (not to speak of your life). As Reid Hoffman and Ben Casnocha explain in their book, *The Startup of You*, your career must be in continuous "beta" (a software prerelease phase in which developers identify defects, and collect feedback and recommendations from prospective customers before developing the final version).[16] You must continually reassess where you are going and how best to get there and engage in continuous experimentation. This adaptability must be incorporated directly in your career planning process, as well as in your job and in your life. After all, given the pace of change in today's market, you can't let your career planning get too far ahead of reality. As the book's authors explain, it's probably best to think two career steps in advance, not ten.

Let's now look at my additions to P21's list.

Insatiable curiosity and a passion for learning is a trait that, while always desirable and helpful, is becoming indispensable. The primary reasons: the pace of change has become so fast and unpredictable, and the body of human knowledge has become so large and specialized, that anyone who does not have this passion is destined to fall behind. Changes, no matter how sudden and dramatic, can often be discerned from (or at least suggested by) earlier clues. This can be anything from a war to the failure of a company, or the automation or outsourcing of a particular job. Although not all changes are telegraphed, those who understand what to look for and who continually look for clues have a better chance of anticipating, hedging, and preparing for them. Better yet, those who anticipate and position themselves ahead of emergent trends have the potential of getting in on the ground floor of new industries or companies.

> The pace of change has become so fast and unpredictable, and the body of human knowledge has become so large and specialized, that anyone who does not have insatiable curiosity and a passion for learning is destined to fall behind.

Just as importantly, the state of human knowledge is expanding exponentially. Every field, regardless of how specialized or obscure, has hundreds, if not thousands of specialists whose lives are devoted to extending the boundaries of their fields. Some fields such as medical genetics are just emerging. Even mature fields such as financial trading and materials science are being continually revolutionized (such as by high-frequency trading and nanotechnology, respectively). You can't escape progress. Any professional that does not keep up is destined to watch as they and their skills become obsolete. While it used to be that corporations could usually find a role for those who couldn't or wouldn't keep up, few now have the luxury of retaining dead wood.

Self-restraint, or the patience to wait for deferred gratification: Self-restraint can be a foreign concept in a society obsessed with instant gratification and living for the moment. It can also be a critical foundation in any effort to build a career, start a business, or even just succeed in a job.

A plan is, of course, the foundation for building a career plan. It entails determining what you want to accomplish sometime in the future, identifying the steps that are required to achieve your objective, and then taking those the steps (leavened with, of course, a big dose of flexibility and adaptability) required to achieve this goal.

The same is true of starting a business. Before you leave an established job (especially if you depend on that job to pay your rent) and commit your and your family's savings to a new business idea, it's probably a good idea to have a plan. You should at least have a vision for your business, have initial financing lined up, and have a pretty good idea as to your target market and means of reaching that market. Ideally, you may even have a prototype for a planned product and have initiated conversations with potential customers or investors. All plans, of course, must be subject to change, and you must have the flexibility and adaptability to change or even abandon your plan. But just as failure is a critical learning experience, so too is planning and the self-restraint it imposes upon you.

Just how important is this self-restraint? Two Yale professors just wrote a 2014 book, *The Triple Package: How Three Unlikely Traits Explain the Rise and Fall of Cultural Groups in America*, that attempted to determine why some minority U.S. immigrant and cultural groups (Jews, Mormons, Chinese, Indians, Iranians, and others) consistently outperform national norms.[17] They boil their explanation down to a combination of three traits:

1. Insecurity, which results in a drive to continually prove oneself;
2. A superiority complex, or a belief in some form of their own exceptionality (and therefore abilities); and
3. Impulse control, which they believe may be the single most important.

Although the authors acknowledge that each of these is contrary to many contemporary American attitudes and sensibilities, they contend that this combination drives success not just of minorities, but any individual from any background.

Learning and Applying 21st-Century Skills

Although P21 has taken the most comprehensive approach for defining the skills required to succeed in the 21st century, and for identifying the type of learning environments and processes by which they can be learned, it is by no means the only effort to identifying the skills required for success.

Books from authors including Daniel Pink[18] and Thomas Friedman[19] and Harvard Graduate School of Education professors Howard Gardner[20] and Tony Wagner[21], for example, propose their own lists. Most such examples and lists, however, implicitly incorporate many of P21's themes. Education provocateur and reformer Tony Wagner, for example, effectively foreshadowed P21's work in his still provocative 2008 book, *The Global Achievement Gap*.[22] This book highlighted seven types of skills:

1. Critical thinking and problem solving;
2. Collaboration and the ability to lead by influence;
3. Agility and adaptability;
4. Initiative and entrepreneurialism;
5. Effective oral and written communication;
6. Assessing and analyzing information; and
7. Curiosity and imagination.

Employers tend to agree with such requirements for success. According to a 2013 Hart Research survey, the six most important capabilities employers are looking for in graduates are: critical thinking and analytical reasoning; the ability to analyze and solve complex problems; oral and written communication; the ability to locate, organize, and evaluate information from multiple sources; and the ability to innovate and be creative.[23]

Dilbert cartoon creator Scott Adams, in his 2014 career guidance book *How to Fail and Everything and Still Win Big*, suggests a much more pragmatic list of everyday skills: public speaking, psychology, business writing, accounting, basic design, conversation, overcoming shyness, second language, golf, grammar, persuasion, hobby-level technology, and voice technique.[24]

But whatever the list, you still have to ensure that you not only learn but also continually apply, refine, and enhance these skills. After all, as Wagner explains in his most recent book, *Creating Innovators: The Making of Young People Who Will Change the World*, knowledge is now a commodity, available over the Internet.[25] "The world," he claims, "no longer cares how much you know; the world cares about what you can do with what you know." "To succeed in the 21st-century economy, students must learn to analyze and solve problems, collaborate, persevere, take calculated risks, and learn from failure."

> The world no longer cares how much you know; the world cares about what you can do with what you know." "To succeed in the 21st-century economy, students must learn to analyze and solve problems, collaborate, persevere, take calculated risks, and learn from failure."

But exactly how do you apply these skills to developing your career?

It's true that a small percentage of people—those with truly exceptional skills in a particular area, such as analytical skills and/or with exceptional understanding of particularly important areas—will continue to be sought after, retained, and rewarded for their analytical skills alone. The vast majority of us, however, need to combine multiple skills. You must, for example, have:

- The imagination to identify new opportunities;
- The skills to build compelling business cases around them;
- The interpersonal and communication skills required to sell these ideas;
- The determination to achieve your goals, regardless of the obstacles you face; and
- The adaptability to continually reassess progress, search out and incorporate new evidence into your evaluations, and continually tune and adapt your goals and your approaches to achieving them.

But if these traits and skills are so important, why aren't schools organized to teach them? Why haven't they created academic curricula, or even formal courses around them? Although P21 and the Common Core Initiative hope they will do exactly this, the current opportunities for learning most of these skills are, at best, scattered.

You can certainly take courses in which some of these skills are taught, such as communications or information technology. And plenty of classes and books claim to teach productivity, culture sensitivity, and creativity. Creativity and innovation, as discussed above, are becoming some of the most sought-after and in-demand disciplines in schools such as the Stanford D-School and the MIT Media Lab. Then of course, there are the proliferation of courses and programs in entrepreneurship, such as those identified in Chapter 9.

But what school, book, or seminar can teach you initiative or accountability? Or can they be taught at all? Perhaps some skills and some personality traits can only be learned by experience and by trial and error.

Until the educational system acknowledges the importance of such skills and develops an agreed upon process for helping you learn them, you will have to take responsibility for learning them yourself. Luckily, however, life is filled with opportunities for developing and practicing these and all types of other skills. However, you have to search out and take advantage of these opportunities—and make sure that you learn the appropriate lessons from them. Plus, learning these skills yourself provides you with a number of advantages. First, you can do so by focusing on opportunities in which you have an interest and are motivated to explore, rather than having someone assign them to you. Second, you can learn these lessons in whatever way is best suited to your own learning style, rather than the way someone decides they should be taught.

> Until the educational system acknowledges the importance of such skills and develops an agreed upon process for helping you learn them, you will have to take responsibility for learning them yourself.

Sure this will take work and may result in many mistakes along the way. That, however, is probably all for the best since the very process will help you learn other skills, such as initiative, self-direction, accountability, and flexibility. Taking responsibility for this part of your education will also give you good practice for many of the other things you will have to do in building and managing your career. For example, they will be good practice for what you will have to do to identify and create your own brand, for building and managing your own network, and for designing and managing your own education.

Lifetime Skills Development

Developing these skills, graduating from school, and getting a job are only the first steps in building your career. Keeping the job—not to speak of succeeding in it and using it as a springboard to building a successful lifelong career (much less building two or more different careers)—requires far more than in the past.

As discussed throughout this chapter, the skills required to get and succeed in a job in today's concept-driven creative economy are very different from those required for jobs in the information-based knowledge-based economy. Just as important, the jobs in this new economy will change at a much faster rate than had been the case in previous economies.

Rapid change is uncomfortable. It presents you with a critical choice: you can either:

- Live by the skills you developed in school, and risk career stagnation and possible obsolescence; or
- Anticipate how jobs and skill requirements will change and develop these new skills in advance, thereby positioning yourself for promotions and, especially, for the jobs of the future—including those in entirely new disciplines and industries.

This later course will require lifetime education. This education can be formal or informal, depending on the skills you wish to enhance or develop, the learning style that is most effective for you, whether or not you need some form of certificate to demonstrate your skills, and your own schedule and budget. It may come simply from reading, participating in clubs or groups, or from pursuing a hobby. More likely, it will include at least some more formal components. It can entail the taking of a few additional college or graduate classes, completion of a MOOC course or program or even a new degree. Or perhaps your employer will offer and pay for courses.

Whichever approach you choose those who hope to grow, or at least to remain fresh in their careers, have no alternative. They must continue their education. And now, with the proliferation of free information across the Internet and the availability of free MOOC-based college-level courses that can be completed at any time and from any location, you also have no excuse for not doing so.

CHAPTER 4

Twenty Steps to Your Dream Career

You cannot escape the responsibility of tomorrow by evading it today.
—Abraham Lincoln

Key Points

- Career planning can be divided into three broad stages: Identifying a career that's right for you; developing the skills you need; and getting and capitalizing on your first job.
- Among the key steps, you must:
  - o Identify your driving passion, assess and determine how to apply your skills to your passion.
  - o Identify a few ways of using your unique passions/skill combinations to real-world needs.
  - o Prepare for a complementary "safety career" just in case your dream career doesn't work out or doesn't last.
  - o Select and fully utilize your first job as an indispensable foundation for a long-term career.

Getting your first career-track job out of school is tough and it is not likely to get much easier for at least the next several years. And if getting an initial job is tough, the requirements for keeping these jobs—not to speak of steadily advancing your career or changing your career path along the way—are tougher yet.

Tough, but certainly not impossible. But you need a plan. To paraphrase Lewis Carroll, "If you don't know where you're going, any road will take you there."

This chapter identifies a three-stage (20-step) approach that you can take to identify the types of jobs that are best suited to you, the skills these jobs will require and how you can develop them, what to look for in your first job, and, most importantly, how to design and control the career of your dreams. And just to be safe, it offers some suggestions on how to prepare for the possibility that your dream doesn't quite work out as you planned.

Does this sound too good to be true? Well, it will take work, not to speak of considerable self-reflection, research, and preparation. But whoever said that building a dream career and maintaining control of your life would be easy?

Ready? Let's dig in.

Creating Your Career Plan

Why is it that some college graduates get to choose among multiple attractive job offers and others struggle to get a job at Starbucks or Wal-Mart? There are many reasons: everything from the school you attended to your major, your grades, your internships, and—as much as we all hate to admit it—who you and your parents know. Then, of course, there's luck. But you can turn all of these criteria—including luck—to your advantage. This, however, requires planning.

You're probably asking yourself, how can I make a plan when the world is changing so rapidly and in so many unforeseen ways that even experts often fail to anticipate fundamental changes? How can I figure out what type of work will energize me when I've never had a chance to experience it? Why plan for or even bother to fantasize about my dream job when my desires may change in 5 or 10 years, or even five or ten days?

The answer: It doesn't make sense if you just fantasize. As Thomas Edison roughly said, vision without execution is hallucination. You have to objectively assess your dream to understand what you need to do to attain it.

Sure, no plan guarantees success. There is, however, one guarantee: If you follow a logical set of steps in choosing your career and then work to develop the skills you will need for it, you will have a big advantage not only in getting a good career-track job out of school but also in building the foundation for a rewarding, high-value career doing what you love. Just as importantly, the skills and habits you use in developing and executing on this plan will pay big dividends throughout your entire career, regardless of how many twists, turns, and detours that career may take.

It all comes down to creating a plan, doggedly working that plan and continually adapting it on the basis of experience and new evidence.

Three Stages to Building the Career of Your Dreams

Although every individual, job, and career is different, there are common steps you can take to maximize your chances for getting the job you want. At a high level, these steps are divided into three primary stages, each of which has a number of steps. While subsequent chapters will explain and help you go through these steps, let's take a high-level look at each of these steps, each of which will be discussed in detail in Chapters 5 through 10.

Stage One: Identifying a Career That's Right for You

1. **Identify your passions and your interests:** Which are the classes and activities you enjoy the most? In which areas are you most anxious to learn more, what new experiences would you like to have? Don't worry about not having a single driving passion. Dig into and learn as much as you can about the areas in which you have interest. Passions, after all, often come from experience and success in a particular area. And speaking of experiences, even if you already have a passion, create a list of new things you want to experience—and set a schedule for experiencing them.
2. **Identify and objectively assess your primary skills:** What do you see as your greatest skills? What do objective people (teachers, managers, coaches, and so forth) see as your skills? What do tests or assessments show? In which courses and activities do you do well?
3. **Apply your skills to your passions and interests:** Identify many ways (not just one) of applying each of your skills to these passions and interests. Don't worry, at least initially, whether these matches are likely to lead to jobs or careers. That will come soon enough.

In the meantime, applying your skills to your passions will provide an incentive to further develop these skills, lead to new areas of interest, help develop confidence in your abilities, and will ideally lead to accomplishments that will bolster your resume.

4. **Prioritize and target a few of these combinations:** Identify those in which you have the greatest interest and pursue them with passion. Learn as much as you can about them, practice them, develop school projects around them, join or create clubs and interest groups, explore opportunities for part-time or summer jobs or internships. If none of these opportunities exist, create them yourself. But while you're doing this, continue to search for new interests and ways to apply your skills to them.

5. **Begin to define your brand:** Once you identify your skills, interests, and passions, you can begin to define your own unique "brand"—an identity that will initially guide your education and ultimately lead to the differentiation you will need to demonstrate the unique value you can bring to employers and clients. While this brand will evolve throughout your education and your career, the sooner you begin to define it, the sooner you will be able to begin shaping your education, your activities, and your self-image around your planned career.

6. **Validate career opportunities:** Search the wide range of government and private sector sources to determine current and anticipated job availability in these fields, the skills and credentials you need both to get into and succeed in that field, how these jobs pay and so forth. Use this information to narrow your focus to two or three fields—ideally synergistic fields that when combined can give you a big advantage over those with just one of these skill sets. For example, engineering combined with strong oral communication skills can lead to a career in technical sales. Deep skills in computers and statistics can be combined into one of the most promising segments of the next decade—Big Data analytics.

7. **Create and cultivate a network of advisors and mentors:** Such people can be instrumental in helping you identify and assess education and career opportunities around your skill, interest, and passion combinations. They can include teachers, managers, guidance/career counselors, your and your friends' parents, people you meet

on career and interest-based social networks, college professors, and people you meet that work in these and related fields.

8. **Search for breaking waves:** It is possible to build a rewarding career in virtually any field. However, it is typically much easier to break into a field or an industry that is growing rapidly, searching for people and especially one that is young, but on the cusp of big growth. Such a field is easier to enter, and more likely to offer a range of long-term growth and advancement opportunities than a field that is mature or in decline. Once you prove your value in your first job in a high-growth area, it is also typically easier to get promoted, transfer into another department within your company, move to another company, or better yet, invent a position around your unique skills and interests, rather than being fit into a preexisting slot.

9. **Plan for contingencies:** Select and focus your energies on two or three synergistic career opportunities. Possessing relatively deep skills in two or more complementary fields can yield big advantages over deep skills in a single specialty. At one level, it allows you to hedge your bets by targeting jobs in a backup Safety Career, just in case you can't get or don't succeed in your dream job or if that job doesn't meet your expectations. It can also give you a big advantage over candidates with demonstrated skills in only one field. Examples can include applying skills in psychology and acting to public speaking or sales, or legal skills to healthcare.

Stage Two: Developing the Skills You Will Need

10. Create a skills development plan: What skills, education, and credentials will you need to prepare for jobs in each of these fields? Which can you develop independently or via part-time jobs or online courses? Which require formal education, an apprenticeship? What internships and part-time jobs can you target to enhance your skills, demonstrate your commitment and experience, and, possibly, to line up a full-time job before you graduate?

11. **Create an education plan:** Virtually all high-skill jobs require education, and possibly some form of certification beyond high school. Some have formal or informal educational requirements such as a

two- or four-year degree or graduate school. Others may accept less formal qualifications, such as work experience, online or independent study, or the completion of projects that demonstrate your skills. You must determine what is required for your chosen fields and which type of learning (e.g., lecture, seminar, reading, independent study, hands-on work, and so forth) is best suited to your learning style. Also, which is in your budget.

12. **Take charge of your own education:** Once you identify the skills you must develop and the credentials you will require, you must take responsibility for developing them. You must decide which school is best suited to your specific learning and occupational goals and which can offer the most help in lining up internships, interviews, and introductions to potential employers. You must also determine how to best mesh two or more of your skills (and ideally your interests and passions) into an educational program, as via special projects, major and minor declarations, dual majors, or graduate school. If the school doesn't offer the combination you need, how can you create your own program? You must build relationships with key professors; identify the extracurricular and social activities and organizations you can join; and identify and line up internships, externships, or part-time jobs that will help you learn about and gain experience in fields in which you may be interested.

13. **Complement a degree with a certification:** When an employer hires someone with a degree, it is often at least as much for that person's potential than for the value they can deliver today. But, as I previously discussed, employers are increasingly looking for people who can deliver value today, as well as grow into new jobs in the future. For example, if you have a degree in graphics design, you might consider attending boot camp or enrolling in an online program that grants a certificate in desktop publishing. Similarly, if you have a degree in engineering or economics, a business boot camp can give you an advantage over other candidates without business experience. But while certificates may help, real-world experience (as through a previous job or internship) is even better, especially if your accomplishments can be demonstrated by examples of your work, by references, or by awards or recognitions.

14. **Learn critical life skills:** Your education and initial work experience, whatever forms they may take, should help you do more than just learn the type of skills you will need to get and succeed in your first job. They should also help you develop the type of communication, teamwork, and leadership skills that you will need in any job (not to speak of in your personal life). It should form a foundation for the social and professional networks that you will need as well as the perseverance and adaptability that will be instrumental in achieving any of your long-term goals. It should give you plenty of chances to fail, so you can learn to recover and learn from your experiences. Most importantly, it should help you not only to "learn" but also to "learn how to learn" and especially to "love to learn." After all, in an era of rapid and continual change, you will have to continually refresh your skills, develop new ones, and understand how to anticipate and prepare for the unexpected.

Stage Three: Getting and Capitalizing on Your First Job

15. Identify your target career options: Which types of jobs are best suited to your career objectives? Which industry and company is, as mentioned in Step 8, likely to experience the most growth and create the best immediate job and long-term career opportunities? What type of organization is best suited to your needs and your work style? Should you look for a large company or a small one, an established company or a start-up—or should you start your own business?

16. **Selecting the right first job:** Your first job should ideally be one of the most important in your entire career. Be sure that you know exactly what you should look for in this job and how to prioritize your objectives. Understand what you should learn from this job, the opportunities it will create (both within and outside the organization), the opportunities for finding and cultivating mentors and sponsors, and how the industry and the company will mesh with your self-image and your lifestyle. And oh, by the way, you also want to confirm that the salary and the benefits are at least comparable to those of similar jobs in other organizations.

17. **Set and achieve your own goals:** These goals should not only meet but also far surpass those that your employer has for you. Your first responsibility must be to do every job you are asked to do, and do it better than anticipated. Just as importantly, you should continually search out additional opportunities to learn and to identify ways that you can deliver additional types of value. This can entail volunteering to participate in interdepartment projects, identifying and volunteering for new tasks that will bring value to your organization, and, ideally, increasing and improving the visibility and image of your manager and your department throughout the organization.

18. **Expand your network:** Who in your current network can best advise you and refer you to others who may be able to help focus or advance your search? How can you extend these networks in a way that will help you zero in on the best opportunities and introduce you to other people who can help? How can you find not only the people who are looking to hire but also those who can create a position specifically for "just the right person?" And, even after you get a job, how can you keep these people involved in your career network?

19. **Build relationships:** This is included in, but goes far beyond building a network. This is about increasing the depth, rather than just the breadth of your relationships. While this may include forming close friendships, it is more about forming business relationships based on mutual respect and trust. Build relationships with peers, managers, and others (ideally a couple of levels up in the organization) who know and trust your work, your standards, and your character. Find people who will not only advise you and serve as references but also proactively advocate for you within the organization, bring you into their own professional networks, and, ideally, bring you along with them as their own careers advance.

20. **Expand your professional presence beyond your own company:** Think about memberships and active volunteering in professional and trade organizations, charitable and community groups, alumni organizations, and other groups such as world affairs or current affairs groups that draw other professionals. You will not only expand your network but also develop skills that you will need throughout your career and your life.

Applying the 20-Step Model

Dream Careers and Safety Careers may be a nice theory, but what if you don't have a passion? What if you don't know what your real strengths are or how they can be applied to your dream career? How do you get all the way from a vague vision of what you would like to do to a rational career plan and a job offer? That's where the 20-Step Program fits in.

The good news is that the younger you are the easier and less expensive it is to engage in this process. It's much better to identify and plan for options now than after you have gone through college, have a mortgage, and a family to support.

And you're never too young to begin this process. In fact, looking back with 20:20 hindsight, I should have begun recognizing clues as to my skills, interests, and passions back in fifth grade, when I wrote my first report (on the country of Chile). If I had recognized my deep interest in and abilities to research and write back then, or even in middle, high school, or college (rather than in my mid-20s), I could have focused and developed my skills much more effectively and established a much more solid career foundation.

This is certainly not to say that I have any complaints about my career. As it turns out, I did manage to establish myself as a "high-value, differentiated brand" and build an incredibly exciting and fulfilling career by applying my skills to one of my passions. (I am pursuing other passions in subsequent careers—including the writing of this book.) But again from hindsight, I may have saved myself considerable angst if I had recognized or thought about nurturing my skills back then!

But whenever you begin the process, understand that it will take work, soul-searching, and perseverance. The sooner you accept these responsibilities and begin to seriously examine yourself and your options, the greater your chance of ensuring that you will be the master, rather than the victim of your own career.

> This will take work, soul-searching, and perseverance. The sooner you accept these responsibilities, the greater your chance of ensuring that you will be the master, rather than the victim of your own career.

The remainder of the book will take you through each of these 20 steps in more depth:

- Chapter 5 focuses on Steps 1 and 2, identifying your passions, interests, and skills;
- Chapter 6 broadly addresses Steps 3 through 9, examining ways of aligning career choices around this combination of passions, interests, and skills, identifying the skill gaps that you must address to position yourself to address your career objectives, and by explaining ways in which you can "future-proof" your career by building contingency planning into your career plan;
- Chapters 7 to 9 examine the broad range of options for addressing Steps 10 through 14; the different postsecondary education options for developing the skills and obtaining the credentials you will require not just to get your first job but to succeed in that job and to give you the flexibility to extend or change your career plan in the future;
- Chapter 10 focuses on the six remaining steps; how not only to get your first job out of school but also to succeed in that job while simultaneously positioning yourself for subsequent jobs and careers.

A couple of caveats before you dig into these chapters. Although I hope that identifying these points as steps will help you prioritize the tasks you must undertake to develop a plan, it is somewhat artificial. First, tasks such as assessing your passions and your interests, creating education and job search plans, and developing your brand and network can't be relegated to discrete "steps." They and a number of other steps must be applied throughout the entire process, all the way up to the time you eventually retire from your last career. Second, while some steps, such as identifying your passion and developing your brand, require detailed attention, others, like expanding your presence beyond your own company, barely require additional mention. Meanwhile, some requirements, such as choosing a job you will enjoy and assessing a company's atmosphere and culture before you take a job, are important, but don't really constitute formal steps.

I have, therefore, organized the following chapters as narratives that highlight what has to be done in each of these steps (and what has to be done as part of or in addition to these steps), but that do not precisely follow the steps. This being said, I have generally noted which parts of the narrative refer to which steps of the process.

CHAPTER 5

Discovering Your Passions, Your Skills, and Yourself

Steps 1 and 2

The two most important days in your life are the day you are born and the day you find out why.

—Mark Twain

Key Points

- Building your dream career requires continual introspection, focus, and coordination with reality.
- Passion is critical, not just for living your dream but also for providing the motivation required to master a field.
- Passion accounts for little unless you have the skills and the persistence required for mastery.
- Search continually for new experiences from which new interests and passions may arise.
- Discovering your passion, interest, and skills provides a perfect opportunity to begin building your professional network.
- Don't know your passions, interests, or skills? Seek out the tests and books that can help you discover them.

To paraphrase Confucius, every journey starts with the first step. Sometimes, this first step is the most difficult. So get the hard part behind you and begin the journey. This chapter will guide you through the first two steps of designing and building a rewarding career. After a brief overview of different ways of thinking about your career, it suggests ways in which you can begin identifying the types of passions around which you can build a career that you will love. Just as importantly, it discusses the importance of continually expanding your interests as a means of finding new passions and of identifying complementary career opportunities. It then examines the critical link between passions, interests, and skills and how a viable career plan requires the melding of all three.

This requires an inventory and objective analysis of your skills and limitations, and a plan to proactively develop your skills (especially by applying them to your passions) and address or compensate for your weaknesses.

Then, in case you are finding it difficult to identify, assess, and prioritize your passions, interests, and skills, the last section provides a partial list of some of the many resources that can help you through the process.

What Do You Want to Be?

You can take many different approaches to identifying potential career directions while you are still in school. You can, for example:

1. Roll the dice, as by taking whatever courses are easiest, that your friends take, or are of interest, but with no real idea or plan as to where they will take you. Then when you finish school, applying for any job that is open.
2. Drift into a career (as I first did) by identifying something that sounds interesting (such as law or medicine) and, without deeply exploring what a career in this field actually entails, assessing the employment prospects, or following a prescribed set of steps for preparing for that career;
3. Keep your options open by preparing for multiple careers, and then deciding, toward the end of school, which way to go;
4. Follow your passion wherever it may lead and focus on developing your skills in the area, with the expectation that once you get good enough, you will find a way of turning that passion into a career;

5. Objectively plan for a career by identifying the fields that are most likely to offer the best job prospects and then diligently prepare for and pursue an entry position in your field; or

6. Identify what you are good at and love to do, explore a broad range of options for careers in that field and then prepare for a few related jobs—all while simultaneously gaining exposure to other fields and disciplines and developing skills (as via minors, dual majors, or grad school) in multiple areas of interest.

There is no real right approach and each has pluses and minuses. Option one is certainly the easiest. It is, however, also the most likely to result in a "career" of standing in lines at the unemployment office. However, even with this approach you can "luck" into an ideal job and career.

The other five options also have advantages and disadvantages. While option two worked for me in the mid-1970s, it is much more problematic in a time of high unemployment, slow growth, and intense competition for the best jobs. Option three may also yield success, while simultaneously providing you with the type of multi-disciplinary perspective that will serve you well in your life and your career. However, it could also put you at a disadvantage relative to others who have single-mindedly pursued a particular course of study and who demonstrate demonstrable skills in and a commitment to the field in which they are looking for a job.

Option four can provide the incentive and the discipline required to master a set of skills. It, however, also has dangers, such as in limiting the number of fields and experiences to which you are exposed and by leaving all of your eggs in a single basket that may not offer employment opportunities. Say, for example, that your passion is basketball; but you don't grow taller than 5′2″ and can't dribble or hit a free throw to save your life.

What's the value of single-mindedly pursuing a passion if it won't lead to a job? Or if you find out that your "dream job" comes with a number of day-to-day responsibilities that you don't enjoy or aren't very good at? Or that, after years of single-minded, diligent preparation, you discover another passion that turns out to be even more compelling, but in which you have not developed the required skills?

Overall, options five and six are the most likely to prepare you for a job in your chosen field. Option five may provide the best chance of getting a good job out of school, but at what cost? Committing to a particular course of study too soon could foreclose your options. Worse still, it could prevent you from searching for or identifying even better options.

Option five also has more pragmatic drawbacks. No matter how much diligence you exercise in finding a career that offers the best employment prospect, who has a clear crystal ball to guarantee that the job market will actually turn out as anticipated? And even if it does, will it result in a job you will enjoy—not only initially but also over the course of your entire career? After all, how many adults do you or your parents know that have become locked into a career they had single-mindedly pursued only to find that their one-time passion burned out and they are stuck with a job that has become a chore.

Option six also has the inherent drawback of being a compromise solution. It invites you to spread your time and efforts so thinly that you don't develop sufficient skills in your primary area of interest. It is an attempt to thread the needle—pursuing a passion, while simultaneously keeping your options open: Focusing on this passion while simultaneously exploring and developing other interests and skills: Balancing your passion with the realities of the cold, cruel job market. But if you carefully plan, you can take this path to pursuing your dream while simultaneously providing the foundation for one or two safety careers (see Chapter 6) that may provide greater potential of landing a job in a field that is closely aligned with your passion.

But no matter how carefully and thoroughly you plan, as 18th-century philosopher David Hume once said: "*Stercus Sccidit*," which is Latin for "Shit happens!"

You will always run into unanticipated obstacles. Say you diligently prepared for and got the job of your dreams, but what if that career path you had so carefully crafted is suddenly blocked or eliminated by an industry-wide restructuring? What if the job is offshored or, more likely, eliminated or totally transformed by technology?

Getting a good job out of school is tough enough. Building a high-value and sustainable career doing something you love is even tougher.

Still, you have to attempt to accomplish both of these goals in an era of unprecedented volatility, where assumptions and rules can change overnight.

This requires a diligent pursuit of your goals, but also the flexibility to adapt to changing circumstances. It requires an idealistic pursuit of your aspirations, but also brutal realism in assessing your prospects.

Finding Your Interests and Passions (Step 1)

Regardless of what career you hope to pursue, your first step should be get to know yourself: Who are you? What are your passions, your interests, your skills, and your weaknesses?

Why should this the first step in identifying and planning a rewarding career? It all goes back to one of the most valuable life lessons I ever learned from my father who told me to:

Find a way of doing what you love. You will you enjoy your work and you will do it much better than something you don't love.

I built upon this and added my own tweak to his advice:

Identify your skills and weave them into your passions in a way that will establish you as a highly differentiated, high-value "brand."

> Find a way of doing what you love. Then, identify your skills and weave them into your passions in a way that will establish you as a highly differentiated, high-value "brand."

But passions are double-edged swords. When carefully nurtured, developed, and managed, they can bring meaning and joy to your life and your career. If not, they can lead to a spiral of hedonistic disaster, as by using them as a justification for blindly following a path that is highly unlikely to ever lead to a career or personal fulfillment. You must keep your eyes open and maintain a genuine willingness to learn from and adapt to your experiences.

> Passions are double-edged swords. When carefully nurtured, developed, and managed, they can bring meaning and joy to your life and your career. If not, they can lead to a spiral of hedonistic disaster.

The first step is to identify your passion—and hopefully, your passions. In an ideal world, you should begin identifying, diligently pursuing, and building a solid foundation around your interests and passions when you are in middle school. But even if you are well past that point in school, it is never too late for you to figure out exactly who you are, what your skills are, and what you love to do. The problem with beginning late is that it will probably take a lot of work and much time to hone your skills in your chosen field and develop the background you will need to compete for your dream job with those who had a head start in preparing themselves.

But whenever you begin, identifying your passions is a great first step, not only in identifying a career that will allow you to pursue and live that passion but also in developing the skills and the personal attributes you will need to succeed. And if your passions change? No problem! The very act of diligently pursuing your passion (whatever that passion may be) will help you develop skills and especially many of the critical personal attributes (initiative, self-direction, perseverance, adaptability, curiosity, and so forth) that, as discussed in Chapter 3, will be required for success in virtually any career or careers in which you eventually find yourself.

Forget for the time being about practicality and your ability to find a job in the field in which you have a passion. That comes later. Don't limit yourself to "practical" interests or even things you can do now, or are ever likely to be able to do. Do you love to play music or basketball, but know you will never be good enough to play professionally? No problem. Do you think you would love to travel, even if you have never left your home town? That's fine. So too are things such as spending time with friends and family, or even playing videogames or keeping up with friends on Twitter. Think broadly—as if there were no limits to what you might be able to do.

And if nothing quite qualifies as a passion, what interests do you have? Do any of them have the potential of becoming passions?

Don't yet have a passion or deep interest? Find one! You can focus on and begin to develop some of your current interests that have the potential of growing into passions. You can look for new experiences that may, once you learn more about them, evolve into passions.

Where do you begin your search? Everywhere. Think about subjects that you enjoy in school, hobbies, extracurricular activities, jobs of family members or acquaintances, things you read about or see on television or on the Internet that you find interesting.

Now that you may have identified things that might intrigue you, how do you narrow it down? By asking yourself a few questions:

- What do I currently do when I have some free time or extra money?
- What would I most want to do if I could do anything I wanted for a full day? For a month? For a year?
- What are the things that I do in which I "lose myself"— get so involved and interested in what I am doing that I lose track of time or lose consciousness of what is going on around me?
- What are the things in which I am most driven to excel?
- What do I consider my single, most overriding passion? What secondary and tertiary passions?
- What other things do I enjoy?
- What are the types of things that I used to love doing, but in which I have lost interest or no longer have the time?
- What other areas do I find of interest that may have the potential of becoming passions if I were able to explore them?

Running out of ideas? Think broadly. Ask friends and family what they see as your passions, your interests. Don't limit yourself. As I discuss in the next chapter, many of the best career plans may be based on a combination of two or even three interests and passions.

Brainstorming to create a list of what your passions are or may be in the future is relatively easy. Now it becomes a little more difficult.

Take your list and rank them, from those that you are most passionate about to those that have the potential of being passions in the future.

Then comes the more difficult part—what specifically is it about each of these passions that you most enjoy? That most inspires you? That most drives you to excel?

If you get a particular type of self-satisfaction from doing something well, exactly what is that "something"? Is it the satisfaction of solving a complex problem? Learning new things? Developing mastery? Escaping from the demands of day-to-day-life? Gaining the respect and admiration of friends, families, or teachers? The more specific you can get about the rewards you get from pursuing each of these passions, the better. For example, if you get satisfaction out of solving problems, what type of problems? Qualitative, quantitative, physical, or social?

And what is it about doing these things that you most like? Is it the act itself? A particular component of the act? Or is it the self-satisfaction or the external validation you get from accomplishing something? All, as you will see, are important questions that you must think about.

Great start. Now it's time for some matching exercises:

- What are the commonalities or similarities among these passions?
- What are the common themes among the types of satisfaction I gain?
- Which types of satisfaction do I find most rewarding?
- What other things that I do or enjoy provide similar types of satisfaction?
- Are there any other areas beyond my current passions and interests that I think have the potential of providing similar types of satisfaction?

Exploring and Nurturing New Interests (Step 1, Continued)

By now you may have narrowed down your passions and interests and think you are ready to write your career plan. Right? Wrong! First, don't be afraid to continually reassess your passions as you have new experiences.

After all, your life is just beginning. Once you leave the confines of school and enter the "real world"—and especially if you move from one country to another country, or from a small city to a large city—you will be exposed to far more experiences and stimuli than you can imagine.

When I completed graduate school and moved from Syracuse, New York, to Chicago, Illinois, for my first professional job, it was like a rebirth. I was exposed to so many new cultural, social, work, and academic experiences that the number of my interests exploded. I developed lifelong passions in areas that I had not previously heard of, much less learned about or experienced. The interests I developed over the first 24 years of my life were swept away, many never to resurface. From hindsight, many seemed to be insignificant in comparison with my new interests.

Not only did these new experiences enrich my life, they totally transformed my career—away from tax law to marketing consulting in the still emerging computer industry. And this is for somebody that hated, and barely passed the only computer programming course I had been required to take.

My wife, meanwhile, could have never dreamed that her initial passion for teaching French would have ever transformed into one for retail marketing, or that she would develop an even longer career in helping professional services companies plan and finance their growth.

Nor did either of us imagine that our few high school and college trips would morph into a consuming passion for global travel, or that lunches at McDonalds would evolve into passions for fine food and wine. And where did our interests in art, theater, and architecture come from? Or my fascination with international business and political science (which led me to yet another graduate degree)?

The point is, no matter how much you think you have experienced, and no matter how consumed you are with your current interests and passions, you don't know what you don't know. The more you search for and embrace the opportunity to experience new things, the more interests and passions you will discover.

This search for new interests and experiences is, and certainly should be, a lifelong mission. At no time in your life, however, it is more important than when you are young. It is at that age that you have the best opportunity to nurture these interests into passions, to study and build extracurricular activities around them, to meet new people and learn of the opportunities for careers in their field, and to develop the type of resume that will give you a leg up over less prepared applicants for scholarships, fellowships, internships, and, of course, jobs.

But why focus all this time and effort on a passion or interest that may be a flash in the pan? Something that may be superseded by your next big interest? For many reasons, including:

- You never know where this focus and effort may lead. Even if you lose interest in it, it may spark an interest in something else;
- You may meet new and interesting people;
- Persistence, especially to the extent that it results in some type of accomplishment or mastery of skills, is a great addition to your resume (especially one in the form of a digital portfolio); and most importantly
- The journey, as Greek philosopher Homer said, is often its own reward. The very process of rigorously pursuing your passion provides purpose and helps you develop the 21st-century skills and traits you will need for career success: especially traits such as self-motivation, initiative, discipline, persistence, and, if you use your focus to continually push your personal boundaries, patience, self-control, and resilience (see Chapter 3).

> The very process of rigorously pursuing your passion provides purpose and helps you develop the 21st-century skills and traits you will need for career success.

This, however, is not to suggest that you should find a passion and then focus all your energies on it. While single-minded commitment to one and only one thing may pay-off for a handful of incredibly talented people, it can foreclose more opportunities than it opens. It can make you one-dimensional, limit the perspective required to make informed and balanced decisions, and severely constrict the size and scope of the social network that, as discussed in Chapter 9, is so critical in finding and capturing job opportunities. As with virtually anything, you must balance focus against a continual quest for new experiences and the development of skills in a broad range of areas.

You should, of course, look at school as an opportunity to develop the knowledge and the core skills that will be required for success in any field. You must, however, also look at school (and indeed, your entire life) as a means of exploring as many new areas as possible to discover a broad range of interests and passions—then to drill more and more deeply into a few.

Why drill down into a few interests, rather than just one? First, as mentioned, it will make you a better rounded person and often lead to a richer life. More pragmatically, a thoughtful combination of disciplines can, as discussed in Chapter 6, be one of your most effective strategies for building yourself into the type of high-value, differentiated brand that will maximize your chances of providing value to an employer or client, and of controlling your own career. And of course, pursuit of secondary and tertiary interests can also serve as a hedge in case you lose interest in the first.

On the other hand, an attempt to focus on too many interests is no focus at all. The whole point of focus is to allow you to drill down into a particular area—to dive beneath the surface to discover hidden secrets and ideally achieve some level of mastery.

But before jumping from passions and interests into career choices, you have to take a slight detour through reality. Although passions and interests are a great way to engage your interests, they do not provide a sufficient foundation on which you can build an entire career plan. The next step, and in some ways the most critical, is to objectively assess your skills, your aptitudes, and your personality.

Who are you? What are your greatest strengths, your weaknesses? What is your nature or personality type? Such questions are profoundly important in helping you understand not just what you enjoy, but what you are or can be good at, and in what type of careers you are likely to have the greatest chances for success.

Skills as the Critical Link Between Dreams and Reality (Step 2)

So, you've explored the passions that get you up in the morning and the interests that occupy your days. That's a good start in your quest for a potential career. Unfortunately, passion alone does not make a career path.

Remember the boy who has a passion to play basketball, but is only 5′2″ and can't shoot? His chances of making a living by playing basketball are somewhere between zero and nil. But does this mean that he should forget about basketball and his passion for the game? Not at all. You don't have to be a great player to be a great coach. Or if not a coach, an official, a trainer, a sports doctor, a player's agent or lawyer, or an accountant or marketer in a team's front office. Your opportunities to play the game may be limited to occasional pick-up games (like those of Barack Obama), but you can still build your career and even live your life around this passion, and be an integral part of the sport you love, albeit in a somewhat different role than you originally planned.

The same holds true for most other high-value professions. Not everybody can be a doctor, an astronaut, or a movie star. Anybody, however, can develop a professional career around these professions: a career that allows you to be deeply involved in similar work and experience similar types of job satisfaction. And who knows, just your very involvement in the music industry and day-to-day work with artists and producers may even improve your chances of being discovered. Training and working as a nurse or a nurse practitioner may help prepare you for and ease your way into medical school. Or maybe, after working as a nurse, you may decide that you prefer the personal relationships you can form with your patients over the very different rewards of being a doctor. Or perhaps you discover that your interests lie more in, and that your skills are better suited to being a hospital administrator. Or, who knows, maybe a patient, so impressed with your knowledge, your dedication, and your empathy, may offer you a job in her new start-up company.

In fact, one career book author, Cal Newport contends that most people's passions can't be readily transformed into dream jobs. He believes it is best to find something you are good at, work at it to get even better, and then trade your "career capital" in for the lifestyle you want.[1] Dilbert creator Scott Adams goes even further, insisting that "passion is bullshit": that you to have a greater chance of success, and indeed are likely to more enjoy pursuing a career in a field in which you have skills, than one for which you have a passion.[2] The logic is that doing something well results in self-satisfaction and recognition by others. This, as mentioned above, creates a self-reinforcing feedback loop through which you will come to love what you do well. Fruitless pursuit of a passion for which you do not have the requisite skills can become demoralizing drudgery.

On one hand, I agree that finding something you are good at can be a great start to developing a career. Moreover, success can turn into a passion. On the other hand, being good at something does not necessarily mean you will enjoy doing it, or that you will have the temperament to do it every day. In my mind, it is better to find a way of applying your skills to your passion, rather than hoping passion will somehow emerge. After all, the idea is to find something to which you will dedicate the time and the effort to develop competence, and eventually, mastery. It's a lot easier to motivate yourself to mastering something you love, than to something you know you should or have to do. After all, if author Malcolm Gladwell is right, the key to success in virtually any task, be it surgery, pitching a baseball, or playing a violin, is to practice that task for at least 10,000 hours.[3] That's a lot of time to devote to something you don't enjoy.

Besides, I believe that it is possible to build a financially, as well as a psychically rewarding career around virtually any passion. Some may be much more difficult and take far more work than others, but if you get good enough at your passion, explore enough options, and build a really good network, you can dramatically improve your chances. No, you may not have the skills required to play first violin in a world-renowned symphony orchestra, but you may well be able to pursue your passion (and possibly even earn a living) by playing in a local string quartet. Besides, even if you don't ultimately succeed, do you really want to go through life continually wondering if you could have done it?

Passion, especially if based on skills and honed through practice, is great. But just in case you can't earn a living, or decide that you can be just as happy playing music for yourself or for friends, you should also seriously consider preparing for a reliable safety career (possibly doing something in the music industry)—ideally one based on some combination of your other skills. (See for example, my Chapter 6 discussion of contingency planning and safety careers.)

But, while I generally disagree with Adams and Newport as to the value of pursuing your passion, I totally do agree with Newport's advice that:

> If you experience and develop skills in enough new things, you will find it, or just as likely, it will find you. So pursue your interests while aggressively exploring others. In fact, set an annual agenda of at least five or six new things you want to experience, plus another five or six that you want to learn about or do over the next year—continually monitoring your progress and ensuring you address your goals. Set goals aggressively. Not just dabble in something, but to really learn it.[4]

But I digress. The point is that passion and interests are only one part of a complex equation that you—and you alone—must solve to identify and launch yourself on the career path of your dreams. You must also determine for which type of role your skills and temperament are best suited.

Unfortunately, passion alone does not make a career path. You must also determine for which type of role your skills and temperament are best suited.

Identifying and Validating Your Skills (Step 2 Continued)

Your first step in assessing your skills, like that in assessing your passions, is to determine exactly what you think your skills are. Not that your own assessment is necessarily objective or correct, but it is a good starting place. So, just what do you believe you're good at?

- Which subjects do you enjoy or do well at in school?
  What capabilities and attributes do you think make you

particularly good in these fields (in addition to enjoying them)? Pay particular attention to things at which you are good, but do not particularly enjoy. Why are you good at it (innate aptitude, shear determination, etc.), what about it do you not enjoy (too rigid a methodology, too much memorization, etc.)? Hopefully, if you can discover why you don't like something, and work with parents and teachers to find a way around this issue, you can turn a strength into an interest, and possibly even a passion. While it may not necessarily become the foundation of your career path, an interest in something you do well can always be leveraged into an advantage, somewhere down the line.

- Which sports? Do you have any particular skill in this area, such as speed, agility, anticipating teammate or competitor actions, anticipating which plays are appropriate, team leadership, and so forth? If so, you can probably leverage them into other activities, including some that may offer better career prospects than professional sports. Even if not, disciplined pursuit of a sport can always help you develop some of the career skills discussed in Chapter 3: skills such as teamwork, responsibility, adaptability and persistence.

- Which school and extracurricular activities—class leadership, yearbook, theater, photography, and so forth? What do you do particularly well in these activities?

- Do you work? Which jobs and at which parts of these jobs do you think you are particularly strong?

- Do you have any particular social skills? Meeting and establishing friendships with a wide range of people, public speaking, working in teams, leading groups, empathy, and so forth?

- Do you feel you have any attributes that are of particular help in your schoolwork, hobbies, and day-to-day life? Curiosity, planning, perseverance, organization?

- What about attitudes? Are you outgoing, thoughtful, usually know the right thing to say in a difficult situation, optimistic, and so forth?

- What do others think you're good at? Ask your friends, family members, and especially objective third parties, such as teachers, coaches, and managers for their opinions—they might surprise you!

Identifying what you believe to be strengths is a good start. It is, however, only a start.

What are the particular aspects of a skill at which you excel? Why do you think you are good at each of these? What are the commonalities or linkages among these strengths?

Say, for example, that you are good at golf. What does that mean? Do you have good hand–eye coordination? Are you patient and thoughtful about planning your shots? Are you diligent in reading about and practicing the game? Are you good at forming meaningful relationships with others in your foursomes or on your team?

What else do you enjoy and are you good at? Reading, writing, math, science, acting?

Next, go through the same type of exercise to assess your limitations. Yes, everybody has some—even you.

Self-assessment is always a good starting point. But let's face it, no one can be totally objective in assessing themselves, especially their faults and limitations. You must, therefore, look for objective, nonbiased help in discovering, or at least in validating, your limitations. This means you have to ask. After all, while people may spontaneously mention or complement you on your strengths, few will volunteer their views of your limitations.

Your parents, siblings, friends, and relatives may be a good starting point. However, even if they are objective in identifying and judging your limitations, they may be tempted to shade the truth, to complement you, or to not offend you. Therefore, you must seek feedback from others that do not have these types of vested interests. What do your teachers say? Your coaches? Your employers? Your guidance counselors? What other people know you well enough to assess your strengths and limitations in particular areas—and are willing to tell you the truth?

If few friends will volunteer to tell you about your weaknesses, even fewer third-parties will do so. Explain what you are looking for and ask for their help. You can, for example, tell them that you are trying to do a self-assessment of your skills and limitations as part of your efforts to think about college and career goals.

But rather than putting them on the spot and having them provide off-the-cuff responses, it may be best to give them time to think about it. Ask if you can set an appointment.

When you do sit down with them, begin with general, open-ended questions, rather than lead them in a particular direction. For example, ask what they see as your strengths; your limitations? What do they think you do well and what skills do you have to work on? Then, after they give their opinions as to your strengths and limitations, drill down. Ask for examples of how they saw this. Ask what areas of study and what types of careers they think may best employ your skills. You can then ask specifically about strengths and limitations that you see in yourself, or that others have already brought up.

Asking is important. It is even more important that you recognize that anyone that is willing to give you an honest assessment is doing you a huge favor. Do not—I repeat "DO NOT"—get defensive, make excuses, or begin to argue with them. Instead, ask them to explain and give examples, ask for any recommendations they may have as to how you might begin to address these limitations. Then, thank them for their candor and honesty and ask if you can speak with them again after you have had a chance to think about what they have told you.

It's then time to go home and think long, hard, and objectively about what they told you. If you agree, come up with a plan for addressing these limitations. Ask others, such as parents, guidance counselors, psychologists, or ministers how you may address them. If you disagree, or simply do not see these traits in yourself, ask others.

If these objective parties validate your own views of yourself, great. If not, you should understand why not. But remember, no matter how great they believe your strengths to be, and how great you believe they are, be sure to keep it into perspective. You may be valedictorian of your high school or all-county quarterback. But when you move on to the next level, everybody may be a high school valedictorian or all-county quarterback!

You will be required to assess your own capabilities and performance relative to others through your entire career. Significant and/or repeated errors in these assessments can lead to big disappointment, severe embarrassment, strained relationships, and can seriously limit your career.

Testing Yourself (Steps 1 and 2 Continued)

Although this chapter focuses primarily on self-assessments and the seeking of other people's opinions, you can also find all types of tests to take to get independent validation and, hopefully, new insights into your interests, your skills, and how they can be employed. These tests include:

- Intelligence tests, such as Raven's Progressive Matrices, Wechsler Adult Intelligence Scale, Wechsler Intelligence Scale for Children, Stanford-Binet, Woodcock-Johnson Tests of Cognitive Abilities, and Kaufman Assessment Battery for Children, and those from high-intelligence societies, like Mensa;
- Periodic state-administered high school exit and assessment exams[5] and international PISA tests[6] that compare your and your school's performance in specific subject areas to those of students in other districts and countries;
- The dreaded SAT college admissions, ACT, college readiness assessment and graduate admission tests[7] that assess your ability to apply your intelligence and learning in specific subjects, and your broad quantitative and qualitative reasoning skills as assessing your readiness for college and different graduate programs; and
- Collegiate Learning Assessment (CLA) tests, which assess capabilities such as critical thinking, analytical reasoning, and communication, rather than knowledge.

And for those who are less interested in specific measures of intelligence and performance relative to grade level or readiness for advanced study, there are scores of skills assessment[8] and aptitude tests[9] that help assess your suitability for specific occupations. Such tests can be helpful in suggesting interests and directions that you may not have considered.

Speaking of tests, there is another category of test that assesses not your intelligence, capabilities, or interests, but your personality type. Tests such as those from Caliper or Myers-Briggs assess an individual's temperaments, predispositions, and character as a means of, in the case of Myers-Briggs, dividing people among one of 16 personality types, based on an assessment of how they fall on each of four continua:

- Extraversion or Introversion: how you relate to the world, through others or internally, through your own mind and thoughts;
- Sensing or Intuition: how one best takes in information, through their five senses or through the discerning of patterns;
- Thinking or Feeling: how you make decisions, objectively or through your own perceptions; and
- Judging or Perceiving: how you see, live in and interact with the world, via a structured or a flexible perspective.

You can use such personality types to assess your own predisposition toward and suitability for different types of professions, what type of personality types are most and least likely to work together in marriages and in partnerships, and how a parent, a manager, or a salesperson can most effectively work with children, employees, or customers based on their individual types. An entire mini-industry has grown up around Myers-Briggs, in particular, with dozens of books (I particularly recommend *Please Understand Me II*[10]) and consultants[11] who specialize in these assessments and can help you assess the type of occupations for which you may be best suited or the type of education that is best suited to your particular learning style.

Now that you think you understand the areas about which you are passionate, your interests, and your strengths and limitations, you're ready for the next step: taking an initial cut at identifying potential careers, career paths, and your own professional brand—the aspirational identity by which you hope to portray yourself to employers, managers, peers, clients, and customers.

CHAPTER 6

Crafting Your Career Goals and Your Professional Brand

Steps 3 Through 10

Don't compete, Find what's uniquely yours
> —Arsenio Hall (when asked how he planned to compete in the crowded late-night television market)

Find out who you are and do it on … purpose.
> —Dolly Parton

Key Points

- Identify a range of potential careers that apply your skills to your passions, and narrow them down to a few potential dream and safety careers.
- Identify leverage points around which skills and passions can be applied in different ways, to different fields.
- Begin developing deep knowledge and skills in these areas by working intensely on self-directed projects.
- Craft and continually tune your unique professional brand around your skills, passions.
- Research and validate market opportunities for people with your skills in your intended fields.
- Plan for contingencies, as by targeting leverageable and high-growth fields, breaking waves, and by preparing for a complementary safety career.
- Balance determination and flexibility in pursuing your dream career.bv

Now that you've identified what you love doing, what you like doing, and what you're good at doing, you're on the path to making an informed decision as to the type of career that you will both enjoy and, hopefully, in which you have the capabilities to thrive.

But before getting into the next step, any responsible planning process must also account for the fact that you can't fully predict the future. You must absolutely develop a plan based on your reasoned, best estimates of what will happen. And solid preparation for that planned future will often increase the odds of it occurring. But regardless of how well you plan or how thoroughly you prepare, remember the age-old adage, "Shit Happens." You may, for example, be unable to find a good job in the field for which you prepared. And even if you get the job, you may realize that you don't enjoy it, or that you are not as good at it as you thought you would be.

Or, your job may be redefined (as by technology or reorganization), eliminated (as by offshoring), or even obsoleted (as by automation). Or advancement in that career may involve taking on tasks and responsibilities that you don't enjoy. For example, if you are a research scientist who is promoted into management, you may find yourself doing less of the hands-on research that likely led you to pursue that career in the first place and spending more time managing other people, calculating budgets, playing politics, and doing other things you don't enjoy. Or your passions and interests may change. Or a new, totally unanticipated opportunity in another field—an opportunity that is too good to pass up—may fall into your lap.

In other words, anything can happen. You must, therefore, build your plan around another old maxim: "Be Prepared." No matter how certain you are (or believe you are) that you have discovered your calling, develop the type of skills that will prepare you for a range of potential careers and be adaptable enough to change.

And, since I'm peppering you with trite (but still valuable) aphorisms, here's one more: "Keep your options open." True, some people contend that this is absolutely the wrong advice: That once you make an informed decision that you should commit totally to that decision and not look back.[1] Perhaps this is true if the outcome is totally in your own control. But not everything in today's job market is in your control. Even if you're the next LeBron James, what if you blow out your knee before reaching the pros? You still need to protect yourself by keeping your options open and having one or possibly two safety careers (which are discussed in Step 9 in this chapter), in addition to your dream career.

Translating Your Passions into Career Options (Steps 3 and 4)

The idea of planning a career around your passion may sound pretty straightforward. If you love chemistry, plan to become a chemist; if you like writing, become a journalist or novelist; fixing cars, a mechanic; building things, a carpenter; healing people, a doctor or a nurse; helping people learn to think, a teacher. Or perhaps you know someone with a job that sounds like it may be fun, interesting, and rewarding—like practicing medicine. You may see somebody as a role model and aspire to their career. Or maybe all you really want to do is to sing, play a violin or become a professional tennis player, or golfer.

Hopefully, you already have an intense desire for a field that comes from your heart and your passion, rather than something another person tells you should become. It is, after all, your life. You may as well follow your own dream.

But even if a career sounds like the perfect, or even the only logical fit for your passion and skills, don't jump to conclusions. After all, how many people, at any age, much less someone who has not even landed their first full-time job, understand all their options? For example, suppose you absolutely, positively want to become a chemist. That's a good start, but Chemistry is a big field, The American Chemical Society, for example, lists 37 different career options:

- In which of these multiple branches of chemistry do you have the greatest interest? Bio, nuclear, food, forensic, or polymer?
- What type of job? A chemical technician, a research chemist, or a chemical engineer?
- What are the day-to-day job responsibilities of each?
- What are the educational requirements for each? Will an associate or bachelor degree suffice, or will you need a PhD?

- In what type of organization would you ideally like to work—a university, a government laboratory, a corporation?
- Which positions, fields, and organizations provide the best employment prospects?
- What type of salary do they offer?

It is certainly possible that you will know exactly what you want to do by the time you are in high school—say an astrochemical engineer based in an Antarctic observatory that studies the composition of stars.

For the most part, however, it's best to begin your career planning with a very broad idea. First, your career ideas will almost certainly change, probably many times, before you have to make a firm decision. You can, for example, have a goal of becoming a writer, without deciding if you want to write newspaper articles, technical manuals, academic research papers, or novels. Whatever your initial thoughts, however, you should begin to learn as much as you can about your proposed field, take courses and join organizations or clubs that will allow you to gain hands-on experience, and begin talking with people who work in the field. And, given the difficulty of finding a job in today's (and probably tomorrow's) environment, you should do this with great purpose and discipline.

A Guide for the Passionless (Steps 3 and 4 Continued)

What if you don't have, or have not yet discovered, your dream or your passion? Do you really need one? It depends on your circumstances.

If you're already "Acing" all your courses, star in your high school's sports teams, and are involved in extracurricular and community activities, don't rush into a specific passion. You probably already have most, if not all, of the drive you will need. If you want to or are inspired to dedicate extra effort to an endeavor in which you have a particular interest, go for it (as long as your grades and efforts in other areas don't suffer).

On the other hand, if you are plodding along with average or slightly above average grades, haven't found any area in which you are particularly interested or in which you excel, you have to push yourself. This is especially true if you, as I did in high school and college:

- Did reasonably well without putting in any real effort; or
- Devoted far more attention and energy to fun and socializing, than to learning or attempting to master some discipline or function.

When I graduated from college in the early 1970s, only about 12 percent of working-age Americans had college degrees. Practically any type of BA, from almost any college, was probably sufficient to get some type of college-level job. By the time I got my JD and MBA degrees (at the top of my business school class but in the bottom half of my law school class), I had a choice of decent (not from top law firms or corporations, but still decent) offers for jobs that combined both law and business.

This, however, is not your father's or your grandfather's job market. Today, unless you graduate from a Top 10 school, earn a degree in a high-demand field (especially in many STEM disciplines), or have some special distinction or accomplishments, you may, as discussed in Chapter 1, be lucky to get a job that even requires a college degree, much less a good job in your field.

If you are like I was in the 1970s, just drifting through school, waiting for inspiration to strike, you better get moving. You have to redouble your focus on those subjects and activities in which you currently have interest and actively search for something—almost anything—that will spur your passion to learn and to master some field. Whether you are preparing for college admission or a job out of high school, you have to at least have one or, ideally, two or more skills and accomplishments that demonstrate your ability to focus on and to reach a challenging goal.

> This is not your father's or your grandfather's job market. If you are just drifting through school, waiting for inspiration to strike, you better get moving. You have to redouble your focus and actively search for something—anything—that will spur your passion to learn and to master some field.

As discussed in Chapter 5, this initial passion can be just about anything— as long as you have the motivation to master and to excel in that field.

The next step is to establish some type of initial career vision around this passion. Don't worry about building a long-term career around your initial passion as your passions and your goals will almost certainly change many times as you learn more of that field and discover others.

Nor is it necessary that your initial passion have anything to do with your ultimate career. The important thing is that you begin thinking about how you can convert your interests and skills into career options, laying out the steps you will have to take to turn these options into job offers—and to begin this process NOW. The longer you wait, the further behind you will fall and the more options that will be foreclosed to you. Besides, just like in chess and soccer, the more you learn and practice the underlying skills, the better you are likely to perform in the actual match.

Don't know where to find the motivational spark? One of the aptitude or personality tests discussed in Chapter 5 could be a good place to start. But whatever road you take to discovering your passion (or some other type of motivator), don't use the fact that you don't know your ultimate career goal as an excuse for delaying the process. After all, you probably won't know your ultimate career goal until you are in your 30s, 40s, or even older (hopefully after fulfilling jobs or careers in one or more fields).

Creating and Cultivating Your Professional Brand (Step 5)

Once you've identified your passions, taken an inventory of your interests, and objectively validated your skills, you are ready to begin creating the personal, and eventually, the professional "brand" that will help guide and position you through your entire career.

This brand is essentially a concise, abbreviated form of your identity—a few carefully selected words, images, and attributes that you want people to think of when they see you or hear your name. This branding process can begin when you are in elementary and middle school. In its initial iterations, it can represent your current identity: a combination of who you are, what you love, and what you're good at. By the time you're in college, however, your brand should represent your aspirational identity: not only who you are, but what you want to do, how you want to be perceived, and the type of value you want to be seen as providing to employers or clients.

Just as importantly, this brand must be specific to you. It must differentiate you on the basis of your unique skills, capabilities, and personal traits. Counting on your degree in marketing or biology to provide sufficient specialization may not get you very far. To really differentiate yourself:

- Your skills should be highly specific. This may come from an incredibly deep focus in a specific field (something of a "microspecialty") or by combining two of your core skills or college majors in a way that gives you a competitive advantage in your field and that makes you particularly attractive to your target employers or clients. Examples of this type of interdisciplinary "macrospecialization" may include a mechanical engineer with a well-integrated dual major in urban transportation; a law degree with a mechanical or bioengineering undergraduate to prepare you to practice intellectual property law; or a software architecture degree with a specialty in statistics and the analysis of the type of "Big Data" that is being generated by today's technology.[2]
- Your traits should include those that let you deliver your unique value proposition in the most effective way. Thinking back to the Core and the High-Value Skills discussed in Chapter 3, for example, they can include the cognitive and creative skills that enable you to address problems in new ways, the leadership and collaboration skills that will allow you to bring teams to consensus, or the determination and organizational skills to see complex projects through to the end.

Your professional brand should represent your aspirational identity: not only who you are, but what you want to do, how you want to be perceived, and the type of value you want to be seen as providing to employers or clients. This brand must differentiate you on the basis of your unique skills, capabilities, and personal traits.

You should also be able to validate the depth of these skills (as through certificates, recognitions, awards, and by documentation in your digital portfolio) and most importantly, explain exactly how you can apply these skills to provide a high level of unique value to your prospective employers or clients.

Brands, however, cannot be stable or immutable. Just as your passions, your skills, and your career objectives will evolve, so too must your brand. After all, brands, like bread, can become stale. They should be in a continual state of evolution, continually adapting not only to changes in your own skills and interests but also to changes in the economy, in the market, and in new learnings from your experiences and from the feedback that you receive.

Consider, for example, the ABZ planning concept set forth by Reid Hoffman and Ben Casnocha in their book, *The Start-up of You*:[3]

- Plan A is your current path;
- Plan B is an adaptation in which you adjust your original plan to account for changes in your goal or to new learnings that suggest your original plan may not quite work as anticipated; and
- Plan Z is a fallback position in the unfortunate case where, after going through multiple iterations on Plan B, you decide that your plan just won't work and that it is time to try something else.

But regardless of how many or how dramatic the shifts you make in your objectives, your education, or your career, you must be able to explain these twists, turns, and setbacks in a way that will present even the most seemingly obscure and damaging shifts as part of a logical progression or invaluable learning experience that will allow you to deliver even greater value to a prospective employer.

Remember, however, that just as brands must be continually polished and tuned, they can also be tarnished or destroyed, as by poor performance on a job or a project, an insensitive remark made public, or by an unfortunate Facebook post.

This brings up the entire topic of social media. When used properly, tools such as LinkedIn, Facebook, and Twitter can be incredibly powerful and valuable tools for communicating and enhancing your brand and for building your network. When used poorly, they can sideline even the best plans.

Validating the Market (Step 6)

Although developing a passion or some type of motivational spark is important, you have to perform a high-level reality check before you go too far. For example, are you capable of developing the skills that you will need to meet the minimum bar for entry into the field? Do you have the required physical attributes? Are you capable of and willing to endure whatever course of study or training is required?

Once you identify a broad career that you think has the potential of allowing you to live your passion, you have to objectively assess the opportunities for actually scoring a job in that profession. Not just this, but also how viable these jobs are likely to be in the future, how forces such as technology and globalization will likely affect them, how well they are likely to pay, and the ability to build a long-term career in your preferred field. You should also objectively assess whether you, of all the people who are likely to be competing for the same entry-level job, have a reasonable potential of getting the job. This is all before you begin to develop a plan as to how to prepare for that job.

I'm not suggesting that you should automatically dismiss a career where your odds of entry (much less success), the pay, and opportunities for a long-term career are low. But before you commit to a particular field, you need to understand the odds of getting a job, and be prepared to make deliberate tradeoffs as to how much time and effort you should put into achieving this particular goal, at the expense of your other goals. Also recognize that your first job is likely to be only a temporary stop on your way to a long-term career that may have little to do with your initial position. To the extent that you have begun thinking about your longer term options, you may wish to begin thinking about the types of skills you will need for them and, if appropriate, how you may be able to use your first job as a steppingstone into a future career.

> Before you commit to a particular field, you need to under-
> stand the odds of getting a job, and be prepared to make delib-
> erate tradeoffs as to how much time and effort you should put
> into achieving this particular goal, at the expense of your other
> goals.

Think back to Chapter 5's 5′2″ aspiring pro basketball player example. We know, at least intuitively, that the odds of making a pro-sports team are infinitesimal. And even if you make it, your career may be short and, contrary to the image of league stars, may not result in sufficient money to fund your retirement.

This being said, many sports have relatively structured winnowing processes that will allow you (not to speak of your current and prospective coaches) to assess your prospects along the way. If you can't make your high-school junior varsity team, your odds of a pro career are probably pretty slim. But if you star in high school, win a scholarship from and star for a top-ranked college, make All-American teams, and are heavily recruited by the pros, you can track and adjust your plans along the way (all while still recognizing that not all star NCAA (National College Athletic Association) players make it in the pros, or even semipros).

The same is true in some other professions. If you want to be a doctor, you must first get into and do very, very well in college and a demanding regimen of very technical courses. Then you must be admitted to and get through medical school, survive 80-hour per week internships, be accepted into one of the highly competitive residency programs, pass your boards and so forth.

While most professions have less formal and less structured programs, if you pay attention, you can usually pick up hints as to how you are faring relative to others. Although you shouldn't allow a few cases of negative feedback to derail your plans, a series of setbacks should prompt you to think more deeply about your objective. You may, for example, decide to double down and work harder (persistence), adapt your approach to achieving your goals (adaptability), or to stop beating your head against the proverbial wall and try something else and go on to Plan B, or Plan Z.

Selecting, pursuing, getting a job in and advancing through a career path is an iterative process. You must try an approach, collect feedback, assess the results, and plan your next step.

The good news is that there's typically more than one single path to success in virtually any career. Even if you don't follow the traditional path, lightning may strike. Prospective lawyers don't have to attend the best law school or even pass the bar exam on your first try (or even in the first state in which you attempt it) to become a great trial lawyer or judge. An aspiring athlete who is not drafted still has the potential to earn a walk-on try-out. Nor do you necessarily have to graduate from college (much less have a Harvard MBA) to create your own social networking company or become CEO of a major corporation. Even the greatest obstacles can be overcome with skill, determination, and hard work.

Determine what you have to do to achieve your dream. Objectively evaluate your prospects and the potential for and likely cost of failure, as well as the rewards for success. If, after this, you're still committed, go for it!

But just because there may be a possibility of achieving your goal, it doesn't mean you should bet your entire future on it. Remember, as the ubiquitous NCAA commercial says, "there are over 380,000 student-athletes. . . . and just about every one of them will go pro in something other than sports." The same can be said of premed students and aspiring artists and entertainers.

The Costs of Following Your Passion
(Step 6 Continued)

Even, after thoughtful deliberation, you may decide to pursue your dream. Then another piece of reality interferes—money!

Financial considerations come in many different flavors. We all know about the incredibly steep and rapidly rising costs of a college (much less a graduate school) education and the burdens that are imposed by the growing mountains of student loan debt. (See Financing Your Education in Chapter 8.) There are also opportunity costs. Assuming you can get a job in the first place, you will forgo salary and advancement opportunities while you are in school and also might earn no or very little money while you are waiting for your dream job to materialize, or at least to pay off.

Many of these dream jobs, however, never materialize at all. Or when they do, they may not pay very well. Humanities graduate unemployment rates, even after more than three years of economic recovery, still range between 9 and 10 percent.[4] And while graduates with such degrees often incur student loan debt that must be repaid, humanities' graduate salaries (for those who manage to get full-time jobs) tend to average only about $40,000 per year.[5]

Meanwhile, we all know about starving artists, bands that are forced to play for tips on street corners, and aspiring poets and novelists who scrape by waiting tables or driving cabs. But how about starving philosophy and anthropology PhDs who are living on infinitesimal post-doc or adjunct professor salaries in hope of securing a coveted, but increasingly rare, tenure-track position?

They can incur more than $500,000 in costs during four years in college and five-to-seven years of grad school. Post-graduation debt payments can be crippling, even for the small percentage who do manage to earn an Assistant Professorship. Not, of course, that they have many choices. There tends to be little demand for humanities PhDs in the corporate world.

Or how about starving lawyers? Law school graduates typically require seven years of education and routinely rack up loans of $100,000 or more. Those who get jobs at top national law firms often start at about $160,000 per year. Those few who make partner can pocket over $1 million per year. In reality, however, fewer than eight percent of all law school graduates win such coveted positions. According to the American Bar Association, the median salary of those 2012 grads who got full-time jobs is $61,000.[6] Such figures, however, have little meaning for the 15 percent of 2012 law school graduates who were unemployed at the time of the survey, or for the 35 percent who were unable to get jobs practicing law.

Anyone looking to choose a career should understand the employment prospects for their chosen field. What percentage of those who graduate with a degree in your major—and from your school—end up getting a job in that field, or any other full-time job? What types of salaries do they typically earn? How do such results vary among different colleges? By major in that college? And how much debt are you likely to incur—and what portion of your anticipated salaries will be consumed by debt repayment?

> Anyone looking to choose a career should understand the employment prospects for their chosen field.

A number of private sector companies (including Manpower and Monster. com), nonprofit organizations (The Pew Foundation, the National Association of Colleges and Employers and others), and government agencies (especially the Bureau of Labor Statistics, or BLS) regularly publish reports that provide glimpses into these and a range of other statistics. ACT (the organization that develops the college admissions test), for example, offers tools that allow you to understand the nature, salaries, and requirements of jobs[7] in different fields, what you should look for in colleges[8] and what different majors[9] entail. O*NET, meanwhile, provides detailed information on the responsibilities and primary activities, knowledge and skill requirements, wage ranges and employment growth projections, lists of current job openings for hundreds of different occupations, and suggestions of related fields.[10]

Meanwhile, a handful of companies, states and most recently, the U.S. Department of Education (DOE) have introduced scorecards. DOE's College Scorecard, for example, now compiles and publishes data on the cost of getting a degree in a specific field from different colleges and universities, the rates of graduation, average debt loads, and loan default rates.[11] They plan to add employment and salary data later this year.

The ability to systematically compare such data by college, by major, and by profession will be a great help. However, by their very nature, such comparisons are based on historical data. As we have seen over and over again, history does not necessarily provide a roadmap to the future. The number of jobs being created in individual industries and professions, and the salaries they pay, can vary greatly over a few years based on factors including economic, demographic, and technological trends. How then can a high school student, or even a college freshman, get a glimpse of future employment and salary before they decide on a college or select a major?

Although nobody's crystal ball is particularly clear these days, the Commerce Department's Bureau of Labor Statistics attempts to forecast such information in its comprehensive, bi-annual Occupational Outlook Handbook (of which the 2012/2013 edition is the latest), and its veritable blizzard of interim updates and analyses.[12] These include specialized student information[13] and regular drilldowns into specific industries[14] and occupations.[15]

These BLS reports provide projections including the growth rates and the number of jobs likely to be created (and in some cases, eliminated) in 580 different occupations, the type and amount of education and training required for each, and the range of salaries that entrants in the field can expect. They summarize those occupations that are likely to produce the greatest number of jobs, grow at the fastest rates, and pay the largest salaries as well as provide regular updates of helpful drilldowns into some of the more popular occupations. Although any such projections must be taken with a grain of salt, they can be indispensable resources.

Information Networking (Step 7)

Speaking of indispensable resources, there is another invaluable source for the type of career information or suggestions that you seldom find in published studies—a resource that you can't afford not to take advantage of—individuals who know or work in the field in which you have an interest.

Can't think of a career option that suits you? Can't narrow the list to a number of choices that are manageable? Or perhaps you do have some thoughts about potential careers and have read all about them, but still can't decide which choices are best for you or how to proceed? That's where an information network comes in. In fact, this type of network may be even more valuable to someone who knows exactly what they want to do. These networks can help you really learn what these careers entail, provide opportunities to see people actually working in these fields, or even put you in a position to be offered or to apply for an internship or work part time.

Many of us may initially learn about a career, such as detective work, lawyering, nursing, or cooking, from watching a program or movie or by reading a book. Whatever the source, you probably begin with a highly selective, often glamorized view. What is it really like to work, day after day, year after year, in the career you imagine? What are the day-to-day requirements? Think about the practice of law. You may want to know:

- What percentage of law school graduates actually get jobs at the major law firms?
- How many even manage to get jobs that require a law degree?
- What are the opportunities for those who graduate from law school, but never get a job practicing law? How much of a lawyer's actual time is spent in research, writing, or administrative work, rather than in court? For that matter, what percentage of lawyers in various disciplines ever even see a courtroom?
- How many hours a week will you be required to bill and how many total hours of work will this require?
- What are the ethical dilemmas you may face in accepting or representing clients with whose views you may not share?
- How will the growing role of contract workforces, automation, and outsourcing affect long-term job prospects?
- What are the odds of making partner and how long will it take?
- What are the opportunities for the vast number of associates who do not make partner?

You are not going to get answers to most of these questions by watching television or by reading law school brochures or searching the web. But to truly understand the opportunities and pitfalls of practicing law, you should actually speak with those who practice, those who used to practice, those who prepared for a career in law but ended up not practicing, and those who began practicing law but then changed to another profession.

Remember back in Chapter 5, where I discussed the importance of developing a network of objective people to help you objectively assess your capabilities and your skills? That is only the first of many, many needs you will have for a network in your effort to develop a lifelong career. The second is to develop a network that can help you assess your potential career interests.

How do you begin building this network? A perfect place to start is if one of your parents, your relatives, or your parents' friends practice law. Also, remember the teachers and counselors you spoke with about your strengths? They too may make good starting points. Although they may not necessarily know anything about the field you are exploring, they know people who do. Or they may know people who know other people who know someone in that field. At the end of any of these conversations, ask whether the person you are speaking with can recommend other people with whom they think you should speak. Ideally, they may even be able to make an introduction.

Or, you can search the Internet to find someone in the profession you wish to explore. Contact them, tell them what you are looking for, and ask if you can talk with them or, ideally, meet them at their offices.

Once you find these people, you can ask specific questions about the profession, what it's like to work in their field, what the job entails, what types of skills are required, what education they needed to get the job, and so forth. They are also among the people you want to ask about the requirements for entry into this field, the types of courses and activities that may best prepare you, the books you should read, and of course additional referrals to other people in their field, in complementary fields, or other areas that they may recommend. There is, after all, no such thing as having too much information about a field in which you may spend your entire career.

Effective career planning requires deep research, as through publicly available materials, networking and if possible, actual experience in shadowing or in assisting someone in your anticipated field. There is, after all, no such thing as having too much information about a field in which you may spend your entire career.

Are you reluctant to contact a professional in a field you do not yet know, especially if you are still in high school? Don't be. Most people are honored to be asked for their advice. They will be happy to spend a half hour with you and share their opinions. This is particularly true if you have done preliminary research and demonstrate that you ask perceptive questions that you are serious. Not only will most be happy to speak with you, many will be happy to refer you to others. If someone refuses your request, don't take it personally. Try someone else.

The primary goal of such information interviews is to better understand the opportunities and the actual work involved in the profession—and whether it will be a good match for your passions and your talents. They may occasionally yield unexpected benefits. Who knows, if you sufficiently impress the interviewee (and if they have a need), they may even consider offering you an opportunity to assist in their office, or to shadow them to see what they do in a typical day. Or, if you are really ambitious, when you find a firm that is particularly interesting and in which you particularly like the people, you may even venture to ask if there may be any opportunity for you to volunteer or intern on a temporary, part-time basis in return for an opportunity to see, first-hand, what the work is like.

True, any such tasks will be very basic and the pay (if there is any) will be minimal. Even so, this could provide an unparalleled chance for you to see the day-to-day work, give you an opportunity to ask more questions as they arise, and provide you with relevant experience to put on your resume. And who knows, if they are really impressed, it may even result in a full-time job offer.

But no matter how focused you are on a particular field or profession, life offers few certainties. You may lose interest, or discover another field that sounds even more interesting. You may discover that the field is shrinking and offers few employment, much less long-term career prospects. You may not be willing to devote the number of years, or afford the cost required to prepare for the job you envision.

Building Flexibility into Your Plan (Step 8)

One thing is certain: No matter how carefully you plan your life and your career, it will not work out as you planned. Nor should you want it to.

Sometimes these surprises are sprung upon you from outside; sometimes you change your mind or your passion; other times, new information or insight prompts you to tweak your plan. Some, such as an inability to get a job in your chosen profession, a layoff, or a serious illness, can force you to change your plans in ways that you do not want.

Others, such as a decision to pursue a new passion or a surprise offer of a new career opportunity, can be exhilarating.

Since you know things will change, why not build shock absorbers directly into your career? There are, as discussed here, many ways of doing this. Examples include:

- Developing skills in high-demand, highly leverageable professions, such as nursing, software engineering, or finance. These fields offer enough opportunities that virtually anybody with the requisite qualifications can probably get a good job. It may not necessarily be in the particular specialty, the city, or the company you prefer, but you will almost certainly get some type of decent job. And even if you can't get one specifically in your field, these skills can be valuable in and give you a big advantage in getting another job. Nurses, for example, are often valued and can help you get a job in medical insurance companies, pharmaceutical companies, or medical device manufacturing companies. Software engineers can find plenty of opportunities (although not necessarily at Twitter or Google) in fields including corporate software development, technical service, sales, and IT management.

- Searching for the type of breaking waves that will create a broad range of ways in which you can apply your skills to your passions. These waves can be created by the emergence of new technologies, new industries, sweeping taste, or demographic trends or any other type of big change. If you can get into this new field early, you can ride its growth. Working for a fast-growing company, as discussed in detail in Chapter 10, can provide great opportunities for the fast advancement or for changing roles in your company. Experience in a new field can also make you an attractive recruit for other companies in this industry or even provide you with the germ of an idea for launching your own company.

- Planning for uncertainty, as through the type of ABZ planning that facilitates not only the modification of an existing plan but also a fallback position in case plans, A, B, C, and so forth, just don't work out.

- Preparing yourself for a safety career that, as discussed later, not only provides a vehicle for working in a field in which you have a passion (even if you can't get your dream job) but may also open a number of alternate career opportunities.

> No matter how carefully you plan your life and your career, it will not work out as you planned. Since you know things will change, why not build shock absorbers directly into your career? Developing leverageable skills and preparing yourself for a safety career are among the most important of these.

Let's begin exploring these shock absorbers by looking briefly at some of the ways you can develop and use complementary and leverageable skills to not only expand your career options but also develop the type of specialized skills that can form the basis for the type of high-value specialization that will allow you to create your own highly differentiated brand.

Career Leverage Points (Steps 8 and 9)

Some courses of study are more leverageable than others. Law, as mentioned, can be leveraged into all types of fields. There are, however, many other examples.

- Biology is critical for virtually any professional job in healthcare—one of the largest and fastest growing sources of jobs in the world, not to speak of the country.
- Business degrees can help in virtually any field, in preparing to start or run your own business and in many segments of your nonbusiness life (such as in preparing budgets, working in teams, and in assessing the implications of current events).
- Software engineering is and will continue to be one of the hottest and most lucrative job markets in the country for decades to come. But even if you don't become a programmer,

this skill will probably be valuable in almost any career you end up in. You should, at the very least, be able to quickly write a basic program to access and analyze information that will help you in your actual job, whether it is in marketing, economics, psychology, or virtually any other type of knowledge work.

- Math and statistics skills are becoming increasingly valuable in virtually every industry as the Internet begins to generate huge volumes of data that must be analyzed and acted upon. Such skills are becoming increasingly critical in areas such as marketing (as around web marketing campaigns), civil engineering (as sensors and actuators become incorporated into structures), and even medical research (as in assessing the incidence and concentrations of diseases, effectiveness of different treatment regimens, and so forth). Even if you don't directly create or analyze these data, you will have to interpret the findings of these professionals and understand how to apply them to your own work.

- English, although not offering many direct career opportunities, is valuable in virtually any job in which you have to communicate, whether by writing or speaking.

But what about other areas of study, such as many of the fine arts, liberal arts, and humanities disciplines that don't necessarily prepare you for a specific job, and are generally less valued by employers?

First, these fields are often much better than many of the career-oriented programs in helping one develop the conceptualization, critical thinking, creative and writing skills writing skills that everyone will need to compete in the 21st century economy (see Chapter 4). Even if they won't directly prepare you for many jobs, they can provide good foundations for law school or for graduate business school.

A degree—virtually any degree—should, therefore, be viewed not just as a qualification for a potential job, but as a foundation on which to build a range of complementary skills. It is this combination that will form the foundation of your own unique brand—the type of brand that will give you an advantage in:

- Differentiating you in your effort to secure your dream job;
- Preparing you for jobs in a broad range of jobs that are related to (not to speak of many that are not directly related to) your dream job; and
- Providing a unique perspective on, and making unique contributions to any field you may eventually enter.

You can, therefore, usually find a way of incorporating virtually any interest, any skill, and any college major into your career plan. It may require creative thinking and some particularly creative explanations, but you may even be able to turn your unique combination of interests and skills into an advantage in getting a job. This is particularly true if you can integrate deep interests and skills in two or more complementary areas into a unique qualification.

The question, therefore, isn't whether a degree in a particular field will prepare you for a job. It is how you will use this degree as a foundation on which you can build your own differentiated and highly marketable brand.

> The question isn't whether a degree in a particular field will prepare you for a job. It is how you will use this degree as a foundation on which you can build your own differentiated and highly marketable brand.

Of Dream Careers and Safety Careers (Step 9)

I have mentioned the concept of a safety career in previous chapters. But just what is a safety career and why is it so important to have one? To understand, start with the generally self-explanatory concept of a dream career. A dream career is just what it sounds like—a career that allows you to do what you love. This can be playing golf or basketball, acting, writing, finding a cure for cancer, designing robots, saving the environment, or helping elderly people manage their day-to-day lives. It can be anything for which you have a passion and a commitment. The key is in discovering and nurturing your passion.

But even if you have a passion, building an emotionally engaging, financially secure (if not necessarily financially rewarding) career around a dream job can be challenging. Some passions, like playing professional basketball, can be psychically rewarding and pay extraordinarily well, but the odds of making it into the NBA, much less of establishing a solid, long-lasting professional career, are tiny. So too with acting, music, art and even a number of rigorous academic pursuits, such as philosophy or anthropology.

At the other extreme, it is very easy for most people to get a job helping elderly people—especially with the nation's rapidly growing aging population. However, finding a job in this field that will allow you to earn a living wage can be difficult. Building a career around the dream of finding a cure for cancer has its own challenges, not the least of which are earning and paying for the type of M.D. and/or PhD degrees that are generally required to get a job in serious cancer research.

The bad news is that pursuing a career based on one's passion can be a long, expensive, and frustrating pursuit. The good news is that no matter how long the odds, you can take a number of steps to dramatically improve your odds of landing your dream job and building your dream career.

This, however, is not to suggest that you put all your career eggs in a single basket. Commitment and perseverance are certainly critical (not just in your dream career, but in many other life pursuits), but you also need to be realistic and adaptable. You need to balance commitment and perseverance with realism and objectivity and go into it with your eyes wide open. You must, for example:

- Objectively assess your chances and the obstacles you will face in getting your dream job;
- Fully understand and balance the time and cost of preparing for this career with the job satisfaction and the income you can realistically expect; and
- Ensure that you will have the broad skills, the experience, and the credentials that will not only prepare you for this job but also give you an advantage over other applicants.

You must then develop and embark on a systematic effort to get and succeed in your dream career. But everyone, regardless of how deep your commitment or how strong your chances of getting your dream job, needs a contingency plan. What if, after years of trying, you don't reach your goals? What if you achieve these goals but, after a short career, you lose that job or discover that your dream job is not really quite as dreamy as you had imagined? What will you do next?

Career contingency planning is important throughout your entire career. It is particularly critical at the very beginning of your career; before you really know if you will be able to get a good job in your chosen field; before you have the experience to understand what working in that job will really entail; and before you take on the type of financial and family commitments that increase the risk of career change.

That's where a safety career comes in. A safety career is one:

- For which jobs are most likely to be available (such as accounting, finance, and sales jobs as well as many STEM, healthcare, or primary and special education fields); and
- That builds upon some of your particular interests and strengths (writing, speaking, empathy, creativity, cognition, etc.).

In other words, a safety career is something of an insurance policy; like applying for a safety school in case you don't get into the college of your dreams. It is however, much more. Unlike the case with applying for a safety school, the very approach of simultaneously preparing for both a dream and safety career can improve your qualifications for and your chances of getting a job in each of these fields by preparing you to provide more value to an employer. Just as importantly, it can also put you in a better position to control your own career, rather than leaving that control in the hands of an employer or the economy.

> Simultaneously preparing for both a dream and safety career can improve your qualifications for and your chances of getting a job in each of these fields. It can also put you in a better position to control your own career,

Ideally, this safety career may also be tied into your passion. Say, for example, that you love and know everything there is to know about sports, but question whether you will make it into the field, or be able to earn a living as a pro. What are some of your other interests and skills? How can you apply them to sports in a way that will allow you to build a career out of them?

Sounds a bit abstract? Let's look at a few examples of potential safety careers.

If You Can't Get in the Front Door, Find a Window (Step 9 Continued)

Say you love and are great at golf and you and your golf coach see a potential for you to go professional. You should work hard—very hard—at your game, but not to the exclusion of all else. After all, what if you don't make it in the PGA, or you can't earn a living from it—or your passion for golf fades as you get older and experience more things? What will you do when you're too old for the tour, or if an injury shortens your career?

That's where your other interests and skills come in. Even if you aren't destined to be the next Tiger Woods, you can still build a career around golf in a number of other ways. If you enjoy and are good at teaching, what about becoming a teaching pro? If you're good at forming relationships and negotiating, perhaps a sports agent? If you like math, perhaps become an investment advisor or accountant specializing in sports? Analysis and writing? You might like to be a sports attorney. If you are also interested in business, you might consider managing a golf course, a country club, or running golf tours. Computers? What about working on the PGA website? Chemistry or physics? Think about becoming an engineer designing next-generation clubs or balls.

What if none of these appeal to you right now? You might be surprised. Take some time to learn a little about them. Read and talk with more people to find ideas. Options for designing safety careers around a dream career are virtually endless. The more you explore these options, the more other additional possibilities will appear.

That's exactly what you want: To identify a few potential fields that mesh with your passion, to learn about them, to decide what you like and don't like about each, examine how well they are suited to your needs (and you to theirs), and to identify and explore other areas. The more you learn and explore, the more options you will discover—or better yet, identify opportunities or market needs that have not yet been identified or are not currently being addressed and come up with a totally new way of addressing them.

Perhaps none of these options will result in a life in which you spend every minute golfing, but they may have the potential of allowing you to develop a viable career that will allow you to live—and earn a living—in and around the world of golf.

The concept of safety careers applies to any field.

- What if you planned a career in law, but ended up one of the 35 percent of law school graduates who can't get a job practicing law and you don't want to open your own practice? First of all, virtually every career will benefit from the research, analysis, reasoning, and writing skills that you hone in law school. Even if you don't work specifically in law, combining this background with an undergraduate or graduate degree in accounting or finance can position you very well for a career as a tax accountant. Work in contracts can help in all types of careers, such as banking and real estate. Law degrees, meanwhile, have also become almost a de facto qualification for a career in politics. True, three years spent in school plus well over $100,000 in tuition may be costly insurance, but you will almost always get some value from law school.

- Want to be a doctor, but can't get into—or can't pay for— medical school? You could leverage your undergraduate pre-med studies into a job as a nurse or a nurse practitioner (both of which will continue to experience huge demand) and then apply for medical school in the future. Or you could apply to dentistry, optometry, or veterinary schools. If you love medicine, but can't pass Chemistry 101, think about being a hospital administrator, a pharmaceutical salesperson, or a malpractice attorney. Or even a hospital orderly or home healthcare aide.

The point of this long discussion of contingency planning is that you can no longer just plan for a career. You also have to plan for contingencies—virtually all contingencies. Nor can you limit the type of skills you develop because you don't expect to need them in the future. Possessing a broad range of skills is critical for almost any job in the creative economy. It is also instrumental in preparing you to capitalize on unanticipated opportunities and in recovering from unanticipated career or life shocks.

> You can no longer just plan for a career. You also have to plan for contingencies. Nor can you limit the type of skills you develop. A broad range of skills is critical for almost any job in the creative economy. It is also instrumental in preparing you to capitalize on unanticipated opportunities and in recovering from unanticipated career or life shocks.

Having these skills can even create new opportunities. A friend or colleague, from the extensive network that you build and cultivate, may present you with a new opportunity of which you had never dreamed. Or you may be reading something far out of your primary area of focus that ends up sparking a new passion. Such opportunities can cause you to rethink your entire career plan, or they may provide complementary experiences that will allow you to resume your original career with an entirely new (and differentiating) perspective or set of skills. They can also expand your network, which can present even more new opportunities.

Although a career plan is critical to getting on the first rung of a promising career path, no career will ever develop exactly as you have planned. Nor should you ever expect or want it to. You must always be prepared to:

- Modify or totally discard a plan that isn't working as you expected;
- Recognize and take full advantage of an opportunity that you had not previously anticipated, even if it is totally contrary to your plan; and
- Convert every one of your career setbacks into a new opportunity.

From Skills Requirements to Skills Development (Step 10)

Now that you have identified a set of initial leverageable and complementary career opportunities that apply your skills to your passions, you have to determine the skills and credentials you will need. Not just the skills that will be required to qualify you for your target job, but those that will differentiate you from and give you an advantage over others that will be applying for the same job. Then when you add in the skills and personality traits you will require across your entire career (Chapter 3), you can begin to identify the type of post-secondary education and training you will need.

Some professions, such as teaching, engineering, the practice of medicine, or one of the many other branches of healthcare science, have strict requirements as to courses you must take, the certifications you must get and even the schools that are accredited to teach these courses. The vast majority of high-skill professions, however, offer far more flexibility. Even the practice of law, which still requires that you graduate from an accredited law school and pass a state bar exam, does not require a specific undergraduate field of study, provides total flexibility in courses beyond the first year (usually including courses from complementary graduate schools [business, public policy, and so forth]). Some state bars are even considering making the third-year of the law school courses optional, in favor of a one-year apprenticeship program.

Most high-skill professions, however, have even fewer requirements. Many, such as software development and management, even permit the substitution of informal education and demonstrated competence as an alternative to a formal education.

The good news is that there are now far more options for getting an education than ever before: Trade schools, boot camps, online classes, and many other options. Many colleges even allow you to substitute work experience, apprenticeships, independent study, and online courses for course-based credits. The bad news is that there are more options than ever and that some of the most popular—especially colleges—are becoming so expensive as to become cost-prohibitive for many families.

So what type of post-secondary education is right for you, with your own specific interests, career goals, learning style, and financial considerations? What type of education will not only prepare you for your dream and safety careers but also give you the long-term flexibility you will need to pursue new careers, as your interests or circumstances change—and simultaneously to maximize the value you can deliver in whichever career you choose?

Chapters 7 through 9 lay out the growing number of educational options, explain the roles, advantages and limitations of each, and provide guides to help you get the most out of each.

CHAPTER 7

The College Conundrum

Steps 10 Through 12

Education is what remains after one has forgotten what one has learned in school.

—Albert Einstein

Key Points

- College grads on average have more fulfilling, enriching, and stable careers than those without degrees.
- Occupations that require an advanced degree are growing faster than jobs with lesser educational requirements.
- Although a four-year degree is the most common and socially accepted path to a fulfilling and enriching job, it is not the only path and isn't well-suited to all.
- There is serious question whether college is fulfilling its core missions and especially if the costs outweigh the benefits.
- There are more credible options to college than ever before.
- One of the worse reasons to go to colleges is that you're expected to do so.

You now know the types of jobs that are likely to offer the best career opportunities (Chapter 2) and the broad range of skills that will be required for success in today's Creative Economy (Chapter 3). You have assessed your own passions, interests, and skills (Chapter 5) and have developed an initial idea of the types of jobs and careers that are best suited to them (as well as their employment prospects, skill and credential requirements, potential salaries, and their long-term growth potential)

(Chapter 6). You now need a plan that will not only ensure that you have the qualifications to prepare you for entry into your chosen field but that will also:

- Differentiate and provide you with an advantage over other candidates for landing your first—and ideally your first few—dream jobs; and
- Prepare you for long-term success, not just in your first few jobs, but through your entire career (in whatever field that career may turn out to be) and in your life outside of work.

This is a complex task which is complicated by the fact that your educational opportunities are exploding. In the "old days," you learned the requirements for most careers by learning, either formally (as through an apprenticeship program) or informally (as by being thrown into a new position or by working under or with people with more experience). The career preparation process changed with the creation of formal primary and secondary schools and curricula and, especially, with the creation of colleges and graduate schools.

There are now literally hundreds of different types of college and graduate programs. Some schools, such as community colleges, many for-profit schools, and boot camps, combine elements of classroom education and apprenticeship-like training. Community college educations, meanwhile, can blend into four-year college degrees and new types of education, such as Massive Open Online Courses (MOOCs) and Gap Year programs, can be used as part of or substitute for any of these more formal educational programs.

Given all the options and the blurring of distinctions among them, it's not possible to examine the education section of the plan (Steps 10 to 14) sequentially. I am, therefore, dividing the examination of educational issues across three chapters, aligned generally by type of institution and program and the complementary and competing ways in which you can use each to achieve your goals.

- This chapter focuses broadly on the growing debate surrounding the role and value of a college education and the growing number of alternatives to a four-year degree;

- Chapter 8 is for those who have chosen or are considering a four-year college or university, looking at the considerations of choosing a school; majors, minors, and other courses; and graduate school. It also looks into some of the broader issues surrounding a college education, such as the tradeoffs between preparing for a job and developing broader life and career skills; the tradeoffs among academics, social life, extracurricular activities, and internships; and the increasingly critical issue of the cost of a college education, who can afford it, and how to assess the value of your degree.

- Chapter 9 examines the exploding range of options to a four-year degree. It begins with community colleges (and the multiple roles they play) and how they blend with and compete with apprenticeships; the growing range of structured, semistructured, and unstructured options to college; and different means of supplementing a college degree with more career-focused programs.

Thinking about Your Education Options

College is certainly the most common, the most socially sanctioned, and the most employer-recognized path to preparing for a high-skill occupation. And, in an era in which the nature of jobs is changing so quickly, college has become one of the most trusted indicators that you have the core knowledge, skills, and persistence required to do the job for which you are being hired. Just as importantly, in a slow growth market in which employers have a choice of many applicants for each job, many are demonstrating a strong preference for a college grad, even for jobs that do not actually require a college degree.

This being said, college is not the only path to a rewarding, high-skill, high-value career. Many good jobs don't require college. Different careers require very different types and amounts of education and training—ranging from effectively zero to eight or more years of formal postsecondary education, plus multiple years of on-the-job training. (See the Bureau of Labor Statistics [BLS] Education and Training Assignment site for an overview of these requirements for different occupations.)[1]

Nor may college be the best path for you. College, after all, is just one means of gaining the knowledge, developing the skills, and creating the network you will need for your career. As discussed later, many people with more than enough intelligence and persistence to succeed in college are better suited to much less formal, much more personalized learning environments.

> Although a four-year college degree is the most common and most widely recognized path to preparing for a high-value career, it is not the only one. And it may not be the best one for you, your particular needs or for the type of job you are targeting.

This being said, college, or some other form of disciplined higher education (whether formal or informal and self-directed), will be one of the primary means by which most young adults will develop not only the qualifications but also the certifications that employers will look for in new employees. This education will also form the foundation for the type of self-directed analysis, critical and innovative thinking, communication, and life skills that you will need in all aspects of your life, as well as in your career.

While Chapters 8 and 9 look specifically at the advantages, limitations, and roles of various types of postsecondary education, this chapter looks broadly at the roles of various types of education in preparing you for the jobs of the future, the relative advantages and limitations of each, and provides a means of thinking about the type of education that may be best for you.

The College Advantage

College graduates, as I have discussed throughout this book, are still having a tough time finding jobs that make use of their education. Although larger percentages of graduates are now getting jobs than during and immediately after the recession, many of these jobs neither require degrees nor pay the salaries or provide the training or advancement opportunities of those that do require degrees. But if you think it's tough for college grads, consider the plight of those who don't earn college degrees.

College grads (and especially advanced degree holders) are far more likely to earn more money and are far less likely to experience unemployment at some time during their careers. For example:

- Ninety-four of the BLS's Top 100 paying occupations[2] require a four-year degree or higher;
- Pay for college graduates has risen 15.7 percent over the past 32 years (after adjustment for inflation),[3] while income of workers without college degrees has declined by 25.7 percent:
- Lifetime earnings of high school graduates average about $973,000 in 2009 dollars, compared with $3.6 million for those with professional degrees (associate and bachelor's degree holders fall in between, at about $1.7 million and $2.3 million, respectively).[4]

These disparities aren't new. However, they are becoming much more pronounced, especially during and in the aftermath of recessions. As shown in Table 7.1, those adults with higher levels of education enjoy higher rates of employment than do those with less education, regardless of the state of the economy. Just as importantly, these employment rates tend to fall much more slowly for those with higher levels of education during and after a recession than for those with less education. In fact, the last recession saw the employment rate for high school educated individuals fall more than twice as much as for those with bachelor degrees.

Table 7.1 Employment rates by education level: 2007–2012

	High school degree	**Associate's degree**	**Bachelor's degree**
Before recession	55%	64%	69%
During recession	51%	62%	67%
After recession	47%	57%	65%
Percentage decline from before to after recession	16%	11%	7%

Source: Adapted from "How Much Protection Does a College Degree Afford?" (2013), Figure 2, p. 11. http://www.pewstates.org/uploadedFiles/PCS_Assets/2013/Pew_college_grads_recession_report. pdf (Figure 2, page 11)

As shown in Figure 7.1, wages are also increasing much more rapidly for the most highly educated workers than for their lesser educated counterparts. In fact, after adjusting for inflation, the wages for those who did not complete college have barely risen over the last 40 years and have fallen significantly from their peak in the early 1970s. Those for people with less than a high school degree have actually fallen. In contrast, wages for college grads have risen handily.

But, as dramatic as this Council of Economic Advisors' chart is, it masks one of the greatest disparities of all. By combining Bachelor's degree holders with those with those with a Graduate degree, it somewhat overstates the differential between Bachelor's and Associate's degree holders and significantly understates the differential between Bachelor's and Graduate degree holders. A similar chart by economists Daron Acemoglu and David Autor separates the results for these degrees. It shows that the salary gap between those who earn Bachelor's and Graduate degrees has

Dollars (2010)

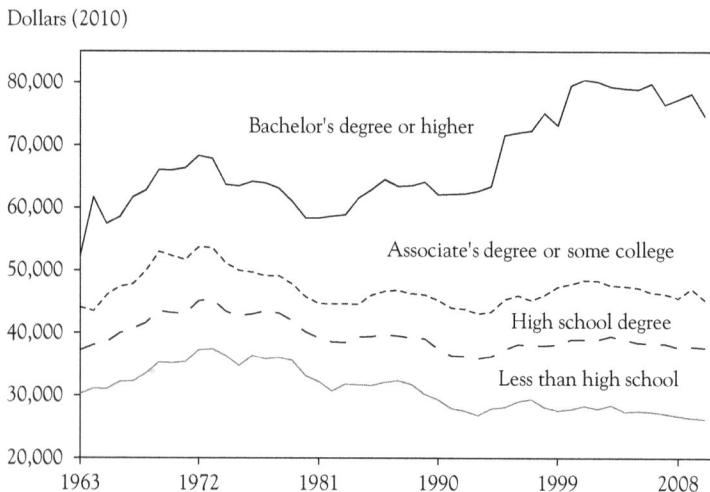

Figure 7.1 Average annual earnings by worker education, 1963–2010

Note: The sample includes workers aged 25–65 who worked at least 35 hours a week and for at least 50 weeks in the calendar year. Before 1992, education groups are defined based on the highest grade of school or year of college completed. Beginning in 1992, groups are defined based on the highest degree or diploma earned. Earnings are deflated using the CPI-U. Calculations are based on survey data collected in March of each year and reflect average wage and salary income for the previous calendar year.

Source: Council of Economic Advisers calculations using March Current Population Survey.

grown even wider than the gap that separates Associate's and Bachelor's degree holders.[5] One recent study, in fact, found that the gap between those with Bachelor's and Graduate degrees has grown from almost zero in 1963 to 27 percent in 2010.[6]

These disparities have continued throughout and in the aftermath of the recession. As shown in the 2013 Pew Research Trusts study referenced in Table 7.1 above, four-year college graduates (and to a somewhat lesser extent, those with associate degrees) not only had continually higher rates of employment than high school graduates, but that they were less likely to lose their jobs during the recession. They also had greater success in finding new jobs after being unemployed and suffered much lower declines in wages (5 percent) than did those with less education (10 percent for high school and, somewhat paradoxically, 12 percent for those with associate degrees).

The advantages of a college education, while already great, are growing.[7] Median weekly earnings of college-educated, full-time workers are now 79 percent above those for similarly aged adults with high school diplomas. This premium has increased from 48 percent a mere 30 years ago. And this does not even include the fact that college grads are more likely to be employed in full-time jobs.

> While inflation-adjusted wages for those who did not complete college have barely risen over the last 40 years and those with less than a high school degree have actually fallen, those for people with college-and especially graduate degrees have surged. College-educated workers now earn 79 percent more than those with just high school degrees.

Table 7-2 Employment rates by education Level—2007–2012

	High school degree	**Associate's degree**	**Bachelor's degree**
Before Recession	55%	64%	69%
During Recession	51%	62%	67%
After Recession	47%	57%	65%

Source: Pew Charitable Trust

These wage advantages continue over one's entire career. According to the Georgetown University Center on Education and the Workforce, by the time the average four-year college degree holder retires, he will have earned $960,000 more than his counterpart with a high school diploma.[8] And, for STEM graduates from prestigious schools such as MIT and Caltech, these lifetime premiums can be even greater—about $2 million according to a 2013 PayScale analysis.[9]

Those with two-year associate degrees, meanwhile, earn an average of about $425,000 more, and those with some college (but not a degree) earn more than $240,000 more than those with just a high school diploma. The Brookings Institution Hamilton Project expresses the value of a four-year college education in terms of a return on your investment in college tuition and room and board.[10] It estimates that graduates earn an average 16 percent annual return, even after accounting for lost earnings during college.

As great as these economic differences may appear, they do not even begin to account for the noneconomic advantages that college grads are likely to have over their less-educated counterparts. For example, they tend to have longer life expectancies, lower divorce rates, fewer single-parent families, and lower rates of smoking. Grads also tend to live in safer neighborhoods and their children attend better schools and achieve higher levels of academic and economic achievement. In fact, a number of studies show that U.S. intragenerational and intergenerational wealth mobility (the ability for individuals and their children to move from one economic class to another) has fallen dramatically, with the United States now having one of the lowest levels of mobility in the developed world.[11] The best way to improve both your and your children's economic fortunes, according to another Pew Charitable Trust study, is for you to earn a college or, better yet, an advanced degree.[12]

This education is becoming more important and more prevalent than ever. A record 33.5 percent of Americans aged 25 to 29 now have at least a bachelor's degree (up from 24 percent less than 20 years ago) and another five percent have an associate's degree.[13] The problem is that almost half of these people do not have jobs that require a degree.[14] But if you think these graduates have it tough, think about those a bit further down the educational ladder. They are losing or being displaced from traditionally non-college jobs by people with degrees.

Higher-Education: High-Skill Holy Grail?

At first glance, given all the employment, income, and other disparities, it may appear that any student with a real choice in the matter should get at least a bachelor's degree and, ideally, a master's. Although only one-third of all jobs currently require more than a high school degree, jobs that require more than a high school degree are expected to grow significantly faster than those that do not.[15] As shown in Figure 7.2, the fastest growing will be those that typically require advanced degrees (especially master's) and those that require either an associate degree or some form of postsecondary certificate. Although jobs that require bachelor's degrees are expected to grow at a faster rate than those that do not require any postsecondary degree or certification, they will experience the slowest growth of any of those jobs that do require post-secondary education. And which single job is likely to experience the fastest percentage growth over the next decade—organizational and industrial psychologists, whose ranks are expected to grow by 53 percent.[16]

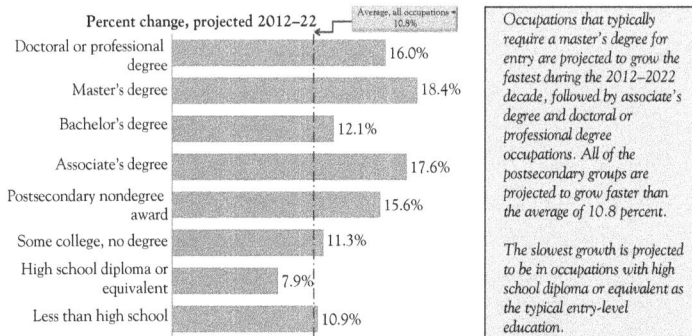

Percent change, projected 2012–22

Average, all occupations 10.8%

Education category	Percent change
Doctoral or professional degree	16.0%
Master's degree	18.4%
Bachelor's degree	12.1%
Associate's degree	17.6%
Postsecondary nondegree award	15.6%
Some college, no degree	11.3%
High school diploma or equivalent	7.9%
Less than high school	10.9%

Occupations that typically require a master's degree for entry are projected to grow the fastest during the 2012–2022 decade, followed by associate's degree and doctoral or professional degree occupations. All of the postsecondary groups are projected to grow faster than the average of 10.8 percent.

The slowest growth is projected to be in occupations with high school diploma or equivalent as the typical entry-level education.

Figure 7.2 Percent change in employment, by education category 2012–2022 (projected)

Source: U.S. Bureau of Labor Statistics (2012), Chart on p. 2. http://www.bls.gov/emp/ep_edtrain_outlook.pdf (Chart on page 2)

Clearly, not all fast-growing, high-skill, high-pay jobs will require a master's, or even a bachelor's degree. Apprenticeships, as discussed in Chapter 9, can also be good onramps to good jobs. In fact, BLS estimates that jobs requiring apprenticeships will grow at an even faster rate than those that require master's degrees—22.2 percent.[17] There are, however, some important common threads among all types of good paying, high-growth occupations—virtually all will require some form of formal postsecondary education or training and many of the fastest growing, highest paying of them will require some form of STEM skills.

Questioning the Value of a College Education

Although the rewards of a college education can be great, they can also be speculative. You have to pay for these educations upfront, before you know what type of job you will end up getting upon graduation. Given the experiences of the last seven years, it's of little surprise that many prospective students are questioning the value of a college education or the ramifications of the debt they will have to take out to pay for their educations.

Prospective students and their parents, however, aren't the only ones questioning the value of a degree. A 2012 McKinsey Center for Government study found that only 42 percent of surveyed companies and 45 percent of recent graduates thought that colleges and universities had prepared graduates for today's jobs.[18] (In something of a startling disconnect, 72 percent of surveyed colleges thought their graduates were prepared!)

> Although only 42 percent of surveyed companies and 45 percent of recent graduates thought that colleges and universities had prepared graduates for today's jobs, 72 percent of surveyed colleges thought their graduates were prepared!

Some academics are also questioning what students actually learn from their college experiences. Richard Arum and Josipa Roksa's 2011 book, *Academically Adrift*, questions whether colleges deliver what they promise, or whether they even teach the right skills.[19] They demonstrate that many colleges are not delivering on their primary missions of teaching the types of critical thinking, complex reasoning, and effective writing skills (much less inspiring the type of self-discovery and reflection and instilling the type of lifetime love of learning) that have been the traditional hallmarks of higher education. In fact, their analysis of the results of College Learning Assessment test results suggests that 45 percent of graduates have no appreciable gain in critical thinking skills from a four-year degree![20] Claudia Goldin and Lawrence Katz, in their book *The Race Between Education and Technology*, agree that many graduates leave college without the high-level reasoning skills needed to succeed.[21]

Arum and Roska's study spreads the blame among schools, professors, and students. For example:

- Many schools and professors offer too many courses with minimal requirements and lax grading; and
- Students take too many courses with minimal reading and writing requirements and have dramatically reduced the time dedicated to homework in favor of social activities.

But while the majority of students from a majority of schools show little gain in critical thinking skills over their college career, the study does find exceptions. Not too surprisingly, students whose parents went to college, those who had better grades in high school advanced placement courses, and those in more selective schools tend to show greater Collegiate Learning Assessment (CLA) gains over their college careers than do others.

Other academics, such as George Mason's Bryan Caplan, contend that many colleges are becoming little more than diploma mills for certifying a graduate's intelligence and competency (at least in the type of memorization and categorization skills and self-discipline that schools, from primary through college, typically teach, test, and reward). The sorting process, he contends, has become more important than the learning process.[22] How and why has this happened? Students are increasingly looking for easy courses and social opportunities; parents for a road to their children's career; and businesses for skills that can deliver immediate value. UCLA, which has conducted surveys and studies of incoming freshmen over the last 40 years, provides support for such assertions. As New York Times columnist David Brooks explains, these statistics suggest that high school graduates arrive at college with very different expectations and habits than did those in the mid-1960s.[23]

First, incoming freshman enter college expecting much better grades for much less work. In 1966, for example, 19 percent of incoming freshman graduated high school with A or A- averages. By 2013, 53 percent had these averages. That is despite the facts that recent graduates have done less homework (in 1987, nearly half of high school students did at least six hours of homework per week, compared with fewer than 33 percent in 2006) and were less diligent in attending class (In 1966, 48 percent of students said they sometimes showed up late to class, compared with more than 60 percent in 2006). But despite this, recent graduates rate themselves much more highly than past generations on leadership skills, writing abilities, social self-confidence and so on.

They also arrive in college with different expectations of what they hope to gain from college. In 1966, 86 percent of college freshmen believed that developing a "philosophy of life" was very important, compared with fewer than 50 percent today. Money, however, has become more important, with the percentage of freshman "going to college primarily to allow them to earn more money" increasing from 50 percent in 1976 to 69 percent by 2006.

While many colleges seek to fulfil traditional objectives (helping students discover themselves, learn critical high-level skills, develop philosophies of life, become good citizens, and so forth), they also have to cater to current student and parent expectations and accommodate the engrained habits of today's students. Columbia professor Andrew DelBlanco, in his book, *College: What it Is, Was and Should Be*, questions whether any school can ever address such conflicting needs.[24]

These conflicts, combined with new challenges, such as the need to reduce ballooning costs and challenges based by Massive Open Online Courses (discussed in Chapter 9) has prompted a team of academics, working under Harvard Business School professor Clayton Christensen, to conduct a study on the future of colleges. The study, entitled "Disrupting

College," questions whether the current university model is even sustainable—except for the largest, richest, most prestigious schools.[25]

Some critics go further. The unschooling movement in general and the Thiel Foundation[26] and the UnCollege[27] organization, in particular, argue not only that college doesn't deliver value, but that it can be downright detrimental. Colleges, they claim, don't even attempt, much less succeed in teaching the real skills that are required for success. Thiel provides $100,000 grants to select students who skip college to focus on work, research, and self-education. UnCollege and a number of similar organizations provide encouragement, direction, and now, even formal programs to help young adults pursue self-education. (A number of such programs are discussed specifically in Chapter 9.)

Still, for all the drawbacks and questions, college continues to reign as the overwhelmingly preferred model for preparing for a career—not just for what you learn, but as a final opportunity to mature, for whom you meet, and not inconsequentially, for the credentials and the image that college confers.

Higher education, therefore, is becoming more and more popular, even as it becomes less and less credible, and probably, less and less viable. For example, as of October 2011, 68.3 percent of 2011 high school graduates were enrolled in colleges or universities—just below the record high.[28] The actual number of attendees—21 million—has been climbing relatively steadily since the Great Depression. Meanwhile, as mentioned previously, the percentage of young adults graduating from four-year colleges has now reached an all-time high of 33.5 percent. And these figures do not include more than 500,000 students who were enrolled in nondegree-granting postsecondary institutions, such as technical training and certificate programs.

But even graduation is often not enough. A 2013 Accenture survey[29] of 2011/2012 graduates, for example, found that while current college students generally believe that their degree will allow them to get and succeed in the job they want, those who had recently graduated and are in the job market have very different opinions:

- Fifty-two percent of grads with a two-year degree said they will need to get a four-year degree in order to get the job they want;

- Forty-two percent of four-year college grads expect they will need to pursue a graduate-level degree to further their career;
- Forty-eight percent of unemployed graduates said they would have fared better in the job market with a different major, and 57 percent expect to go back to school within the next five years.

Is College Worth It?

Unfortunately increased enrollment, or even national graduation rates, do not necessarily translate into improved college performance, much less increased employment. According to the Institute of Education Sciences, only 59 percent of full-time, first-time students who enroll in four year colleges actually graduate within six years and a depressing 31 percent in two-year programs graduate in three years.[30]

Those who leave without earning their degrees end up reaping the worst of both worlds. Although employment rates and earnings are somewhat higher than for those who do not attend college at all, they paid for the college experience, may have racked up debt, delayed their entry into the workforce (at least assuming they could have gotten a job), and probably suffered a blow to their egos.

And this does not even begin to consider the astronomical costs of getting a college degree and the sometimes crippling burden of student loan debt, both of which are discussed in gruesome detail in Chapter 8.

One thing is for sure. If you do decide to go to college, you must know exactly why you are going, what you intend to get out of college and then be sure that you get everything out of college that you intend. Getting a job should not be the only or even the primary objective of a college education. That being said, college requires too big of an investment to not consider how well it will prepare you for a career. After all, while the "average" college graduate more than recoups the out-of-pocket (tuition, etc.) and the opportunity costs (lost wages while they are in school) of going to college, everyone is not average. The PayScale survey that found the huge college premium earned by MIT and Caltech grads, for example, also found that humanities graduates from lowly ranked colleges may actually learn less than those who never attended college.[9]

Although college is too big of an investment to not consider how well it will prepare you for a career, getting a job should not be the primary objective. But whatever your objectives, you must know exactly why you are going, what you intend to get out of it and then be sure that you get everything you intend.

The "Major" Question

Deciding whether you go to college and where you go are critical questions. But, as suggested by the above example, the question of deciding in which field you major is becoming almost as important. This comes down to a couple of questions. For example, what do you really hope to gain from college (at least academically)? Do you want to prepare for a job; to "learn to learn" and to "love to learn," to become an informed and well-rounded person; or some combination of these and others.

This can be a critical question. After all, the selection of your major is probably the single most important determinant of whether a college graduate will even get a job that makes use of their education.

- On one hand, as shown in the 2012 BLS College To Career report, graduates with degrees in healthcare, education, engineering, IT, and business tend to have the greatest success in finding jobs.[31] Those with degrees in social sciences, and especially in humanities and the arts, generally have the least success.
- On the other hand, liberal arts and humanities programs are often seen as being more intellectually rigorous, providing the greatest breadth of learning experiences, and as being more effective in helping you develop the type of interdisciplinary, critical thinking, and communication skills that will be required throughout your career and your life. This being said, according to the Gallup-Purdue Index, while STEM and business graduates are much more likely than social sciences and humanities graduates to get full-time jobs (more than

60 percent compared with less than 40 percent), those of the latter who do get jobs are slightly more likely to find their work engaging.[32]

The question partially comes down to a question of what you really want from college. What are the relative values you put on pursuing your passion, getting a job, and developing long-term life and career skills?

As for the jobs question, the facts are hard to dispute. Those majoring in nursing, education, engineering, math, biology, computer science, accounting, and economics are not only far more likely to find jobs, they are also more likely to get jobs in their field. And except for education majors, they are also likely to earn higher salaries. Social sciences and humanities majors: much less so! (A more dated BLS report looks specifically at starting salaries for a range of liberal arts majors.)[33]

> The selection of your major is probably the single most import-
> ant determinant of whether a college graduate will even get
> a job that makes use of their education. Nursing, education,
> engineering, math, biology, computer science, accounting, and
> economics are likely to offer the best prospects.

This being said, liberal arts graduates from highly selective Ivy League and other tier-one schools typically have much greater success in finding jobs than do graduates from less selective schools. This is almost regardless of major. The vast majority of these graduates either go on to graduate school or land jobs before graduation.

Particularly attractive liberal arts graduates of less selective schools—those with the most in-demand majors, the best grades, the most relevant experience and accomplishments, the strongest references, and so forth—may also fare well in scoring good jobs. Morgan Stanley, for example, expects to hire 25 to 30 percent of its bachelor-level hires out of liberal arts, rather than business programs.[34] But whichever major you choose, you will want to think long and hard about your choice. Some surveys suggest that about half of all recent graduates have come to regret their choices of majors.

The question of majors, what you gain from each, their respective employment and salary prospects—and ways of combining "practical," "passion" and "learning" courses into a single educational program—are discussed in much greater detail in Chapter 8. But before jumping into a discussion of college, it's important to mention some increasingly interesting alternative (or in some cases, additive) approaches to learning life and career skills and yes, even for preparing for and getting your first job.

The Non-College Options

There's no question: Long-term success in virtually any career—much less the ability to shape a career around your dreams and maintain control of your career—will absolutely require education beyond high school. But although a four-year college is certainly the most widely accepted means of beginning this education, it is not the only means. It may not even be the best type of education for a particular individual or career.

After all, of the more than 20 million new jobs that BLS expects to be created this decade, fewer than 25 percent actually require a bachelor's degree or higher.[35] The majority—12.8 million out of 20.4 million total—will still require only a high school education or less (see Table 1.3 of the BLS's Occupational Handbook).[36]

Although the vast majority of these jobs will offer low pay, few benefits, little job security, and few significant training or advancement opportunities, there are exceptions. But, as discussed previously, virtually all except the most unskilled of these will require some form of formal postsecondary education or training. This preparation may include:

- Traditional blended education or training programs for entry into a skilled trade, such as those offered by community colleges or apprenticeships programs;
- Shorter, less formal certificate programs, as for tractor–trailer drivers and cosmetologists;
- New, less-structured MOOC courses and, increasingly, more formalized multicourse programs that may culminate in certificates or degrees;
- Short-term "boot camps" that are intended to provide fast, intensive exposure to a particular discipline, such as basic

programming or starting and managing your own entrepreneurial business; and

- Increasingly popular, increasingly structured non-college programs and gap years.

There are also opportunities to bypass even these educational programs in favor of less formal, self-directed programs. There are, for example, opportunities for especially motivated (and especially extroverted) young adults to go on their own missions of self-discovery, as by travelling, working in different jobs to understand what they entail, and then, as they get a better idea of what they want to do, get jobs (or more likely unpaid internships) in positions and with companies that may lead to a career.

Meanwhile, some companies are much more interested in your accomplishments than in your educational credentials or your chronological age. For example, a growing number of software companies (think Google, Facebook, etc.) are recruiting particularly talented college students well before graduation, showing them how they could learn much more (often $80,000–$100,000 starting salaries) by skipping the rest of college and going directly into a job. Many have already begun to target particularly promising interns who are still in high school.

Nor do you necessarily need sterling technology to score a good job without college. Good salespeople, for example, are always in demand. A bright, ambitious person, with the right training, communication, and empathic skills and a detailed understanding of a product's capabilities and how they can be used to address a pressing customer need, will almost always have a choice of job opportunities. And then there are entrepreneurs. They can come from anywhere—no specific education or training required.

Or you could bypass all of this by starting your own company straight out of high school, or partway through college. After all, it worked for Bill Gates and Mark Zuckerberg. Moreover, one ex-technology magnate even offers no-strings $100,000 grants to particularly promising students who drop out of college to launch their own companies.

These and many other non-college options are discussed in much greater depth in Chapter 9.

Where Do You Go From Here?

So what type of education and experience is right for you? That requires you to answer a number of questions. For example, how did you do in high school? What form of learning is most effective for you? How self-directed are you? What are your career objectives and how thoroughly have you explored and prepared for them? Can you afford college? What are your family responsibilities? Even if you focus primarily on employability and salary, the answer varies greatly by factors including:

- Which career do you plan to pursue and what combination of education, training, skills, and preparation does it require?
- What combination, above the base requirements, will give you a particular advantage in this field?
- What experience and accomplishments do you currently have in your targeted field?
- Which school are we talking about: Harvard or the proverbial Podunk State? What is the educational and employment value of a degree from that school?
- Which major do you plan to pursue?
- Exactly what do you expect to get out of your education and how can you ensure that you get that value?
- Do you have the direction, motivation, and self-discipline required to develop and pursue a nonstructured education program, or do you need a more gradual transition (i.e., college or apprenticeship) from the structure of high school to the "real world"?
- What will be the cost of the degree? Is it a private or public school, what types of financial aid are available, and can you ameliorate expenses such as by living at home or working part time?

Many people are capable of doing quite well without a formal postsecondary education or apprenticeship. This is even true for a handful of people who plan to enter highly demanding, high-skill occupations. This being said, a four-year college education provides much more than preparation for a career. It (along with community colleges and apprenticeship programs) also provides additional opportunities to mature, and more gradual transitions from high school to the world of work, careers, and financial responsibility.

But whatever form of education you prefer, you will need a combination of academic education to develop the technical skills and to understand the processes and the context of your field, and experience to develop the practical understanding of how to perform the work efficiently and effectively. Even more importantly, as stated by Harvard's Graduate School of Education and Innovation Lab's Tony Wagner, "the world no longer cares how much you know; the world cares about what you can do with what you know."[37] And if and when you do graduate, you need more than an education and potential, you also need skills—skills that will allow you to deliver immediate value to an employer.

> The world no longer cares how much you know; the world cares about what you can do with what you know. Getting and succeeding in a good job increasingly requires skills that will allow you to deliver immediate value to an employer—and especially the personality traits discussed in Chapter 3.

In the end, however, you also need something else. You also need the type of personality traits that, as discussed in Chapter 3, that will be increasingly required for success in any field. As Wagner explains, "To succeed in the twenty-first century economy, students must learn to analyze and solve problems, collaborate, persevere, take calculated risks, and learn from failure."[33]

So, with these caveats, let's now take a deeper look into the most common means of preparing for a professional, high-skill career: four-year colleges.

CHAPTER 8

The College Equation

Steps 10 Through 14

23- to 25-year-olds with bachelor's degrees make $12,000 more than high school graduates but by age 50, the gap has grown to $46,500. When we look at lifetime earnings . . . the total premium is $570,000 for a bachelor's degree and $170,000 for an associate's degree.
                                        —Brookings Institution

Key Points

- Although you certainly want a college education that will prepare you to get your first job, it's more important to prepare for success—not just in that job, but in your entire career and your life.
- Selection of your major is at least as important as your selection of a school in getting a job that makes use of your education.
- Healthcare, engineering, computer science, and business majors are most likely to land jobs that require a degree and that are related to their majors.
- Employers are generally more interested in graduates with cognitive, communication, and work skills than in domain-specific content knowledge.
- Even if you're in a professional or preprofessional major, be sure to include a healthy dose of liberal arts classes.
- Although some little-known colleges provide the best returns on your education investments, some elite private universities may offer some of the best college bargains.

College had been an integral part of the American Dream: A veritable ticket to a good job and an upper middle class lifestyle. To some graduates, it is increasingly becoming part of the American nightmare: underemployment or even unemployment, combined with big debts. Former Secretary of Education Bill Bennett, for example, claims that only 57 percent of adults now believe a college degree is worth it, compared with 83 percent in 2008.[1]

But, for better or worse, a college degree is becoming the new high school degree. A growing number of employers now look for applicants with degrees, even for jobs that didn't traditionally require them. Even for jobs where they are not actually required, many employers will almost reflexively choose an applicant with a degree over one without one. This has led to rapid growth in college enrollment (although there was a slight decline in 2012). Even though a pitifully high 36 percent of students who begin at a four-year college don't graduate within six years, a record percentage of young adults (38 percent of those between 25 and 34) now hold some type of postsecondary degree.[2]

The good news for aspiring graduates is that this is nowhere near sufficient to address projected demand. Although close to half of all recent college graduates either can't get jobs or can't get ones that require a degree, a Georgetown University Center on Education and the Workforce study states that 63 percent[3] of all U.S. jobs will require some form of postsecondary education by the year 2018. Although the skills requirements for new jobs is certainly expanding, some of this new demand will likely come from the same type of "job inflation" that has already affected college grads. We are already seeing employers demanding college degrees for jobs that have not traditionally required them. Unfortunately, few of these jobs pay college-level wages or provide college-level career paths.

But, while a four-year degree (or increasingly even a graduate degree) is increasingly becoming a de facto requirement for a growing number of jobs, this does not, as suggested in Chapter 7, necessarily mean that college is right for you. And it absolutely does not mean that you can't get a good job without a degree. In fact, as discussed previously, the number of occupations that require certificates and associate degrees are growing more rapidly—and some of these offer better pay and probably more stable careers than do those that at least nominally require degrees. And there are now many more opportunities for getting solid non-four-year postsecondary education than has been the case in the past.

The educational and job opportunities for these less traditional postsecondary education and training programs are discussed in detail in Chapter 9. This chapter looks specifically at the factors you must consider if you are among the growing number of high school grads that has decided that college is right for you. It looks at everything from how to select the type of college and the specific school that is best suited to your needs, what you should look for—and even demand—from your professors and your courses, the major and minors that are most likely to result in good jobs, and how to deal with the skyrocketing costs of getting a degree.

Finding the School that's Right for You

Colleges and universities have long been the pride of the U.S. educational system. U.S. institutions perpetually dominate ranks of the world's best universities, with 7 of the world's top 10 and 43 of the top 100 in U.S. News current rankings.[4] This being said, overseas schools are making big gains. European (especially UK), Canadian, and Australian schools have long been well regarded and a growing number of Asian schools are now climbing in the global rankings.

Now that a global (and especially Asian) perspective is so important in so many fields, U.S. applicants should increasingly look to such schools for at least part of their education. This may include anything from full-time enrollment in a degree program to participation in an exchange program to some form of work–study experience. It should ideally be in a country in which you have a deep interest, one that is likely to be important in the field in which you hope to build a career, or one with particularly strong growth prospects, such as China, India, or many other countries in southeast Asia, Africa, or Latin America. If in doubt, you can bet that China will play a growing role in your field, almost regardless of what that field may be.

That being said, what should you look for in a college—and how do you identify the colleges that can best provide it and those that will be the best fit for you?

As a general rule, you should probably lean toward the most highly rated school in the field in which you plan to major and that you can get into—and, as will be discussed later, that you can afford.

> As a general rule, you should probably lean toward the most highly rated school in the field in which you plan to major that you can get into—and that you can afford.

Why? First, going to a school that doesn't fully challenge you can lead you to disengage or even drop out. Second, many employers place great weight on the quality of the school. Not necessarily because they deliver better education, but because selective and highly selective schools already provide a good first-level filtering of candidates for some of the characteristics that many companies value. In fact, one recruiter, who was asked who was the most important reference for a potential employee, only half-jokingly claimed that it was the college admissions officer! Indeed, Ivy League social sciences and humanities graduates often get more and better job offers than do graduates of lower tier business schools with better grades.

How do you find the most selective, most highly rated schools in your field of study? While there are many ways of assessing and ranking colleges, counselors can be a great help. U.S. News and World Report rankings are also widely followed, although not always for the best of reasons.[5]

Having said this, you need a college that will address not just your academic needs but also your social and emotional needs. Do you, for example:

- Want an education that will specifically prepare you for a job, one that will prepare you for graduate or professional school, or one in which you can learn a broad range of life skills (see Chapter 3). Examples of these life skills include learning how to learn and loving to learn, critical and innovative thinking skills, social and oral and written communication, adaptability and persistence, and how to deal with and learn from failure and rejection;

- Prefer a liberal arts college or one that offers a broad and deep range of courses in your particular area of interest (recognizing that your interests may well change through your college career);
- Feel more comfortable in a large school or a smaller one, in a large city or a relatively remote campus; or
- Want to or have to stay near home (such as to care for family, to work, or to reduce expenses by living at home) or would you prefer to "escape" your home town and live with your peers.

Beyond that, there are a number of factors to look to in deciding whether a particular school will provide an environment that will allow you to address your specific goals—academic, social, extracurricular, and career. Your chosen school should deliver all of this at a cost that will not break the bank or plunge you or your parents deeply into debt.

Although there is, as discussed below, an intense debate as to most important missions of colleges, students and parents, for better or worse, appear to be in growing agreement as to what they believe is important. According to Eduventure's 2013 College Bound Market Update, career preparation is now the single most important criterion that applicants and their parents look to in selecting a college.[6] This is followed, in declining order, by core academics, academic environment, affordability, and social environment.

Selecting a School

This very pragmatic focus on college's role in preparing students for a career places many schools in an uncomfortable position. Most have held themselves to loftier objectives, such as helping students learn about themselves and the world; critical thinking and complex analysis skills; and especially a love of learning.

They're understandably reluctant to change their curriculum based on what they perceive as a "transitory need for a particular skill." They are particularly reluctant to turn their institutions of higher learning into "vocational schools." And even if they wanted to, how many university professors (outside of business or some science and engineering fields) are close enough to the private sector to really understand and teach the type of skills that companies will need over the next 5 to 10 years?

As a former liberal arts student (philosophy and economics), I see huge value in a traditional liberal arts education. I mourn the decline in social science and humanities in favor of "practical" undergraduate majors and hope that the vast majority of students will understand and take full advantage of the long-term value that can be gained from an interdisciplinary liberal arts education.

Having said this, I believe that schools can and must play a central role in helping their students prepare for a fulfilling career (at least partially to ensure that alumni will be able to financially support and refer potential students to their alma mater). Luckily, a growing number of such schools are getting the message and are increasingly integrating career development into their missions. Wake Forest University, for example, attracted career officers from more than 70 universities to a three-day conference titled "Rethinking Success: From the Liberal Arts to Careers in the 21st century."

If you are looking for a college that will help you prepare for both life and a career, you should look especially to schools that blend theoretical and applied learning, such as by:

- Adapting their academic programs to emphasize real-world applications, as through labs and practicums;
- Integrating IT skills (such as programming, research techniques, and social media) and math (especially statistics and analytics) into virtually every area of study;
- Encouraging interdisciplinary research and course coordination among diverse, but complementary areas of study (such as combining economics and psychology, architecture and urban studies, transportation and mechanical engineering, or biology and chemistry—or any of the above with math and/or information technology);
- Working more closely with the private sector to support and develop curricula around skills that businesses require, such as by inviting companies to engage with professors in joint

research projects and in delivering lectures, by developing case studies across all types of disciplines (in addition to in business schools), and by arranging substantive internships;

- Engaging career services offices, faculty, alumni, and prospective employers in sponsoring web conferences and seminars that discuss career options for different disciplines; and
- Providing proactive coaching to help students design programs that integrate career and academic goals, suggest relevant internships and companies that are looking for particular backgrounds, and track progress.

Some more practically focused colleges, such as Babson, Olin, and Harvey Mudd Colleges, have been doing this for years. Meanwhile, a growing number of liberal arts colleges are taking a more integrated approach to helping students think about and plan for their careers. For example:

- Clark University's Liberal Education and Effective Practice (LEEP) is a four-year program that helps students think through their career goals, integrate coursework with career-preparation workshops and alumni mentorships, and plan internships and research opportunities;
- Wake Forest offers a minor in innovation, creativity, and entrepreneurship (which is now the university's most popular) that is designed to be integrated with a liberal arts major.

Even the University of Chicago, one of the most academic of all liberal arts colleges (85 percent of whose graduates go on to graduate school), is taking an increasingly comprehensive approach to helping its undergraduate students prepare for careers.[7] For example, its Career Advancement Office's:

- Career Exploration workshops encourage students to consider what career options are of interest to them;
- Steps to Success program helps first-year students think about potential careers, craft resumes around these objectives, and

make the most effective use of their summer opportunities and line up meaningful internships;

- Major Madness series helps second-year students conduct personal inventories, think about career paths, and understand the role of different majors in preparing for these paths;
- Taking the Next Step conferences help second- and third-year students explore postgraduation options and meet with alumni who have pursued careers in their areas; and
- UChicago Careers programs help students explore opportunities in specific areas, such as education, public service, healthcare, law, and business.

But, when evaluating colleges, you must consider much more than their ability to prepare you for and help you get your first job. You should look for a college in which you will be comfortable, one that will continually challenge you, and one that will prepare you for many potential careers (including some of which you have never thought of, or even have not yet been invented). You must also look for a college at which you will learn long-term career and life skills (see Chapter 3) and provide you with a varied social experience, as well as one that will prepare you for your first job. Depending on how you learn, you may also want to assess the types of learning options they offer. For example:

- What percentage and types of courses are taught via lecture, rather than in smaller, collaborative discussion-based classes;
- Does the school provide options for taking some courses online, rather than in class; and
- What type of student-to-student and student-to-teacher interaction is offered?

For a college that will help you prepare for both life and a career, you should look to schools that blend theoretical and applied learning, encourage interdisciplinary education, offer proactive career coaching and that teach in ways that you best learn.

Of Majors, Job Offers, and Starting Salaries

In an ideal world, you would major in whichever field you have the greatest interest and find to be most intellectually challenging, and then chose a job that will give you an opportunity to apply your knowledge and skills to the type of real-world problems that you find to be most interesting.

Needless to say, this is not an ideal world. Graduates who hope that businesses will recruit them for their raw potential and then train them on the specific requirements for the jobs are usually disappointed. True, a number of employers used to hire for potential and you will occasionally still find a few such companies. Most companies, however, have reduced their training programs and are now looking for people with the technical (and often the practical) skills required to be productive from day one—in addition to offering long-term growth potential. Although some companies anticipate rebuilding at least some of their training programs, don't expect miracles.

Despite my whole-hearted belief in the value of a liberal education (with specialization coming on the job or in graduate school), this unfortunately appears to be becoming a luxury for all except for those who graduate from the most selective of schools, or for those who plan to go to graduate or professional school.

> This being said, all too many students forgo both the opportunity to use college as a means of developing life skills, and of developing job skills. They totally shortchange their college experiences by forgoing both the long-term value of a challenging liberal education and the practical value of a career-focused discipline in favor of a major and course schedule that won't impinge on their social lives. They select majors and courses that require the least work and promise the highest grades, rather than those that offer the best learning opportunities.

Do not succumb to these temptations! Such choices are likely to come back to bite you in a market where jobs are scarce. After all according to an Associate Press-sponsored analysis[8] of 2011 Labor Department data:

In the last year [college graduates] were more likely to be employed as waiters, waitresses, bartenders, and food-service helpers than as engineers, physicists, chemists, and mathematicians combined (100,000 versus 90,000). There were more [graduates] working in office-related jobs, such as receptionist or payroll clerk, than in all computer professional jobs (163,000 versus 100,000). More were employed as cashiers, retail clerks, and customer representatives than engineers (125,000 versus 80,000).

Why? One of the primary reasons is that, as discussed in Chapter 2, far more jobs are being created in lower skill, lower pay occupations than in higher skill, higher pay fields. Only one of the 20 occupations the BLS expects to have the greatest number of openings over the next decade explicitly requires any postsecondary degree at all.[9] That occupation, registered nurses, who require a minimum of an associate's degree. In fact, only eight of those occupations that are expected to generate 50,000 more jobs explicitly require a bachelor's degree or higher.[10]

Just as jobs that require a college degree are less numerous than those that do not, some also pay less. Although those who earn bachelor degrees do, *on average*, earn more than those with high school diplomas or associate degrees, there are many exceptions. As shown in a 2012 Georgetown University Center on Education and the Workforce study, The College Payoff, 14 percent of people with a high school diploma make at least as much as the median earnings of those with a bachelor's degree, and 17 percent of people with a bachelor's degree make more than the median earnings of those with a professional degree.[11]

Not surprisingly, many recent graduates have had second-thoughts about their choices of majors. A 2013 Accenture survey, for example, found that 48 percent of 2011/2012 graduates said that they would have fared better in the job market had they chosen a different major.[12] Indeed, a 2012 report by the John J. Heldrich Center for Workforce Development found that 37 percent wish they had been more careful in selecting their major, or would have chosen a different major.[13] Of these:

- Forty-one percent would have chosen a professional major, like communication, education, nursing, or social work;

- Twenty-nine percent would have chosen a STEM major;
- Seventeen percent would have selected business; and
- Only 11 percent would have selected social science or the humanities.

---

48 percent of 2011/2012 graduates believe that they would have fared better in the job market had they chosen a different major.

Although this choice of majors is certainly a big setback for those (including me) who find huge value in a liberal, ideas-centered education, it is certainly pragmatic. As shown in Figure 8.1, well over 90 percent of those 2007 and 2008 undergraduates who majored in healthcare, education, engineering, computer science, and business landed jobs. Humanities and social sciences graduates were at the bottom of the list with unemployment rates of 13 percent and 12 percent, respectively. And, as shown in Figure 8.2, liberal arts majors were also far less likely to get jobs that were related to their majors.

Georgetown University Center on Education and the Workforce provides a much more granular breakout for 2010, showing unemployment rates, earnings, and popularity among students for each of 173 different majors.[14] (See also the Wall Street Journal concise overview of these findings.)[15] Although sample sizes for some of the less popular majors are undoubtedly small, and must be taken with the proverbial grain of salt, unemployment rates suggest wide variations among disciplines in the same general field. Engineering unemployment rates, for example, range from zero for geological engineering to 9.2 percent for industrial management. Those in education, from zero for educational administration to 10 percent for educational psychology.

Advantage: STEM

Some majors offer not just better employment prospects than others but also more choices in the type of job, field, and industry in which you work. A separate Georgetown Center on Education and the Workforce

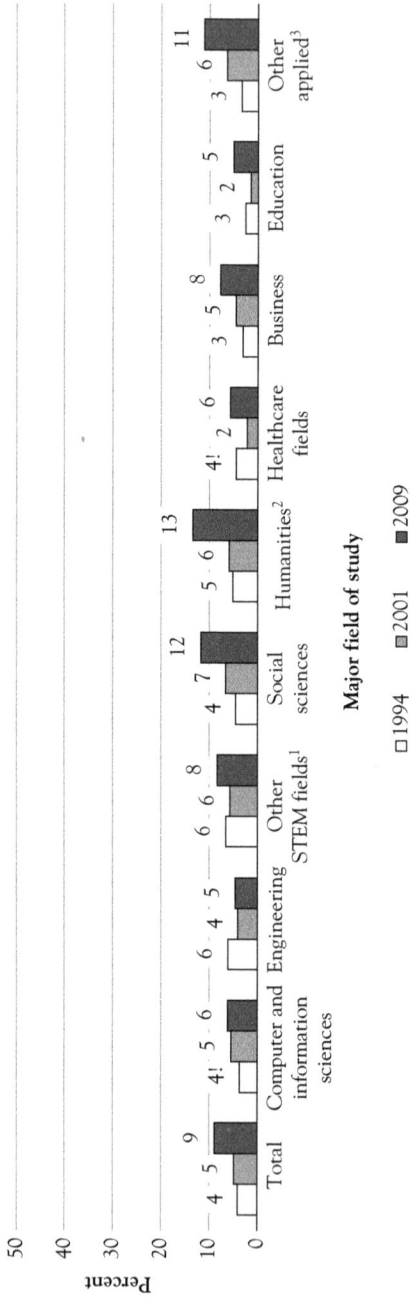

Figure 8.1 Unemployment and major field of study

Source: Graduation (n.d.), Figure 5, p. 8.

Major field of study

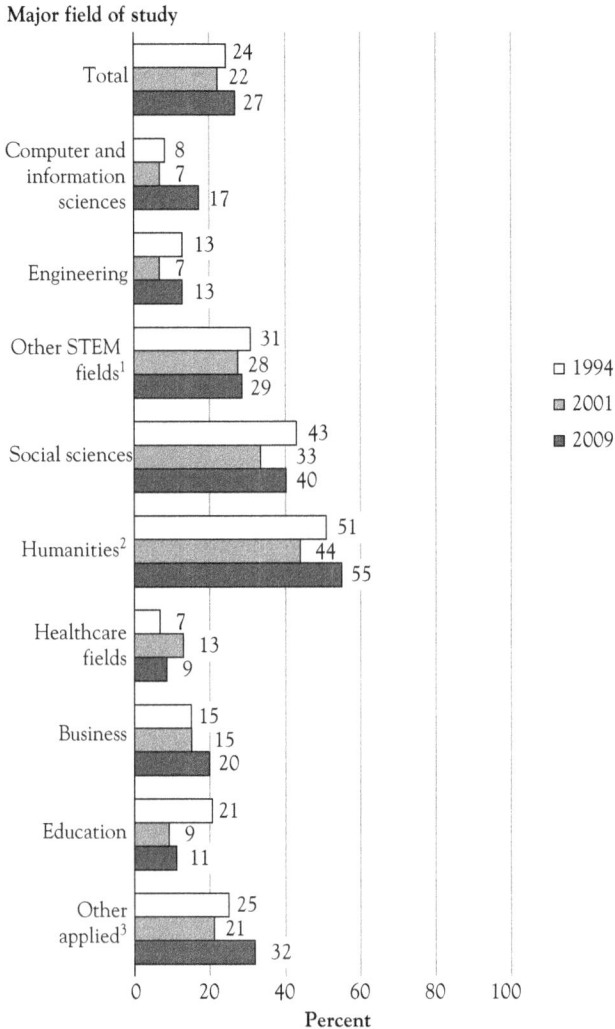

Figure 8.2 Job unrelated to major and major field of study

Source: Graduation (n.d.), Figure 6, p. 9.

report, appropriately named STEM, provides a comprehensive overview of all STEM fields, from definitions to explanation of different types of occupations, to hiring trends, and almost everything you may want to know about STEM wages.[16]

The study also examines the offers received by—in addition to the jobs actually taken by—science and engineering grads.[17] It finds that those who major in these fields not only receive more job offers than those in other fields, but they also have a greater choice of fields in which to work. Fewer than half of STEM graduates, in fact, end up taking jobs in the field in which they majored. Employers look to them to, and grads often choose to employ their skills in jobs that use the skills from, but are not specifically in their field—jobs in areas including sales, marketing, or finance. Why would STEM graduates choose to work in another field? Many may see them as offering more opportunities for social engagement or for offering more varied career paths.

Although the differences in employment prospects among majors are great, the differences in salaries are even greater—much greater. While salary should not be a primary factor in selecting a career or a major (see Chapter 10 for a fuller discussion), it does have to be considered. And, of the 173 majors listed in the Georgetown survey, all of the top 10 bachelors' degree majors yielding the highest median salary were in STEM fields. These were led by petroleum engineering, with a median salary of $120,000—and $189,000 at the 75th percentile.[18] Psychologists occupied the opposite end of the salary spectrum, with counseling psychologists earning $21,000 at the 25th and $42,000 at the 75th percentiles. These salaries were even lower than for oft-maligned humanities degrees, such as visual arts and theology.[19]

Payscale generally confirms the salary premiums that STEM grads can command. Its 2013 to 2014 College Salary Report[20] shows that all of the 10 top-paying majors[21] (all with starting salaries above $50,000 and average mid-career salaries above $100,000) and 37 of the top 40 (with starting salaries ranging from $40,000 to $100,000) were in STEM-related fields. (While a few of these, such as economics and construction management, are not strictly STEM professions, they rely heavily on math.) Only three of these top-paying majors do not have significant STEM requirements: government, international business, and international relations.

Not only do engineering and science grads in most majors get more and more varied job offers, have less unemployment, and earn higher salaries than bachelor degree grads in other fields, they also, according to the Georgetown report, earn more than those with advanced degrees in other fields. According to the report:

Sixty-five percent of students earning bachelor's degrees in science or engineering fields earn more than master's-degree holders in nonscience fields. And 47 percent of bachelors-degree holders in science fields earn more than those holding doctorates in other fields.[22]

STEM degrees also age well, with the wage premium for STEM-educated workers actually growing over time.[23] And this is true, both upon graduation and over a lifetime, regardless of whether you actually work in a STEM profession.[24]

> STEM majors typically get more and more varied job offers, have less unemployment, and earn higher salaries than bachelor degree grads in other fields.

However, by the time you reach the masters and doctor or doctorate levels, healthcare (which requires deep science knowledge) and business (which is increasingly math-intensive), tend to command higher premiums than engineering and computer backgrounds.[25]

As if the competition to hire and reward for STEM skills is not heated enough, both seem to be amping up. As discussed in a 2012 Wall Street Journal article, a growing number of technology firms are targeting premier computer science and software engineering students well before they graduate—using $100,000 to $200,000 packages to persuade them to drop out of college (or at least to commit to the company upon graduation).[26] And this does not even count the 17-year old British high school student that Yahoo just hired as part of its $30 million acquisition of his small software company![27] Google, in particular, has already posted 400 student ambassadors (with plans for more than 1,000) at top universities to identify and recruit prime talent.

If a degree in one of these STEM fields is valuable, combining majors in two fields—especially two STEM fields—can produce even greater benefits, not only in employment and salary but also in flexibility as to the industry and field in which you work, and in the long-term demand for your services. Or you could get the best of both worlds in terms of employment prospects, flexibility, and compensation, by combining a STEM major with an MBA. A broad range of dual major, or major and graduate degree combinations are specifically discussed in the following sections.

Comparing Fields of Study

Let's look at the demands for three broad classes of majors in a bit more detail—STEM, business, and liberal arts.

STEM

The vast majority of students—the 88 percent that do not graduate with STEM majors—are probably getting pretty tired of hearing about the competition for recruiting STEM graduates, and the multiple job offers, high salaries, and lavish benefits that are showered upon them. You had better get used to it.

The popularity and high salaries for STEM graduates should come as no surprise. The surprise is that, with all these rewards, only 12 percent of college students choose STEM majors. This is not all for lack of interest. As I discussed in my December 2011 blog, Expanding the Ranks of STEM Professionals, 30 percent of all incoming 2009 college freshman planned to major in one of the STEM fields.[28] Unfortunately, many of those students who aspire to a STEM career lack sufficient high school backgrounds. Fewer still are prepared for the workloads required of a STEM major. The majority end up switching to less demanding majors.

But not all STEM graduates necessarily share in this bounty. Most STEM fields, especially in most types of engineering, software development, and many of the physical sciences, offer plenty of opportunities for bachelor-level grads. Some, however, such as general science are a bit too broad, and others like animal and neuroscience offer more opportunities for those with advanced degrees. Of all the STEM majors, some form of computer science is probably the most versatile and promising major. At least Stanford undergrads seem to think so, since the school's redesigned, more interdisciplinary major is now the undergraduate school's most popular.[29]

Business

Business is, overwhelmingly, the single most popular undergraduate discipline, accounting for 22 percent of all 2010/2011 bachelor degrees.[30]

This is somewhat understandable given parents' and students' growing desire for "marketable skills." And it can certainly pay off, especially if the degree is in a high-demand quantitative field such as finance, accounting, auditing, and supply-chain management, or in some marketing fields, such as e-commerce.

Unfortunately, many business grads, especially those from less selective schools and with less focused or demanded majors, find that they are less marketable than they anticipated. One reason is that a growing number of companies have begun to question the value of an undergraduate business degree.

As explained in the Carnegie Foundation report, "Rethinking Undergraduate Business Education: Liberal Learning for the Profession," undergraduate business education is often more narrow (focusing on technical mastery of discrete segments of knowledge) and less intellectually rigorous than many liberal arts (much less STEM) curricula.[31] Business courses often lack the type of long essays and class debates that help to develop critical thinking and problem solving and "fail to challenge students to question assumptions, think creatively, or to understand the place of business in larger institutional contexts."

> Although business degrees can result in good jobs (especially in high-demand quantitative fields such as finance, accounting and supply-chain management), a growing number of employers view business curricula as too narrow and insufficiently rigorous.

Given this, a number of those premier (not to speak of the best paying) companies, such as those in consulting, technology, and finance that do recruit bachelor-level graduates, are increasingly targeting candidates with broader, more rigorous academic backgrounds, such as in STEM, economics, and even English. They often find it easier to teach these graduates the required content, than to teach critical thinking and problem solving skills to business graduates.

A number of undergraduate business schools are responding by requiring or strongly encouraging their students to incorporate liberal arts courses into their business curriculum, to integrate historical, psychological, ethical, and sustainability considerations into traditional courses; providing more global perspectives; and by requiring more and deeper written analyses. Even if your school does not require such courses, you should incorporate them into your own program.

Healthcare

Demand is surging and will continue to do so for anyone with an associate degree or higher in virtually any healthcare discipline. Demand and compensation will be particularly strong for nurses (especially those with bachelor degrees or higher) and especially for those with masters, doctor, and doctorate degrees in virtually all segments.

Most of these positions require a minimum of a bachelor of science degree in your target specialty, and most, as mentioned, require some type of advanced degree and state certification. Information on the educational requirements, responsibilities, career opportunities, and salaries for all types of occupations is available in a BLS report[32] on healthcare occupations and on the healthcare sections of sites including Bureau of Labor Statistics,[33] O*Net,[34] and WorldWideLearn.[35]

Careers in healthcare, however, go way beyond those for the actual care providers. Hospitals and HMOs, like any other large organization, also need managers, accountants, IT and human resource professionals, marketers, lawyers, and all types of support workers. Although many of these jobs don't require specific knowledge of the industry, having a specialty or experience in areas such as medical records management for accountants and IT managers, or regulatory compliance for lawyers can provide advantages in getting jobs and in commanding higher salaries. There are, of course, also hundreds of occupations outside, but that work closely with healthcare providers. These include industries such as insurance, pharmaceuticals, and medical electronics.

Liberal Arts

We all know that those with four-year degrees in liberal arts find it more difficult to find a job out of school, are more likely to be unemployed—and especially underemployed—and earn less money than those with preprofessional degrees. Although graduates of elite colleges may get good jobs right out of school, those from less selective schools often end up in lower paying (albeit potentially intrinsically rewarding) jobs such as counselors, social and community service workers, customer service representatives, and in any of the hundreds of professions that do not require college degrees, and do not offer particularly compelling career paths.

A comprehensive 2013 study by The Association of American Colleges and Universities, meanwhile, shows that it takes most liberal arts graduates longer to get jobs out of school and they typically earn about $5,000 less than graduates with professional or pre professional programs.[36] When they do get jobs, however, employers are often pleased with the results, claiming that their broad backgrounds allow them to think critically and work effectively in diverse teams. This may help these graduates advance more rapidly than—and close at least part of the initial salary gap with—business and healthcare (albeit not STEM) undergraduates over time.

Some liberal arts graduates, in fact, end up eventually overtaking salaries of those with business and healthcare (but again, not STEM) degrees. These, however, are primarily among the roughly 40 percent of all liberal arts undergraduates that end up getting advanced degrees.

> It generally takes liberal arts graduates longer to get jobs out of school and they typically earn less than graduates of professional or pre-professional programs. Their intellectual preparation, however, may end up resulting in faster promotions and eventually, even higher salaries.

The lesson from this is not necessarily to shun liberal arts. The perspective and skills derived from a challenging, multidisciplinary liberal education can yield big dividends, in both your professional and personal life. The lesson is that you must be able to show employers that you can make immediate contributions to their business, in addition to providing long-term growth potential. You can do this either by getting a master's degree in a relevant field or by having and demonstrating strong skills in an area in which large numbers of employers always need help, such as programming in popular languages like Python, Java, C++, and Ruby. (See Chapter 9 for a discussion of the growing options for college graduates to learn these and other career-enhancing skills.)

Selecting Your Courses, Majors, and Minors

Career preparation should certainly be an important consideration in selecting courses, major, and minors. It probably, however, shouldn't be your first, much less your only consideration.

For example, if you enter college with a very good idea of your dream and safety careers, you may be inclined to quickly declare your major and to sign up for as many courses as possible in these fields. Bad plan.

Constructing an entire college program around the requirements for a specific career can do more to limit your career, than to enable it. It can lock you into a field in which job prospects are limited by the time you graduate (not to speak of by the time you are ready to retire), or in which you may lose interest. Meanwhile, some fields may focus so heavily on teaching the "tools of the trade" that they deemphasize development of the type of high-level thinking, conceptual and communication skills that will be required to succeed in any high-skill job. Most importantly, however, the first few years of college provide some of the greatest opportunities for discovery that you will experience in your life.

You should absolutely take a few courses in your target fields over these two years. These can help you decide if they are really the areas in which you want to dedicate your career (or at least your first couple of jobs), provide a solid foundation for deeper studies in this area, and allow you to experience and meet professors with whom you will want to engage later in your studies. Your primary objective for these first two years, however, should be to experience as many different fields as possible. Some should certainly be focused around core skills that will be required in any career (introductory computer science, statistics, public speaking, persuasive writing, and so forth). Others, regardless of the field, that will give you experience in skills such as critical reading, creative thinking, logical writing, and teamwork.

As for subject area, go for fields in which you have an interest, a curiosity, or that sound like they may have the potential for engaging you. Most importantly, look for those courses—regardless of the topic—that are taught by the most inspiring professors: Those professors who inspire a passion not just in the topic they teach, but also a passion for learning and for prompting students to do their best work. Search out professors who prompt students to look at the world, themselves, and possibly their career choices, differently.

A couple of years of this type of discovery will not only prepare you to select a major in which you will have a passion but also spur you to work harder and help you to develop deeper skills.

> My recommendation: spend your first two years experiencing as many different fields as possible, especially courses taught by the most inspiring professors. Then, when you select a major, add courses in complementary fields.

Selecting a major will—and should—involve some soul-searching. On one hand, what you learn from your specific undergraduate major will be of little concern (and will probably have little relevance) after your first few jobs. But on the other hand, it can play three important roles in your life. It can, for example:

- Provide a powerful signal of your interests and perspective to potential employers (or graduate school admissions committees) and, depending on the major, play a big role in the type of positions for which you will be considered for your first job;
- Prepare you to pursue your passion, either as a career or as a hobby; and
- Shape the lens through which you view and interpret many of your future experiences due to perspectives and methodologies you learn, the sources and types of information you use to analyze hypotheses, and support your positions and the ways in which you express your opinions and conclusions.

Each of these is very important, but in very different ways:

- The first of these roles is the signaling, and in some cases defining (such as in planning for a career in engineering or for applying to medical school) the type of job or graduate school for which you will be considered. This will play a critical role in determining the options that will be open to you upon graduation. In some cases, however, the decision won't so much define the types of jobs that you are likely to get as it may limit the type of jobs (or grad schools) for which you may be considered. This being said, the importance of a major in your career will probably fade rapidly after your first job (or grad school). By that time, your experiences and accomplishments are more likely to far outweigh what you studied in school in creating future career opportunities.

- The second of these roles—pursuing your passion—speaks for itself; and
- The third—providing you with the perspective with which you view and interpret the world—is likely to play a limited role in getting your first job. It may, however, play a critical role (usually much more than the knowledge you gain from your major) in determining how well you do in your first job, the options that will be open to you in the future, and even how you think about your life.

Ideally, all three will mesh, such as where your major prepares you to pursue a field that you love while also providing a strong learning environment, and simultaneously preparing you for a career in a growing field. Examples may include premed, software engineering, or teaching programs.

Creating Your Own Unique Secret Career Sauce

But what if your passion is art, archaeology, or philosophy? These can certainly be interesting and psychically rewarding passions and are often helpful lenses for viewing the world. But what employment opportunities do they offer? When the three roles of your major don't mesh, you may have to engage in a balancing act between the near-term rewards of maximizing your job opportunities and the long-term rewards of training your mind, shaping your perspective, and pursuing your passion.

That's where safety careers fit in. If, for example, you are intent on pursuing your passion or your intellectual curiosity, despite limited employment prospects in your chosen field, you can choose a complementary field, or at least a field around which you can craft a compelling story as to how deep skills in both areas allow you to provide a type of value that others cannot (see Chapter 6). You can do this in any number of ways, such as with dual majors (which will not only maximize your credentials, but also demonstrate your commitment and perseverance), a major and a strong minor, a major and a boot camp or MOOC program, or even two graduate degrees.

What combination? There's no limit. They can include virtually any combination of two or more academic disciplines (such as English and political science), one discipline with a focus on a particular industry (such as economics and healthcare), or by combining computer science or business with pretty much any discipline or industry you wish. Or say, perhaps, that you have a passion for theater and are also good with numbers? How about a combination of theater arts and accounting, or a course or experience in fundraising.

Love working with computers and good in math? You're in luck. The combination of the Internet, social media, and the growing use of embedded sensors is creating a new opportunity to capture, analyze, and identify opportunities from the vast mountains of raw data that are being accumulated on everything, from shopping patterns to the spread of infectious diseases. Indeed, combination of computer science and math disciplines is among the most sought after and highest paid combinations you can pursue. Opportunities range from earthquake prediction to bioinformatics; from Internet advertising to the pricing of Wall Street derivatives.

The opportunities for complementary combinations are limited only by your imagination, your skills, and your ability to demonstrate the value of your combination to potential employers or clients. Indeed, some combinations have proven to become so valuable and popular that they have merged into their own formal disciplines. Chemistry and biology, for example, have been combined into biochemistry and economics and psychology into behavioral economics.

Whatever you major, consider a complementary area of focus that can improve your marketability, serve as the foundation for a safety career and create a platform on which you can create your own, unique interdisciplinary "macrospecialization."

This trend toward integrating complementary disciplines is also becoming increasingly common in graduate schools. Law schools and business schools have been offering joint degree programs for decades. Stanford Law School, for example, now offers 28 formal joint degree programs plus additional combinations students can tailor to their own interests.[37] So-called science masters are one of the hottest new graduate programs.[38] These hybrid degrees, which are now offered by nearly 140 schools, help students apply a business perspective to their science backgrounds and move beyond laboratories into management positions. The most popular combinations revolve around computer science, followed by information science, environmental science, natural resource sciences, math, statistics, and biotechnology. More than 90 percent of graduates in one of these combinations get jobs in their fields and more than two-thirds earn salaries above $60,000.

But whatever combination of disciplines you choose, you must do your research—and then validate your findings with potential employers. You must, for example, read about the near- and long-term career prospects in your potential field, assess current and anticipated job openings, and speak with everybody you can (including professors, career centers, and especially, practitioners) to objectively evaluate your prospects for getting a job.

It is, of course, also important to line up appropriate internships, part-time jobs, or work–study programs. Such practical experience will demonstrate your commitment to the field, help you hone your focus and skills, and allow you to see what the work actually entails and how you can provide the greatest value to potential employers.

Just as importantly, these positions (especially when paid) can also result in referrals and ideally job offers. A 2013 National Association of Colleges and Employers survey, for example, found that paid interns do more substantive work than those who are unpaid, are much more likely to get job offers (69 percent versus 37 percent—and 35 percent of those who didn't intern at all), and earn higher average salaries ($51,930 versus $35,721—and $37,087 for those who didn't intern).[39] This being said, well paid internships are getting more and more difficult to find—especially among top employers. Goldman Sachs, for example, hired only 350 of 17,000 applicants for its summer 2013 internship program![40]

Don't be too deterred by skeptics who advise you to choose a major that is more likely to prepare you for a job. As discussed throughout this book, any major can prepare you for a job. The question is not *whether* you can build a career around your passion: The question is *how* you are going to do it!

> In the end, the question is not *whether* you can build a career around your passion: The question is *how* you are going to do it!

In summary, you have almost unlimited options in selecting majors and minors. If you select and diligently pursue a field or a combination of fields based on a balance of the previously mentioned three criteria, you will be well positioned for the future—both the near and the more distant futures. The biggest mistakes you can make are selecting fields:

- On a whim or because a friend has chosen it, with no serious thought as to what it will provide you;
- That foreclose options, such as by preparing you for a narrow field with nontransferrable or leverageable skills (see for example, a Princeton Review list[41] of 10 majors that will keep your options open); or worse yet,
- That are intended to produce the best grades with the least amount of work.

The majors and the minors you choose can play important roles in shaping your future. Not just in giving you an advantage in getting your first job, but in shaping your entire life. Don't squander the opportunity—or the real value of an expensive education.

Just as importantly, while you should certainly consider the financial payoff of potential majors, don't get blinded by the money. Selecting majors and minors solely on the basis of their practical value can be self-defeating. What value will you derive from majoring in a field in which you aren't intellectually or emotionally engaged, and in which you won't put in the extra effort required to develop mastery? Consider also the psychic rewards of a particular profession, not to speak of the higher level skills and the love of learning you will develop by taking courses that you find intellectually stimulating. In the end, these benefits will pay much higher career dividends than will what you learn in a particular major.

Designing Your Own Course of Study

Every job has its own specific requirements that relies on its own body of knowledge and employs its own methodologies. But, as discussed in Chapter 3, these differences are relatively small when compared with the skills that most high-demand, high-skill, high-wage jobs of the 21st Century will have in common.

The problem (which you can and must convert into an opportunity) is that these skills are changing much faster than educational organizations' abilities to teach them. Some traditional skills (such as memorization) are becoming all but irrelevant and others are becoming little more than antes for success in tomorrow's jobs. The real winners in tomorrow's job market will be those who can rigorously and critically analyze complex situations and marshal required information and tools (from multiple sources and across multiple disciplines) to solve complex problems in creative and innovative ways.

Just as important as the ability to solve problems is the ability to identify problems that others may not see, to tackle ambiguous situations, and to address complex, unstructured problems that have "no right answer." Few schools really know how to teach these skills, much less the more abstract complementary success attributes such as initiative, accountability, adaptability, and grit.

Where do you find courses for these skills in your course catalog? One way is to look for classes or activities that integrate learning and doing, particularly in project-based settings, where you take the lead in identifying the problem to be solved, the approach by which you will do so, and demonstrate the persistence and the adaptability required to achieve a challenging goal.

A second way is to find professors that inspire and require you to learn and the courses that require deep reading, which entail the researching and writing of longer papers and that give you opportunities to express and defend your ideas and to critique those of others.

Many education experts believe that the best way to develop these high-level competencies is probably through self-directed, experimental project-based learning that combines book and classroom learning with experience in actually performing tasks.

> The best way to develop high-level skills is probably through self-directed, experiential, project-based learning.

This approach is already well established in many apprenticeships, in some community colleges, and in medical internships and residencies. It is also common practice in German engineering schools and is becoming increasingly common in some graduate schools.[42] This is especially true in MBA programs, where corporations partner with B-schools to use students as consultants on actual projects.[43] Meanwhile, some law schools are beginning to structure their third-years as apprenticeships, where students work with experienced lawyers as low-fee advocates for poor and working-class clients who cannot normally afford legal representation.[44]

Unfortunately, most undergraduate programs have been reducing the rigor of their classes—not to speak of their grading standards ("A's," for example, now account for about 47 percent of all college grades). Most undergraduate schools and programs are also late to the "experiential learning party."

You may, therefore, have to search out courses that employ "active learning," such as interactive seminars and cooperative projects, and especially semester-long projects in which student groups work with companies, nonprofits, or government organizations to address real-world needs.[45] Science, engineering, and business schools are generally taking the lead in providing such opportunities at an undergraduate level. Olin College, a small engineering school, for example, offers eight such opportunities over its four-year program.[46] Northeastern University, meanwhile, is known for its interdisciplinary research programs[47] and especially for its co-op programs,[48] in which students in just about any discipline can get up to 18 months of related work experience in the time required to earn a bachelor's degree.

Regardless of your chosen discipline you should drill down into your prospect colleges' commitments and approaches to experiential (aka active or project-based) learning. Not only are you likely to learn more and gain more job-ready skills, you are also more likely to enjoy the process of learning them.

> The winners in tomorrow's job market will be those who can rigorously and critically analyze complex situations, marshal the diverse information and tools required to solve these problems in creative ways and tackle ambiguous situations for which there is "no right answer." Since few schools know how to teach these skills, you have to take primary responsibility for learning these skills.

Another requirement for students in any discipline: take at least introductory courses that teach at least the basic fundamentals of business and entrepreneurism. First, a basic understanding of business will help in any type of organization in which you want to work, including government, hospitals, and not-for profits. Even if you aren't directly involved in functions like accounting and marketing you will have to deal with people who are (including those who define the metrics on which you will be paid and set the budgets under which you will work). Besides, regardless of your plans, odds are that sometime in your career you will either choose or be forced to go out on your own. BE PREPARED!

A basic understanding of entrepreneurism will help not just in these situations, but also in large companies. Most organizations, for example, are devolving responsibility down to entrepreneurial business units and teams. More importantly, as discussed in Chapter 6, effective career management requires that you view yourself as a small, entrepreneurial business. You need your own brand, your own marketing pitch, and the ability to manage your own finances. Basic entrepreneurism courses, which a growing number of colleges now offer, can provide a great way of learning these techniques.

Managing the Surging Costs of a College Degree

We have all heard the horror stories:

- The steep and rapidly rising cost of tuition[49] which, as of 2010/2011, ranged from an average of $8,909 for two-year colleges to $15,918 for public and $32,617 for public four-year universities and $46,899 at a private medical school—up an average of 92 percent over the last decade, compared with 27 percent for the consumer price index;
- The tuitions for once affordable public community colleges and universities are now rising even faster[50] than those of private colleges;
- The crippling debt loads of college loans, in 2010/2011, which now average $29,400[51] for the 70 percent of college seniors who took out loans, but can easily exceed $100,000 for those who earn professional or doctorate degrees—debts that can't even be discharged by bankruptcy;
- The still grim employment prospects for many college (and even business and law school) graduates, with unemployment of new college grads still over 8 percent and underemployment of those who do have jobs at over 40 percent;
- The low pay that many companies that are still hiring are offering.
- And then there are the rapidly growing number of troubling critiques discussed in Chapter 7, in which employers contend that many graduates can't even write coherent paragraphs and leading academics contend that close to half of all graduates experience no appreciable gain in critical thinking skills after four years of college.[52]

What's a prospective college student to do?

While the situation can be grim, you can still get an education on the cheap. You can, as discussed in Chapter 9, take a non-college-like approach to "hacking your own education," as by systematically creating your own experiential learning agenda, by searching out volunteer or no- or low-pay internships, and/or by building your own college program from a combination of free and low-cost online courses and certificate programs. More conventionally, you can spend two years at a public two-year college (average annual tuition of $3,131) and then transfer to an in-state public university (average tuition of $8,665).

You can further reduce these costs through combinations of grants or tax incentives. According to the College Board, about two-thirds of full-time students already receive such incentives.[53] In fact, the average community college student receives enough in grants and tax breaks to cover not only average tuition expenses but also all but $10 of the average $1,230 bill for textbooks and school supplies.

But even if you don't qualify for scholarships, grants or aid, you can slash the cost of a four-year degree. According to a Conference Board study, by the time you add in all the costs associated with going to school (room, board, and books, in addition to tuition and fees), four years of on-campus study at a private, nonprofit college can be expected to set you back the princely sum of $180,000.

There are, however, many ways of cutting these costs. One of the most cost-effective approaches for getting a four-year degree (again, excluding scholarships, grants and aid) is by combining two-years at a community college (approximately $32,000 for two years) with two at an in-state public university (a total of $46,000). Living at home (excluding additional transportation and food costs) can cut this by another $34,000, for a total of $44,000 for a bachelor's degree. (One big caveat, however, is that living at home often comes at the expense of college socialization and networking opportunities.)[54]

Still a lot of money, but remember these are published rates, before accounting for scholarships and aid. While figures differ greatly by school and family income, the College Board calculates that 80 percent of all college students now receive some form of scholarship or grant. Although these packages average only about $1,500 per student, grant aid, on average, covers all tuition and fees for students from families with incomes below $30,000 (in 2011 dollars) enrolled in public two-year and public four-year institutions.[55]

Given the typical costs of attending college, it is of little surprise that the tough economic decade has prompted larger percentages of students to choose the public education option. In fact, over the last 10 years, enrollment in lower cost public universities increased by 28 percent and the percentage going to two-year, rather than four-year colleges, grew by 20 percent.[56]

This, however, doesn't mean that a private school education is necessarily out of your reach. Although these schools certainly have much higher list prices, they often offer much larger scholarships and more aid than public schools. Some are taking more creative approaches to reducing the cost of attending. *The New York Times*, for example, published examples of some colleges that are freezing tuitions, promoting three-year bachelor's degree programs, forgiving part of the tuition for students who take low-end jobs, and some that are entering into academic partnerships with local community colleges.[57] Some are even offering "sales." These include eight semesters for the price of seven (where the last semester's tuition is forgiven for students who maintain 3.5 GPAs) and five years for the price of a four-year degree (again, for those maintaining specified GPAs).

In the end, however, some of the nation's most elite private universities may offer some of the best college bargains of all. In fact, a highly qualified, low-income applicant can often attend a highly selective private university for less than the cost of attending a public university.

Since some of these colleges have some of the richest and most generous alumni, they have the largest endowments—allowing them to offer generous scholarship and financial aid packages. In fact, as discussed in Scholarships.com's blog, some elite schools go so far as covering the entire cost of attending college—tuition, room, board, books, and all— for all four years for students with family income less than $60,000 per year.[58] Those making between $60,000 and $120,000 will pay less than 10 percent of the total list cost of attending Harvard. Northwestern provides scholarships (averaging $15,000) to half of all its students. Duke covers all tuition—plus a summer program at Oxford and expenses—for some scholarship winners.

In fact, one of the growing number of federal government tools for assessing college costs and returns (see the following section) shows that for households with income between $48,000 and $75,000, the average net cost for a student receiving aid at one of U.S. News' top 10 private colleges was only $9,340.[59] This compares with an average net cost of $13,486 at the top 10 public universities. (And, as discussed in the following section, this does not even begin to account for the better employment prospects and higher salaries that graduates of elite universities often enjoy,

It's a pity that more lower income students (not to speak of their high-school counselors) don't know about such programs. A number of these schools, struggling to increase diversity in their student bases, are trying to address this knowledge gap. Some are even sending letters and emails to inform prospective lower income students of such offers in an attempt to attract many who may have not even considered these schools.

So, if you have the grades to qualify for admission to schools such as Harvard, Princeton, and Stanford, but think you lack the resources to pay for them; think again.

Comparing College ROIs

Focusing on just the costs—even net costs—of attending college doesn't give you a full picture. It certainly doesn't account for the fact that employers view different schools and majors very differently.

As discussed in Chapter 7, the most expensive college educations are those for which students pay tuition and take out loans, but do not graduate. They pay for the cost of this education, but receive few of the benefits of lower unemployment, better career paths, higher salaries, and more generous benefits.

According to Harvard's Pathways to Prosperity Project, 46 percent of four-year college freshman fail to earn degrees within six years.[60] Even if they do end up graduating, one-third will lose credits (and therefore money) by transferring to another college. The results are even worse for for-profit colleges. According to Education Trust's 2008 report, The Subprime Opportunity,[61] only 22 percent of these schools' first-time, full-time bachelor's degree students graduated within six years (compared with 55 percent at public institutions and 65 percent at private nonprofit colleges).[62] Worse still, some of these schools, which also have some of the highest dropout and student loan default rates, enroll disproportionately large percentages of minority and low-income students who can least afford them.

To get a comprehensive picture of the true cost of attending a particular school you must look beyond the dollar outlays and factor in the value you are likely to derive from this degree. In other words, you must determine the return on investment, or ROI of a degree in your specific major from each college.

As discussed in Chapter 7, the average college graduate earns far more than the average nongraduate. These averages, however, disguise big differences in earnings among graduates from different schools and with different majors. PayScale's annual College Salary Report lists the average starting and mid-career salary earned by graduates from more than a 1,000 U.S. colleges.[63] It breaks these numbers down by type of school (from Ivy League to Party schools) and allows you to create your own custom comparisons, such as among liberal arts colleges within 100 miles of your home. Not surprisingly, graduates of many of the nation's most elite universities and liberal arts colleges (Princeton, Stanford, Williams, Harvard, and so forth) and those with some of the best known STEM programs (Caltech, MIT, and NYU-Poly) earn some of the highest starting salaries.

They are, however, joined by a number of schools that few may expect: While Princeton is number one on the list, Harvey Mudd College, one of the nation's better STEM colleges, is number two. It is joined in the top 10 by the U.S. Naval and Military Academies, a small liberal arts college (Lehigh), and an undergraduate business school (Babson) that offers a particularly strong entrepreneurship program.

When you compare the cost of attending these colleges with the salaries graduates are likely to earn, you find that a number of tier one schools (including Princeton, Harvard, Stanford, Dartmouth) and a few STEM schools (especially Harvey Mudd and Georgia Institute of Technology) yield the biggest salary bangs for your tuition bucks. If you look solely at the cost, rather than comparing it with the return, you miss the fact that some of lowest-cost colleges also yield some of the lowest returns on your education dollar.

But, as PayScale emphasizes, you can't look at the school alone. Salaries and ROIs are also highly dependent on your major. Graduates of engineering, computer science, economics, and natural science programs, for example, tend to earn the highest returns. Those with degrees in nursing, criminal justice, sociology, and education tend to get the lowest ROIs. To drive the comparison home, the data show that a Stanford computer science graduate has lifetime earnings of $1.7 million more than a high school graduate, after subtracting the cost of education. A humanities major from Florida International University, meanwhile, earns $132,000 less than the average high school graduate. Nor is FIU alone. Twelve percent of colleges in the PayScale study produced negative returns. Thirty percent produced lower returns than you could receive by investing the money you would have paid for college in 20-year Treasury bills!

> To assess the true cost of attending a particular school you must look not only at the cost, but also the salary the degree will allow you to command. Some of the most expensive school yield some of the greatest ROIs—some of the least expensive may even yield negative ROIs. Overall, community colleges offer the greatest bang for the buck.

Pulling all this information together on your own can be a Herculean task. Many colleges add to the confusion by not disclosing or by providing selective or downright misleading information. Some for-profit schools have been called out by the government for making things even worse with aggressive sales tactics and sometimes blatantly false claims.

A small but growing number of sources are beginning to provide accurate, comparative information on the gross and net costs of different colleges, their dropout and graduation rates, and the salaries that graduates can expect to earn. This will be especially true when the Department of Education launches its planned College Navigator (see the following section).[64]

Cutting Through the College Decision Confusion— Where to Go for Help

Choosing the school that is best for you can be extremely confusing in the best of cases. And then there are the challenges of navigating the admission process, assessing scholarship and aid options, obtaining loans and managing the resultant debt, and selecting majors, minors, and extracurricular activities. These challenges can be particularly daunting if you are the first in your family (not to speak of your neighborhood and your high school) to attend college and cannot rely on parents, siblings, or teachers for detailed guidance. But regardless of how much guidance is available to you, you should seek additional help. If your parents didn't go to college, what about family friends or your friend's families? Teachers and guidance counselors can also be of help, and especially those with whom you interacted (in following the steps laid out in Chapter 6) to assess your career options.

Selecting a College

You can also seek advice from third-party professionals. The most comprehensive and personalized support can come from the rapidly growing number of "college consultants" or "college counselors." (You can find one in your area and that meets your needs by Googling these terms.)

These consultants can guide you through the entire college planning, admission, and selection process, or assist you in individual components of the process. Services can include conducting personal inventories, identifying and evaluating colleges that fit your specific personality, learning style and needs, admission test preparation, helping you through the admission process, suggesting essay topics, preparing you for college visits and interviews, identifying financial aid and scholarships, helping you make your final selection, preparing you for your first days of college, and more. Although the right consultant can provide tremendous value, they can be costly: $100 or more per hour and $3,000–$6,000 for a comprehensive engagement.[65]

Need help but can't afford a private consultant? You can use some less expensive options. Unigo provides an online database that profiles and provides student reviews and rankings of thousands of colleges and universities as well as opportunities to speak with students from these schools for $29 per half hour.[66] It offers subscription-based (from $199 to $599) services that include video courses of all stages of the college search, application and admission processes, and opportunities to work with Unigo consultants on individualized programs. Unigo also partners with McGraw-Hill Education to offer a college and career readiness and study curriculum that combines live events, multimedia projects, and mentoring programs.[67]

There are also many even less-expensive do-it-yourself options. U.S. News, for example, offers a free quiz that can help you assess your readiness for college and what types of colleges may be right for you.[68] Meanwhile, a quick search, such as for "book, selecting the right college," will point you to dozens of books that can guide you through the process. These books include the Intercollegiate Studies Institute's "Choosing the Right College"[69] and Consumer Reports' "Find the Best Colleges for You."[70]

Deciding on a Major

You can also get help in identifying a suitable and employable major. The not-for-profit College Board,[71] for example, offers advice and ideas for students looking for guidance on what to study, identifying the schools which are strong in their chosen field, finding colleges that match your goals and lifestyles, and tips on choosing the right major.[72] ACT's Map of College Majors provides similar help. It allows you to see which majors tend to be best aligned with an individual's broad interests and explains what each area of study entails, the degrees that are available and the types of occupations for which they can prepare you. (Its World-of-Work Map, meanwhile, allows you to link these findings to specific occupations, their day-to-day tasks, salaries, and so forth.)

The Bureau of Labor Statistics issues regular reports that compare opportunities for different majors and careers, as well as annual studies that compare job availability and salaries for hundreds of different occupations. Private companies, including Dice.com,[73] provide detailed information on career opportunities for different majors and occupations in specific industries (technology, in the case of Dice) and others, such as PayScale, compare the salaries commanded by graduates from different colleges and in different majors.[74]

A number of university-based higher education research centers also provide guidance on selecting majors. These include Michigan State University's Collegiate Employment Research Institute's 2012 to 2013

Recruiting Trends report[75] and the Georgetown University Center on Education and the Workforce's From College Major to Career[76] website. And if you prefer to do your reading the old-fashioned way (i.e., from a book), a quick web search on "Choosing the Right College Major, Books" comes up with hundreds of titles, including the *2013 Book of Majors*[77] and *How to Choose a College Major*[78], along with hundreds of websites that provide similarly focused advice. *Everything College Major Test Book*, meanwhile, provides a series of tests to help students select appropriate majors.[79]

College Costs and Returns

Getting objective, comprehensive information on and especially finding comparisons on the real costs (gross, net, drop-out rates, and ROI) of a college education is more problematic. As discussed in the previous section on Financing Your Education, sources including Scholarships.com's blog[80] and Payscale's annual College Salary Report[81] provide a good start. The Department of Education also provides a number of tools, including college cost calculator[82] and basic comparisons of net college costs. The most ambitious program, and currently the best tool for assessing and comparing the true costs of different college options, comes from the Department of Education's College Navigator.[83] While this relatively new tool is being enhanced to provide better information on salaries and majors, at least one Senator (Ron Wyden of Oregon) has introduced a bill that would require the federal government to disseminate statistics on a broad range of factors, including graduation rates, salary levels, debt levels, and so forth, on the costs and returns of different courses of study at different colleges.

Whatever help you choose to get (or not to get), you can't count on your consultant, your professors, or your college (not to speak of your friends) to craft the educational experience that will best prepare you for your dream career. You will have to take responsibility for your own education. Nor, as discussed in Chapter 10, will you be able to count on your manager, your employer, or your job counselor or recruiter to manage your career. You will also have to take responsibility for this.

Although you should seek as much advice and help as you can get, some things are just too personal and important to entrust to others.

The Graduate School Decision

Although this book focuses primarily on planning for undergraduate admission and study, I have to at least mention graduate degrees. After all, they are required for some fields and extremely helpful in others. And remember that demand for those with master's degrees is growing faster than for any other type of degree.

But just as many college degrees are being seen by employers as "the new high school diploma," a growing number of graduate degrees appear to be on track for becoming "the new bachelor's degree." This is particularly true for many liberal arts master's degrees that recent graduates have pursued as a means of "riding out" the recession, in hopes of an improved job market. Even as the market slowly improves, many such degrees are likely to provide modest, if any, real employment or monetary value. Although they may provide some help in differentiating you from other applicants from second-, third- and lower-tier schools, there are many, many better ways of spending your postgraduate school time and money (including on many of the nondegree options discussed in Chapter 9).

Decisions on graduate school are similar to, but in some ways easier than, making decisions on college. It partially depends on the type of career you're targeting. Is a graduate degree necessary, as in law or medicine? If so, depending on the degree, are there any advantages and/or disadvantages of pursuing the degree directly out of undergraduate school, rather than working for a few years? Many Tier-One MBA programs, for example, won't even consider a candidate that has not had actual business experience.

In some fields, like psychology and biology, graduate degrees may not be formally required, but are de facto requirements for employment, much less for serious work in the field. In others, like business, nursing, and software engineering, bachelor degrees are sufficient (or in the case of nursing, which requires a minimum of an associate degree, more than sufficient) for most jobs. In fact, since jobs are so plentiful in some of these fields (especially nursing and engineering) and pay so well (in many

IT, math, and some science fields) postponing work in favor of graduate study may incur big opportunity costs. Besides, as mentioned previously, STEM graduate degrees often return less of a salary bump over a bachelor's degree than advanced degrees in business and many healthcare fields.

Although most professions don't require graduate degrees for initial employment (except in healthcare, law, and tenure-track faculty positions), these degrees may be required for long-term certification (as for many teacher positions). For most other positions, graduate degrees can burnish your skills and your resume, and either qualify you for a new position or put you on a fast-track for advancement.

> Occupations that typically require master's degrees are projected to grow faster than those for any other level of education. The demand for most PhD's on the other hand, is problematical.

Graduate degrees, however, may also have their downsides. First of all, they are costly—both in terms of out-of-pocket expenses and, if you can get a job with a bachelor's degree, in opportunity costs. Moreover, even some of the most coveted graduate degrees—the JD and the MBA—are losing much of their luster, at least those from lower ranked schools.

Consider the employment prospects for some of the more popular and coveted graduate degrees.

Law Degrees

We are currently in the midst of a lawyer glut. Only 55 percent of 2011 law school graduates, for example, had jobs that required a law degree within nine months of their graduation.[84] Another 28 percent were unemployed or underemployed. Of those who did get degree-required jobs, only a small fraction (mostly from tier-one law schools) landed one of those highly sought $160,000 per year jobs in the nation's most prestigious law firms. Most ended up in much lower paying positions in small firms, solo practice, corporate law departments, or government or public defender offices.

This lawyer glut is prompting most law schools to reduce the number of applicants they accept. Meanwhile, the American Bar Association and some state bars are now exploring the potential for two-year programs, with two years of class work (after which graduates are allowed to take the bar exam and practice law), plus an optional third year in what is effectively an apprenticeship program (working under experienced lawyers, such as in providing legal services for underserved low- and middle-income clients).

Medical Degrees

MDs are at the other end of the professional degree spectrum. Demand is high, and will continue to soar, especially to meet the demands of an aging population. Although this demand is spread across most specialties, it is particularly strong among some specialties and among general practitioners, especially those who practice in inner cities or more rural areas. The AMA, in fact, estimates a shortage of about 50,000 primary care, and 65,000 nonprimary care doctors over the next decade. Even so, not all specialties are likely to enjoy the same growth rates. This is particularly true in radiology, one of the industry's most desired medical "lifestyle" professions. Given the miracle of modern electronics and communication, images can now be transmitted and read more efficiently and cheaply in large remote centers (both onshore and offshore) that provide services for multiple hospitals (thereby reducing the need for many hospitals to employ their own radiologists). And, as discussed in Chapter 2, computers are also being tested and are beginning to yield impressive results in detecting and diagnosing potential problems.

Given the growing national (actually global) shortage of doctors, one may expect that the government would do all in its power to ease the shortage. Au contraire. It appears to be doing all in its power to exacerbate the shortfall. On one hand, many existing medical schools are expanding capacity, and new ones are opening. However, the federal government, in its infinite wisdom, has slashed the already limited funding that hospitals need to fund residencies (which are required before doctors can practice).[85] This has the potential of leading to the absurd situation of graduating desperately needed MDs who are not allowed to practice medicine.

MBAs

The market for MBAs, which was also in the dumper in the depths of the recession, has improved significantly. According to the Graduate Management Admission Council, 62 percent of 2012 MBA graduates[86] exited school with at least one offer and 2013 hiring and salaries[87] were stronger yet. The most sought after (and most highly paid) of these graduates, however, are from tier-one schools and most of these had at least a few years of experience before entering the program.

But even with the recovery's improving employment prospects, applications for MBA programs have been falling, plummeting 22 percent in 2012 (after a 10 percent decline in 2011).[88] Somewhat surprisingly, these declines are being felt by top-tier as well as lower ranked schools. The reasons are a combination of improving (albeit slowly) job prospects for non-MBAs, the costs (both out-of-pocket and opportunity) of earning a degree, and the explosive growth in interest in alternative, one-year specialized business master's programs that are open to students who just finished undergraduate school, as well as those with experience.

These one-year master of science programs, as discussed in a series of my 2010 blog posts, provide opportunities for graduate degrees in any of dozens of specialties, including virtually all of the business disciplines (marketing, finance, international business, etc.), pretty much any field in which a business background is desired (from sports management to wealth management and real estate development), and all current hot topics (entrepreneurism, sustainability, innovation, social media, and so forth).[89] They require less time and cost less than an MBA, provide more focused learning opportunities and have begun to gain credibility among more and more employers.

IT and Math Masters and PhDs

Some of the hottest areas (which should come as no surprise to those who have read my continual harangues about the opportunities in IT and quantitative fields) are in accounting, finance, data analytics, information technology, and supply chain management. One thing that may be more surprising—a number of these quantitative programs are dominated by Chinese students attending American schools. Some schools, in fact, claim that 80 to 90 percent of these programs' students are Chinese citizens![90]

But regardless of the field, these programs can pay dividends to any graduate looking for differentiation or the ability to compete head-to-head with other candidates who have more relevant backgrounds or better educations.[91] This is especially true for:

- Liberal arts graduates looking to boost their relevance to business employers who also value many liberal arts graduates' breadth, writing and critical thinking skills, relative to those of business undergrads.
- Healthcare majors, where masters' are required for many positions and pay premiums for most; and
- MBAs from highly rated programs, for which jobs are relatively plentiful and often pay big premiums over bachelor's degrees.

Science and Engineering Masters and PhDs

Such advanced degrees are virtually required for particularly demanding research work and for gaining a tenure-track position in most universities. They can also help differentiate a graduate attempting to score a position at a particularly demanding employer, such as Goldman Sachs or Google, which according to Human Resources executive Lazlo Bock, hires 5,000 to 8,000 people out of 2 million applicants per year.[92]

But, as discussed above, other than for such premier positions, STEM graduate job prospects are already so strong that advanced degrees are seldom required—except, as also discussed above, in many healthcare professions. As also discussed, many such jobs already pay so well for a Bachelor's, and the opportunity costs of graduate school are so high, that the incremental return from a graduate degree in these fields is already low. Most scientists and engineers who are looking to earn a graduate degree to improve their career and salary prospects may be better off with an MBA, specialized business master's, science masters or even a law degree.

PhDs

As for PhDs: Buyer Beware. Although universities were traditionally the primary employers of PhDs, hiring for tenure-track positions has been plummeting.[93] Much of the new hiring is for lowly paid adjunct professors. Post-docs, biding their time in hope of a tenure-track position, often live in near poverty, waiting for offers which seldom come. The best employment options are now in the private sector.

Demand and salaries for PhDs are relatively strong in natural science (especially energy related), life science, engineering, and math fields. There is also demand for some social science PhDs, especially in economics, but also in other areas for which there is a need to make sense of huge volumes of polling and online data. And a growing percentage of people with these degrees are going into the private sector, rather than academia. In fact, 29 percent of those 2013 PhD graduates who held jobs at graduation were working in the private sector. These jobs, as would be expected, are concentrated primarily in financial services, technology, and management consulting. PhDs, in fact, accounted for 20 percent of all new Boston Consulting Group hires![94]

As for humanities PhDs, unless you're a superstar who can land one of the infinitesimal number of tenure-track positions for which a few universities may possibly hire, good luck.

One additional note on graduate degrees. Most such programs are expensive and often require loans. Although loans to finance bachelor's degrees average $29,000, a New America Foundation and Wall Street Journal survey finds that these outstanding loan amounts balloon to $42,000 for an MBA, over $50,000 for most other master's and more than $140,000 for law and $160,000 for MD and other health science programs.[95]

But while college remains, by far, the most popular means of preparing for a good job, what if college, much less graduate school, isn't right for you? Or maybe it will be in the future, but not yet. Will you be relegated to a mind-numbing low-skill job that may not pay a living wage and probably won't provide a career path? Not at all. There are already many alternative means of getting the types of educations that will qualify you for higher skill, higher-wage jobs. A few won't even require you to sit in a classroom or read a book. Some even provide some of the benefits of graduate degrees by demonstrating proficiency in a field that is complementary to that of an undergraduate degree. And as discussed in Chapter 9, more and more of these options are being created every year.

CHAPTER 9

Alternative Ways of Getting an Advanced Education

Steps 10 Through 14

College is completely unnecessary if you are really smart and driven . . . I think the evidence speaks for itself when you look at great companies that are being created, how many of those people actually finished college.

—Elon Musk
Founder of PayPal, Tesla, SpaceX

Key Points

- Many high-skill careers, including some that pay very high salaries, do not require college degrees.
- There are a growing number of ways of preparing for a high-value career, other than a four-year degree. Community colleges can directly prepare you for many careers or provide a low-cost entry into a four-year education.
- Apprenticeship, although underutilized in the United States, can prepare you for many lucrative trades and increasingly for some key office jobs.
- Some now contend that college degrees not only are not necessary for, but also may reduce your prospects of launching a successful business.
- Gap Year programs can provide valuable detours before or during college.
- Boot camps and MOOCs can complement or even replace formal education.

Some form of college degree, whether an associate, bachelor, or graduate degree, currently is and will continue to be the most common means of qualifying for a high-skill job. This is especially true in a period of "degree inflation," when a surfeit of applicants for each position makes it practical for employers to make a degree a de facto requirement for jobs that don't really require a formal classroom education.

College, however, is certainly not the only means of developing these skills. Many high-skill trades, and even white-collar professions, don't really require degrees. These include:

- Traditional trades, such as carpentry and electrical wiring;
- "New Age" trades, such as CNC tool programming and operation and green energy installation;
- Artisan trades, such as making wine, cheese, and craft beers;
- Most sports and arts;
- All forms of sales, from consumer retail through many types of expensive and complex capital equipment and some professional services;
- Most IT disciplines, from technical support and website design through network and database administration and software architecture; and, of course
- The all-encompassing category of "entrepreneur," everything from starting a corner store to running a franchise operation to launching the next big social media giant.

Apprenticeships are a time-honored way of preparing for a career in a trade. While these hands-on methods of teaching and learning are particularly entrenched in manual trades, they are also beginning to be used in more professional positions. What, for example, are medical internships and residencies, if not apprenticeships? Some law schools, as discussed in Chapter 8, are moving in the same direction, with proposals to make the third year optional and provide students with the opportunity to work under experienced lawyers, such as in providing legal services for under-served low- and middle-income clients.

Both colleges and apprenticeship programs, however, take top-down approaches to teaching: a professor or master effectively decides what the disciple should learn and feeds it to them. The professor and master then decides whether the disciple learned the required information or skills and can demonstrate that learning in a way the master approves.

One, however, can often develop skills in much less formal, more self-directed ways. In fact, those with experience, demonstrable skills, and recognized accomplishments in a specific field (not to speak of those with a friend or relative who can get the candidate in the door) can often trump a candidate with a degree (at least in fields that do not legally require degrees).

Such skills can be gained through hands-on experience, such as hobbies, summer jobs, or fellowships or even solely by reading. There are now a growing number of additional means of developing these skills in an informal, more self-directed way, and even of demonstrating the degree of proficiency you have achieved and of earning a certification that demonstrates that proficiency. And some of this can even be done without setting foot into a classroom or in some cases, paying a dime of tuition.

This chapter begins with a discussion of more formal alternatives to four-year degrees, including community colleges and, briefly, apprenticeships and how they are being extended into professions that have typically required a college degree. It then discusses some less formal education opportunities, including online courses and Massive Open Online Courses (MOOCs), certification programs, boot camps, and fully self-directed learning programs.

The Community College Option

College does not necessarily mean a four-year school. The United States currently has 1,167 community colleges (1,600 when branch campuses are included). Of these, 993 are public, 143 are private, and 31 are tribal schools.[1] They enroll a total of 13 million students—37 percent of all U.S. undergraduates.

Although two-year colleges are often viewed as something of a poor stepchild to four-year colleges, they play five critical roles in U.S. educational system. They provide:

1. Developmental education, for high school graduates who are not academically ready to enroll in college-level courses;

2. Transfer education, for students that will transfer to a four-year institution to pursue a BS or BA degree;

3. Degree education, where students earn a two-year associate's degree, with no current plans to attend a four-year school;

4. Continuing education, which entails noncredit courses for personal development and interest; and

5. Industry-specific and career education, including certificate- and noncertificate-based vocational classes and programs and in conducting the academic component of many apprenticeship programs.

Their role in developmental education typically entails picking up the pieces of the nation's secondary school system by providing remedial courses to those who graduate from high school, but do not yet have the skills required for college. In fact, 59 percent of all community college students require at least one, and often many more remedial classes before they can begin taking courses that will count toward graduation.[2] These schools also serve as a critical, low-cost "feeder system" for four-year colleges by providing a less rigorous entry into postsecondary education and a means of transferring credits that can be used to obtain a four-year degree. In fact, about 26 percent of students who start at community colleges move on to four-year colleges and 60 percent of them end up graduating.[3]

Many students, however, attend community colleges specifically to get two-year degrees. Associate degrees, after all, are the minimum educational requirement for the occupation that is projected to produce the largest number of new skilled jobs in the country—registered nurses.[4]

Community colleges, as discussed in my 2010 blog series on community colleges,[5] also play critical roles as engines of social mobility. They (at least public, rather than private community colleges), for example:

- Have an open admissions policy, admitting anyone with a high school diploma or equivalent, regardless of grades;
- Cost an average of 63 percent less[6] than those for public four-year colleges and 1/10th to 1/20th the cost of many private four-year schools;

- Cater to disproportionately higher percentages of ethnic minorities (40 percent of total enrollment) and first-generation college students in their families (42 percent);
- Are geographically widespread, with campuses or extension centers within an hour's drive of more than half of the nation's population (which also facilitates commuting, thereby reducing room and board expenses); and
- Provide greater flexibility than four-year schools in accommodating part-time students. Since many of these students have jobs, and many have families, almost 60 percent attend on a part-time basis.

These schools have typically been used largely by high school grads that didn't have the grades or the study habits to succeed in a four-year school. However, the combination of skyrocketing tuition costs and the growing financial squeeze on middle-income families is prompting a growing number of applicants who are capable of university-level work, but are looking to reduce the cost of a four-year education. In fact, a 2011 Brookings Institution study rates community college education as the single best investment an individual can make.[7] Its 20 percent internal ROI even beats out four-year degrees (15 percent) and more than doubles the return from the nation's third-highest return investment, the stock market (7 percent). No wonder that the number of people enrolling in community colleges is exploding—up more than 20 percent between 2007 and 2011.

> A 2011 Brookings Institution study rates community college education as the single best investment an individual can make—better than even a four-year degree or the stock market.

However, the vast majority of people who attend community colleges do not end up earning a degree: only 13 percent graduate in two years and 28 percent in four years. One reason is that community colleges attract and give chances to many marginal students who aren't suited to or ready for college-level work.

Many community college attendees, however, never plan to earn degrees. They go to community colleges for nondegree vocational training, such as individual courses in an area in which they want to learn more, certificate programs, part of an apprentice curricula, or special programs run for local employers or trade unions. In fact, about 35 percent of those who complete their formal courses of study at these colleges earn certificates, rather than degrees.

Community colleges may be uniquely suited to such roles. They are often better attuned to the specific skills requirements of local businesses than are most universities and will often design classes in conjunction with, and serve as training arms for these employers. Such courses can take the form of contracted, employer-designed classes (such as for operating specific robots or computer numerical control, or CNC machines), formal certification programs which focus on a specific discipline (such as accounting, gerontology, graphic design, or CAD), or formal two-year associate degrees (as in management, nursing, culinary arts, and other career-based disciplines). Some schools even allow students to combine courses from multiple certifications into a formal degree program.

Governments also partner with private-sector employers to create vocational programs targeted at specific companies and industries. The State of Kentucky, for example, funded an initiative to help Bluegrass Community College build a replica of a car factory to train employees for jobs at a nearby Toyota plant.[8] The San Francisco Bay Area Workforce Funding Collaborative is a partnership among local governments, business, and community colleges that train workers in areas including biotech, healthcare, and manufacturing.[9] Boston's SkillsWorks trains people to work in healthcare, hospitality, property services, automotive services, and green industries.[10] New York and Chicago have recently created similar centers in transportation, construction, services, and manufacturing.

Graduating from such technical training programs can really pay off. A 2013 State of Texas study, for example, found that graduates of two-year technical programs have first-year median earnings of more than $50,000: $30,000 more than students who completed academically oriented two-year degrees and $11,000 more than graduates of bachelor's degree programs across the state.[11] A Colorado study, meanwhile, found that graduates of Associate of Applied Sciences (AAS) programs earn almost $7,000 more than graduates of bachelor's degree programs across the state.[12]

> A 2013 State of Texas studyfound that graduates of two-year technical programs have first-year median earnings of more than $50,000: $11,000 more than graduates of bachelor's degree programs across the state

But for all of community colleges' contributions and advantages, they also have their share of problems. The Department of Education, for example, found that only 31 percent of those who begin at community colleges earn their intended degrees or credential after six years: 27 percent of first semester students do not return for the second semester.[13] Now, big cuts in state funding are forcing many of these schools to reduce the number of students they accept, eliminate classes, increase class size, and reduce quality.

These cuts have been particularly severe among California community colleges. After years of cost-cutting, they have been forced to eliminate 21 percent of their classes, making it difficult for students to get the courses they need to graduate. So difficult, in fact, that despite the systems' open admission policy (any student with a high school diploma or GED is guaranteed admission), enrollment in California community colleges has declined by 16 percent—so much for the state's educational safety net.

A growing number of four-year schools are now also beginning to offer two-year programs that provide some of the same functions as community colleges, albeit with fewer remedial courses and higher costs. These programs, often called "General Studies," are generally designed for students who do not have the grades or the test scores, or are not otherwise ready for a more demanding four-year course of study. Schools such as Boston University, New York University, Texas A&M, University of Illinois, Emory University, Northeastern, and Columbia now offer programs that focus on interdisciplinary and foundational curricula delivered through smaller, more interactive classes with more personalized assistance. Most are intended as entry points for a four-year degree, rather than as a terminal degree. Many such programs guarantee graduates admission to the school's four-year program. The Boston University program, for one, already accounts for about 15 percent of the university's new undergraduate students.

Certification Programs and Apprenticeships

The majority of jobs open to those with no college education are low-skill, low-wage service jobs. However, a number of above average-paying mid-skill jobs don't require a formal postsecondary degree. Most of these have their own informal or formal training programs.

Certificate programs, which provide formal recognition of the completion of a specified set of courses in a specific area, are the most common of these training programs, In fact, according to the National Center for Education Statistics (NCES), certificate programs were the fastest-growing segment of the higher education market from 2001 to 2010, with the number of certificates doubling. As of 2010/11, U.S. schools awarded more than 1 million certificates—more than the number of associate's (942,000), master's (731,000), or doctoral degrees (164,000) combined.[14]

These occupational certificate programs are available in hundreds of fields, from project management to nurse's aide. While 33 occupations require certificates as a minimum qualification for entry, they are used in dozens of other occupations as a demonstration of experience and ideally, competence. The most common of these, as shown in a BLS report that looks specifically at certificate programs, are in various branches of healthcare, personal services, culinary services, and mechanic and repair technologies.[15]

There is also significant demand for certificates in various segments of law enforcement and firefighting (fields in which employment growth is expected to be slow) and many construction trades (some for which employment growth is expected to be strong). there is also growing interest in IT-related certifications. Fields such as PC repair, website design, and computer security are offering both good employment prospects and salaries.

Certificates can require anywhere from a few months to two years to earn, and cost anywhere from about $6,500 at a public college to more than $65,000 at a for-profit college. They also can potentially yield big rewards—or no rewards at all. The median salary for someone with a certificate in aviation, for example, is $66,000. Those with certificates in food services or cosmetology, on the other hand, have a median salary of less than $20,000.

Overall, a Georgetown Center on Education and the Workforce study[16] shows that certificates represent the highest level of educational attainment for about 12 percent[17] of U.S. workers and that these people earn, on average, 20 percent[18] more than those whose highest education level is a high school diploma. Then there are those in computer and information services.[19] According to the study, men with certificates in this area earn an average of $72,498 per year—more than 72 percent of all associate and 54 percent of bachelor degree holders. Women do even better, earning more than 75 percent more than women with associate and 64 percent of those with bachelor degrees!

> Certificates represent the highest level of educational attainment for about 12 percent of U.S. workers and that these people earn, on average, 20 percent more than those whose highest education level is a high school diploma.

Trade Apprenticeships

Although certificates are the most common form of nondegree vocational training programs, the vast majority of mid-skill jobs are, as shown in Figure 9.1, learned through on-the-job training. This training ranges from short-term, casual training for a couple of hours to much more formal programs of several years. The most formal programs— apprenticeships—typically combine formal classroom study (often at a community college and sometimes culminating in one or a series of certificates) with managed hands-on work. Some of these programs can be quite long and quite rigorous. The BLS, for example, estimates that apprenticeships typically entail at least 144 hours of occupation-specific technical instruction and 2,000 hours of on-the-job training per year over three-to-five years.[20]

Most occupations that typically require only a high school diploma or equivalent also require on-the-job training (OJT) to attain competency in the skills needed in the occupation. In 2012, 91 percent of occupations assigned high school as the typical entry-level education required OJT. OJT includes occupation-specific training, not job-specific training. With occupation-specific training, the skills learned can be transferred to another job in the same occupation.

In 2012, about 45 percent of occupations assigned high school as the typical entry-level education needed moderate education needed moderate term OJT.

Occupations in the high school category by on-the-job training (OJT) assignment, 2012

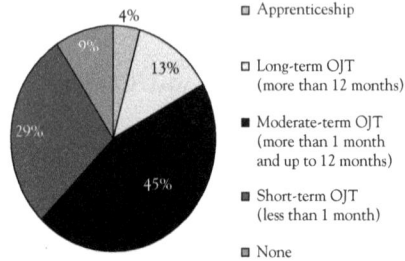

□ Apprenticeship
4%
9%
13%
□ Long-term OJT (more than 12 months)
29%
■ Moderate-term OJT (more than 1 month and up to 12 months)
45%
■ Short-term OJT (less than 1 month)
■ None

Figure 9.1. On-the-job training requirements for high school occupations

Source: U.S. Bureau of Labor Statistics (2012), p. 5.

Jobs that require formal apprenticeships are most numerous and best known in skilled manufacturing and construction trades, such as those for master electricians, plumbers, machinists, and welders. They are, however, also used in some government jobs (such as air traffic controllers and building code inspectors), skilled routine jobs (such as power plant operators and ship mates), creative jobs (fashion designers), green jobs (solar energy installers), and office jobs (paralegals). While many of these jobs offer decent pay (often starting about $15 per hour, with median pay typically ranging between $40,000 and $60,000 per year),some professionals, such as master plumbers[21], pipe fitters, and welders,[22] can easily earn six figures, with some claiming $200,000 per year (for those working on major projects with a lot of overtime).

Workers skilled in many of these trades are also in high demand. As shown in Figure 9.2, for example, the BLS expects occupations that require apprenticeships to grow faster than any single category through 2022. A number of these occupations are expected to grow at more than 20 percent per year, and a few (such as brick masons and insulation installers) are likely to grow by more than 30 percent.

Percent change, projected 2012–22 | Average, all occupations = 10.8%

Occupation type	Percent
Internship/residency	11.2%
Apprenticeship	22.2%
Long-term OJT (more than 12 months)	8.3%
Moderate-term OJT (1-12 months)	8.3%
Short-term OJT (less than 1 month)	9.7%
None	12.9%

With regard to on-the-job training (OJT), the fastest employment growth is projected to be in occupations that typically require an apprenticeship. Most of the apprenticeship occupations are construction occupations. The construction industry was greatly affected by the 2007–2009 recession. Rapid growth is projected for many construction occupations as the industry recovers from the recession; however, this growth represents only a partial recovery of jobs lost.

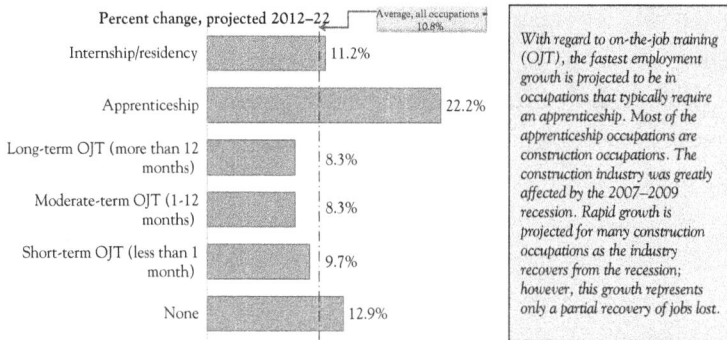

Figure 9.2 Growth in employment in occupations that require a high school degree, 2012–2022

Source: "Education and Training Outlook for Occupations, 2012–22" (2012), p. 4.

> The Bureau of Labor Statistics expects occupations that require apprenticeships to grow faster than any single category through 2022.

Indeed, some of these jobs, such as those in advanced manufacturing and some high-skill construction fields, are desperately in need of skilled workers. A 2011 Manufacturing Institute survey, for example, found that 600,000 manufacturing job openings were left unfilled due to the inability to find qualified workers.[23] And with pending retirements from a rapidly aging workforce, needs are likely to grow. The American Welding Society estimates that by 2020, there will be a shortage of 290,000 welders, inspectors, and teachers.[24] Why are so many good paying and secure jobs going unfilled? Many young people are shunning factory-floor jobs in favor of office work, even when many of these office jobs pay less and are at levels below those for which they are planned and qualified.

Although apprenticeship programs play a very small role in the United States, they remain extremely popular in some European countries. They, for example, currently employ between 50 and 70 percent of all German, Swiss, and Austrian 15- to 19-year-olds and are generally viewed as comparable to college education.[25] These programs are also gaining popularity in other European countries. The United Kingdom, for example, is dramatically expanding its program and about six other countries, including Spain, Italy, and Greece, have asked Germany for help in launching their own programs.

Apprenticeships are, in contrast, almost an afterthought in the United States, where they employ only 7.4 percent of all employed 15 to 19-year-olds and are accorded far less prestige than college degrees. In fact, while European programs are growing, U.S. programs have been shrinking, from 480,000 in 2008[26] to 330,578 in 2013.[27]

Bringing Apprenticeships into the Office

There's another big difference between the United States and European programs. While U.S. programs are overwhelmingly in manufacturing and construction trades, European programs have extended into all types of occupations. For example:[28]

- Swiss programs now cover baking, banking, healthcare, retail, and clerical positions;
- British programs now include commercial pilots, lawyers, engineers, and accountants, with programs that are considered the equivalent of a college education.

Although U.S. firms employ few such white-collar apprenticeships, we are beginning to see a few, such as to train nursing assistants and supply-chain analysts. Computer skills, however, are by far the most common targets of such efforts.

Meanwhile, some state and local governments and private sector businesses are, as mentioned previously, also partnering to help design and fund community college-based apprentice programs. Just as importantly, a growing number of not-for-profit organizations are creating hybrid programs that use different combinations of academic and mentor-led on-the-job, hands-on training programs to prepare people for jobs in a broader range of occupations.

Year Up, for example, offers a one-year program that provides internships (rather than more formal apprenticeships) to high school graduates that not only encourages formal academic study but also requires participants to attend and earn graduation credits at local community colleges.

The first six months of the Year Up program consist of classroom education where students learn a range of technical skills (such as hardware support and repair, operating systems, software installation, security, and Microsoft Office) and soft professional skills (business writing, time management, communication and presentation skills, teamwork, etc.) in the classroom. The second six months entail internships at one of Year Up's 250+ corporate and government partners, where they focus on either computer technology or financial operations. All students have an assigned advisor, a business community mentor and, if required, a private tutor. While Year Up works with a number of community colleges (which typically offer up to 23 college credits for completion of the program), it is now establishing more formal and collaborative affiliations—the first with Miami-Dade Community College.

Students develop marketable skills, earn college credits, and are paid a small weekly stipend. The greatest reward, however, is in Year Up's 100 percent placement rate into jobs that pay an average of $15 per hour or $30,000 per year.

Year Up has graduated more than 6,000 students over its 12-year history and can currently accommodate up to 1,400 students per year across nine U.S. cities. In addition to its perfect placement rate, 95 percent of its corporate partners claim to be satisfied with the program.

Pathways in Technology Early College High School, or P-TECH, is the most ambitious of these programs. The program was formed as a joint venture among IBM, the New York City School District, the City University of New York, and the IBM Foundation, which provided the inspiration, shaped the curriculum, provided hardware and software, and provided the primary funding for the program. While it certainly combines academic education with a practical internship, it reaches all the way back to ninth grade to find primarily lower income students who will go through a six-year program, culminating in an associate's degree in a computer-science-related field—and preferred consideration for a job at IBM. And all of this with no entrance exam, no tuition—and at no additional cost to the city's education system.

> P-TECH, which combines academic education with a practical internship, reaches back to ninth grade to find primarily lower-income students who will go through a six-year program, culminating in an associate's degree in a computer-science-related field—and preferred consideration for a job with sponsoring companies.

The original Brooklyn-based IBM-sponsored high school, which provides an integrated curriculum across high school and community colleges, focuses on a broad range of STEM disciplines while also providing workplace skills in areas such as leadership, communications, and problem solving. Each student is assigned an IBM mentor who will work with the student, their teachers, and advisors to create an academic program that is tailored to the individual student and aligned to college and career requirements. The project-based curriculum will include many opportunities for exposure to the real world, as through guest speakers, regular workplace visits, internships, and apprenticeships.

Graduates receive both their high school diploma and an associate's degree in applied science in either computer information systems or electromechanical engineering technology. While they do receive priority and extra consideration for an entry-level position at IBM, they are not bound to IBM. They can accept positions at other companies or transfer directly to a four-year college.

Since P-Tech is only in its third year, it is far too soon to assess how students will do when they graduate. Interim results, however, are impressive.[29] For example:

- After two semesters, 72 percent of initial students passed both English and math Regents intended for 11th grade students and 80 percent passed after the third semester;

- After two semesters, 48 percent of students met the CUNY college readiness (CR) indicators and 50 percent did so after the third semester;
- After two semesters (9th grade), 25 percent of students exceeded the national average for 10th grade students; and
- Within three semesters, 48 of the 104 students in the first class had completed at least one college course at City Tech. Currently, 74 students (62 sophomores and 12 freshmen) are enrolled in at least one college course.

While the initial P-TECH schools have only about 100 students in each grade, the model was designed to be scalable and to operate with other corporate sponsors. It has already been replicated in eight schools, with plans for 29 more in two years: one in Chicago (with IBM as the lead industry partner) and four others in New York (with Cisco, Motorola, Microsoft and Verizon as lead partners, with another planned by SAP). New York's Governor Cuomo has so-far announced plans for 16 P-TECH schools across this one state alone.[30] The more recently created Chicago school (the Sarah E. Goode STEM Academy), meanwhile, is already ranked number four of 106 city schools in overall student growth and its students have earned an average of eight college credits.

Although IBM originally designed and founded the program, the company enlisted the Center for Children and Technology to produce a guide based on the P-TECH design and early years' experience. The guide, STEM Pathways to College and Careers Schools: A Development Guide has already been used by the other above mentioned IT companies and is available to other companies, schools, and colleges that would like to establish their own private–public partnerships.[31]

Although current lead partners are all in the IT and telecommunications industries, the model is also intended to be applicable to many other fields including healthcare, advanced manufacturing, and finance.

Such programs are only the tip of what will hopefully become a growing trend. A number of the later-discussed Gap Year programs, for example, provide similar programs. The U.S. Office for Apprenticeships, meanwhile, is registering new programs in fields including information technology, healthcare, biotechnology, and geospatial technology.

Incenting Students to Drop Out
and Start Their Own Businesses

Not all white collar apprenticeship programs require college. Many high school graduates (not to speak of some dropouts), who are more than capable of performing college-level work, have little interest in a formal college education. Perhaps they don't enjoy or learn well from structured learning experiences. Perhaps traditional lectures bore them. Perhaps they are looking to design their own learning experiences, or maybe they just want to learn by actually doing real-world work, rather than just learning how to do it. Or maybe they can't afford or justify the cost of a college education.

Whatever the reason, they are looking for an education, but on their own terms. Although people have always had options to college—from informal self-study and travel programs, to formal apprenticeships—the options for gaining a high-quality alternative education are exploding.

Some people certainly manage to do quite well without completing college. Famous dropouts, such as Bill Gates, Steve Jobs, and Mark Zuckerburg, managed to develop pretty rewarding careers without completing college. And, as discussed in Chapter 7, a growing number of IT companies are actively recruiting particularly promising students out of their early years of college, to learn in the real world.

Peter Thiel, a cofounder of PayPal who himself had a sterling education (Stanford BA and JD), has become the de facto champion of the non-college movement. He has vociferously denounced college as a waste of time and money and urges students to forgo formal education in favor of real-world learning experiences. In fact, he feels so strongly that he created a fellowship program that provides a no-strings grant of $100,000, plus guidance, mentorship, and access to professional networks to 25 students per year (60 since the program was started three years ago) who eschew college in favor of developing their own business ideas.[32]

Its goal is to select the type of particularly high-potential young adults that would have normally gone to highly competitive colleges and provide them with an accelerated, nontraditional path to creating their own companies or launching into other types of high-power careers.

But, for all its publicity, the Thiel model also has some high-profile critics. Tech entrepreneur turned academic Vivek Wadhwa, for example, claims that Thiel fully vets and carefully selects students who had already been accepted at elite colleges, puts them through a rigorous qualification process, and then showers the select few with the type of mentors and professional guidance that incubators provide—plus a lot more money—but with none of the results.[33] As he sees it, for all the money and guidance, the program has produced a number of flame-outs, but no significant successes. He also questions the social responsibility of providing a couple dozen high achievers, who are already well on track to a successful career, with a no-cost, no-risk opportunity to accelerate their rise, rather than giving hundreds of disadvantaged youths the opportunity to climb into the middle class.

Self-Directed, Semistructured Gap Year Programs

Although the jury is still out on the benefits of the Thiel Fellowship, a few other nonprofit organizations have bought into the broad idea of alternative educations and are developing hybrids between the apprenticeship and the Thiel entrepreneurship models. Some of these programs are positioned as alternatives to college. Some as semistructured Gap Year programs for those looking for a year of experiential education to, as the American Gap Association puts it, "increase self-awareness, challenge comfort zones, and experiment with possible careers."[34]

> While all Gap Year programs are different, they are typically intended to help participants increase self-awareness, challenge comfort zones, and experiment with possible careers.

Such programs, which can be entered into between high school and college or as a break between years in college, are becoming increasingly popular. The Association, which promotes and accredits these programs, for example, believes that about 40,000 Americans now participate in them. It claims that about 90 percent of participants return to college—typically with more direction and motivation.

UnCollege, which was founded by one of the first Thiel Fellows, provides one such program. It provides free advice and guidelines for anyone looking to design their own alternate education programs, either as an alternative or as a supplement to college.

It is intended to help nontraditional learners identify their own passions and pursue their own paths by helping them define their goals and the steps for achieving them. It guides participants through a process of creating their own individualized learning plans and helps them identify, prioritize, and pursue the life experiences that will allow participants to achieve their goals. It also helps in more concrete ways, such as by helping individuals craft their own elevator pitches, develop strategies for building mentor networks and online curriculum vitae that will demonstrate their competencies. UnCollege contends that this process helps fuel an individual's passion; develops their organizational, creative, and self-motivation skills; bolsters their self-confidence; and burnishes their reputation on the basis of real world, rather than (or in combination with) academic accomplishments.

Information and advice on how to do this is provided in Dale Stephens' book, *Hacking Your Education*, on the organization's website, and through its blog and weekly newsletters.[35] All promote a self-directed approach to learning in which each student (or actually, nonstudent) decides what he or she wishes to learn, actively seeks out the sources and activities to facilitate that learning, and then let the world, rather than a designated master, determine "the grade."

Although initially designed as an alternative to college, UnCollege has added a more formal, year-long blended learning and internship program called Gap Year.[36] Gap Year, like the Thiel Fellowship (and very unlike Year Up and P-TECH, both which are open to all applicants) carefully vets and accepts only select individuals—particularly those with "extraordinary intelligence," "unstoppable motivation," and "unflappable integrity." Unlike Thiel, however, UnCollege does not give participants money. It charges tuition for a relatively informal education program combined with internship or apprenticeship opportunities that it contends will be more effective at preparing students for careers than will college. The year-long program is divided into four, three-month phases:

1. Launch, which consists of sessions, workshops, roundtables, and discussions designed to help participants develop meta-learning and

technical skills, meet mentors, and design their own learning programs and line up their internships;

2. Voyage, where participants will live for three months in a country in which they do not know the language and work in whatever area they believe will most challenge them and help them grow;

3. Internship, with any company or organization that will help advance the individual's specific learning objectives. (UnCollege will help the participant decide on and line up the internship and provide support over the three-month period); and

4. Project, any type of project with a tangible deliverable, which someone will pay the participant to complete, such as a book, an art exhibit, a business plan, or a product.

Gap Year, which costs about $15,000, also includes room and board at a shared house, three months of expenses for living in another country and assistance through all phases of the year-long program. The primary goals are for participants to leave with increased confidence in their own abilities, a range of new skills, a digital portfolio that showcases these skills, and a plan for what they will do next. Most importantly, participants should leave with "the skills and mindset required to build multiple income streams" (such as getting job offers, becoming a freelancer, or creating their own companies)—anything to provide the financial independence that individuals need to remain in control of their own careers and lives.

Enstitute, a two-year program based in New York, is something of a cross between structured white-collar apprenticeship programs and the much less-structured self-directed learning opportunities offered by Thiel and UnCollege. Like Year Up and P-Tech, it is preparing people for entry into mid-skill careers. But like Thiel and UnCollege, it specifically selects the type of people who have demonstrated the skills to succeed, provides them with a relatively unstructured educational program, and provides them with opportunities to develop their skills in apprenticeships.

Enstitute partners with private companies to create apprenticeships in four areas: technology startups, digital media, advertising, and nonprofit or social good. It targets bright, ambitious, entrepreneurial young adults who are either not interested in college, tried college and dropped out, or graduated but are looking for alternatives to graduate school.

The first year consists of Enstitute's own semiformal, modular curriculum that combines online and classroom business courses in disciplines including marketing, sales, business development, operations, human resources, business technology, and design. It drills down into a number of technology areas including systems architecture, front-end systems and user interfaces, programming, and application development and also provides some high-level online academic courses in areas such as English, sociology, and history. These classes are complemented by guest lectures, workshops, and regular (every six weeks) writing assignments. The second year consists of a 40 hour per week apprenticeship, where the student works under a mentor at a sponsoring company.

Although graduates do not receive a diploma, they do compile their own digital portfolios, with examples of the skills they developed, business development deals they've closed, marketing materials they've created, and products they've built. They also receive between 5 and 10 recommendations and, ideally, an offer from the company under which they apprenticed.

While the program just began this year with its first class of 11 students, it plans to expand over the next several years. Students will pay $1,500 in tuition per year (not including room and board). They will, however, receive $1,600 per month stipends during the apprenticeship year.

A growing number of colleges are coming to recognize the value of such programs, often seeing returning students as being more focused and motivated than those who go straight from high school to college. Some not only accommodate students' gap years, they even help cover some of the costs.[37] Schools including Princeton, University of North Carolina, and St. Norbert College now offer formal programs that allow newly accepted students to defer admission for a year, and will subsidize part of the costs of structured programs, such as volunteering for an NGO in areas such as education, economics, health, and the environment. Tufts University goes further than most, paying up to $30,000 to cover participant's airfare, housing, and visa fees.

The Online Education Option

Regardless of which path you choose to developing the skills you will require for your career, that path will increasingly entail some form of online learning. Although computer-based training programs and tests have been around for decades, the explosion and increased sophistication and capabilities of online courses and testing promise to greatly expand the opportunities for learning new skills and qualifying for new jobs.

This revolution is being created by the explosive growth of MOOCs, which are teaching everything from remedial reading to astrophysics. Individuals can listen to lectures, test their knowledge, and even participate in virtual learning teams in which they can question teachers from any computer, at any time that suits their needs. Some of these courses issue certificates of successful completion and even college credits.

> MOOCs, which teach everything from remedial reading to computer programming and existentialism, allow participants to listen to lectures, test their knowledge, participate in virtual learning teams typically for free), and increasingly earn very low-cost certificates, college credits or even degrees.

Online education programs first emerged several decades ago, being used first in in-house training programs and then by for-profit colleges. Their recent popularity explosion, enabled by Internet and broadband connections, was literally born in the closet of ex-hedge fund analyst, Salman Khan, who created the online Khan Academy which is now accessed by about four million people each month. Stanford professor Sebastian Thrun then fuelled the inferno with his massively popular online course on Artificial Intelligence, which registered more than 160,000 students.[38]

There are now thousands of online courses on every imaginable subject, offered by everybody from self-styled gurus to top professors from the most renowned colleges in the country. In fact, dozens of tier-one universities, including Harvard, MIT, University of Pennsylvania, and Stanford, are now producing online courses that are being offered by big, high-budget consortia and venture fund-backed companies such as

Coursera, Udacity, Udemy, and edX. Graduate business schools are also getting into the act. Although a number of top schools offer free introductory or hybrid programs, two top 20 Schools, Indiana University's Kelley School and University of North Carolina's Kenan-Flagler School, now offer fully accredited online degrees.

And the best part—most of the noncredit courses are free. This being said, a growing number of those who complete the required coursework and pass proctored exams want certificates to enhance their employment prospects. While most such certifications currently cost $50 or less, these costs are likely to increase significantly as courses and programs become accredited.

Although courses are becoming available in every field, from calculus to existentialism, the majority are focused on teaching the type of hard skills (as in math, science, and technology) that are most suitable for objective, automated grading. In many ways, this is a great place to start. After all, as discussed in Chapter 3, while computer skills are becoming a basic form of literacy, they are formally taught in only about 10 percent of U.S. high schools.

This borders on criminal. First, virtually every productive member of 21st-century society will require these skills. Second, while BLS estimates that the economy will produce 120,000 new jobs for people with computer science degrees in 2013, few students leave high school with more than basic computer skills or plans to develop them. U.S. colleges, meanwhile, are expected to graduate fewer than 52,000 people with the backgrounds required to fill the millions of jobs that will require coding skills.

Worse still, the United States is lagging far behind many competitive nations in training their youth. Computer science has been a standard part of the high-school curricula in countries including Germany, Denmark, Israel, and New Zealand for more than a decade. England, meanwhile, is now incorporating it into its standard primary school curriculum![39]

Therefore, it is not surprising that a number of for-profit and nonprofit organizations are rushing to teach these skills. Organizations such as Codeacademy, Treehouse, Code.org, Pragmatic Studio, and dozens of others now offer individual courses, full online curricula, and in some cases, formally structured boot camps around all types of IT disciplines.[40] They allow participants to develop skills, and increasingly earn formal certifications in high-demand IT skills such as software development, website design, and computer analytics.

A growing number of organizations are aggregating IT and other types of career-focused courses from thirdparties. SkilledUp.com, for example, provides access to 113,000 courses (ranging from free to $250): primarily skills-based courses in areas including IT, graphics design, finance, and marketing. Apollo Education Group (University of Phoenix) is launching a new online education marketplace called Balloon.[41] It will list open jobs and their skills requirements and refer people to a catalog of about 15,000 online technology classes that will help students develop the type of skills required for these jobs and earn certificates that demonstrate completion.

Google, meanwhile, is already partnering with Udacity to bring its third-party developer programs online and to "fast-track best practices at a large scale." A number of other tech companies, such as Microsoft and Adobe, are preparing similar MOOC offerings, many of which will result in certifications on the vendors' products. AT&T, meanwhile, is partnering with Udacity to train not third-party developers, but potential employees. Its NanoDegree program allows individuals to take classes, designed around AT&T's specific products and methodologies (for $200 per month) to qualify for entry-level positions in the company's IT department.

These are all examples of using MOOCs to help people learn a relatively narrow set of skills that culminate in credentials that qualify graduates for a specific job—sometimes within a specific company. They could also augment or take the place of some companies' work with community colleges.[42] While most such classes currently focus on IT, and especially software development skills, they will soon expand into other areas including energy, healthcare, and manufacturing. Most MOOC courses, however, will continue to focus on teaching a relatively narrow set of skills that culminate in credentials that qualify graduates for a specific job.

Entrepreneurism is becoming another popular field for online study, with a number of courses and predesigned curricula designed around the needs of those looking to start their own business. Examples include Udacity's How to Build a Startup, Y Combinator's Startup Library, and Stanford University's E-Corner. A number of other programs and books teach many of the concepts learned in business school, without the formal B-school experience.[43]

But while MOOCs are still largely experimental, they are beginning to be incorporated into formal college, and even a few high school curricula. High-school adoption may be very slow and limited, but some teachers have begun to assign Khan Academy modules as homework and use class time to review and help students who have problems with the material.

Colleges, however, are moving much more aggressively. Although few of the leading universities that are putting many of their courses online offer college credits for their courses, MIT, in conjunction with EdX, plans to offer a line of low-priced (currently from $275 to $425) XSeries online course sequences that will allow students to earn certificates in subjects including computer science, supply-chain management, and aerodynamics.[44]

A growing number of other colleges are beginning to offer such courses for actual college credit. Some for-profit schools, such as the University of Phoenix, have been doing so for years. Now, a few public colleges such as Washington State, some University of California schools, and Arizona State have begun to integrate online courses into their curricula. Arizona State, in fact, has entered into an agreement with Starbucks, under which the coffee house will pay half tuition for those of its half-time to full-time employees who study for an online bachelor's degree from Arizona State University (and full tuition for those who complete the degree after already having half the credits needed to graduate.) Although many companies offer tuition reimbursement, this program is unique, partially compared with fast food industry standards and partially due to the fact that employees are eligible for assistance from the day they join and are free to leave immediately after they complete their degrees.[45]

Georgia Institute of Technology, meanwhile, became the first major university to offer a formal online degree, a Master's in Computer Science.[46] The program, which will cost about $6,800 for in-state students (compared with $45,000 for an on-campus master's degree), will include access to online tutors, office hours, and other support. It will also require proctored exams. The University will offer these online courses and completion certificates free for those not seeking a degree. The University of Florida is likely to follow with an online bachelor's degree now that the state legislature directed it to offer such programs at about $4,700 for in-state residents, about three-quarters the cost of in-state on-campus tuition.

However, many question whether MOOCs are ready for prime time. Course and exam quality, not to speak of the meaning or value of credentials, are still inconsistent. Completion rates remain below ten percent, with college graduates (presumably due to their existing knowledge base, experience in self-directed study, and motivation) being the most likely to finish. As of now, few courses provide meaningful classroom-type interaction, or an ability to communicate with professors. Providers, meanwhile, are still experimenting with methods of teaching and grading (especially of softer subjects) and of ensuring that people who pass online exams are who they say they are (rather than a friend who takes the exam for them). Few certifications, therefore, yet carry much value and few universities—including those whose professors create these courses—yet offer credit for completion.

edX, therefore, suggests that colleges take a more cautious, "blended" entry into the MOOC world, which would combine traditional and online learning with work experience. Its recommendation: one year of introductory MOOC learning, followed by two years at a physical university, followed by a fourth year that combines MOOC courses and part-time work.[47]

> Although a few colleges already offer full MOOC degrees, edX recommends a blended approach consisting of one year of introductory MOOC learning, followed by two years at a physical university, followed by a fourth year that combines MOOC courses and part-time work

But despite the gaps and the questions, MOOCs are likely to revolutionize virtually every segment of the education market, especially postsecondary. Self-directed learners will have access to whatever courses tickle their fancy. Certificate courses will increasingly move online and gradually gain credibility as the industry begins to agree on standards (such as Mozilla's Open Badges) to confirm the validity of such courses.[48] They will also be increasingly incorporated into college and apprenticeship programs and, as we are beginning to see, form the foundations for entire college degree programs.

They, as mentioned above, are even beginning to creep into some top-tier graduate business programs. While University of North Carolina and Indiana's B-schools already offer online degrees, the University of Penn-sylvania's Wharton School uses its MOOC to attract, and ideally recruit, nontraditional business students (from emerging countries, minority groups, first-generation Americans, etc.). Although completion rate is only about five percent, studies show that many participants are more interested in learning than they are in earning certificates.[49]

Harvard Business School, meanwhile, is introducing a trial, MOOC-based pre-MBA program called Credential for Readiness (CORe) which provides basic courses intended to help liberal arts graduates develop skills in areas such as accounting, analytics and economics. Tuition is expected to be about $1,500 and culminate in a three-hour exam, a grade and a certificate.[50]

MOOC courses will also play a huge role in enabling another critical need of the 21st-century workforces—lifelong learning. They will facil-itate formal and informal updates of work skills, provide new opportu-nities to pursue new hobbies, or prepare oneself for a new job or even a totally new career. True, some of the challenges confronting MOOCs are still to be resolved and it may take time to achieve the type of results that will persuade employers that MOOC graduates actually possess skills comparable to those of graduates from traditional schools and programs (see, however, the latter section on certification). But with all the atten-tion, money, effort, and prestige being invested in these courses, it is almost certainly a matter of time before they gain more credibility.

Post-Graduate Boot Camps

A large—and growing—number of classroom or internship-based sup-plemental education programs are intended to help college graduates sup-plement their education with certificates that demonstrate specific types of marketable skills. The most popular programs focus on specific skills that will equip graduates for entry-level positions in a broad range of industries. Among the three most popular of these disciplines are:

- Entry-level programming which teaches a working knowledge of particularly popular programming languages, such as Ruby, JavaScript, and C++.

- Business basics for nonbusiness majors offer college graduates (primarily those with bachelor's degrees) a high-level working understanding of the type of business terms, functions, and skills that are required to get an entry-level job in a company. Courses may cover areas including finance, accounting, marketing, business communication, organizational behavior, business ethics, and corporate social responsibility.

- Entrepreneurialism, for those planning to launch their own business or to get a job in a start-up. Programs typically include classes on tuning business ideas, writing business plans, and developing pitches to lenders and potential investors. Some of the more in-depth programs also provide basic courses in finance, marketing, website design, and a number of other skills that will be required to manage your business.

A number of classroom or internship-based boot camps help college graduates supplement their education with certificates that demonstrate specific marketable skills in areas including programming, business basics, entrepreneurialism and a growing range of specialized topics.

Coding boot camps are among the most common of these programs, accepting students with little or no programming experience. In return for three weeks to six months of your time and $8,000 to $20,000 in fees, they promise to turn you into an entry-level coder who can command starting salaries of $60,000 or more.

Since I discussed online coding boot camps previously, I'll just briefly mention some of the on-site programs here.

On-site boot camps, from organizations such as General Assembly, Dev Bootcamp, Hack Reactor, and App Academy, can last anywhere from a few weeks to up to six months and cost between $3,000 and $20,000. The longer, more expensive programs often provide premium services, such as personal mentoring and job search assistance and can result in certificates. Some can also be incredibly selective in whom they admit, with some claiming acceptance rates of three to five percent—similar to or even lower than those of Harvard or Stanford. Those who make it into and through the programs can reap some big rewards. Most schools claim placement rates of well over 90 percent and average starting salaries of more than $100,000 in high-demand markets such as the San Francisco Bay Area, New York, Boston, and Washington. In fact, some camps, such as App Academy, are so confident of their alumni's ability to get good jobs that they will forgo tuition in return for 18 percent of a graduate's first year salary.

This being said, there are, so far, no established standards for assessing such claims and some boot camps are retreating from claims that they can turn novices into professional programmers in the equivalent of one semester. Some are expanding their curricula and some, such as Dev Bootcamp, now require students to complete a nine-week preparatory course before beginning formal classes. They are also retreating from their claims of producing "professorial programmers" with statements that although their programs will prepare graduates for entry-level jobs, mentoring and ongoing education will be required to advance in their careers.[51]

Business Basics boot camps are available from a number of schools and for-profit organizations and are intensive, multiweek (typically multithousands of dollars) programs. Many established business schools and colleges, such as Berkeley Haas School and Dartmouth's Tuck School of Business, offer business basic programs to all qualified applicants (remember also the above-mentioned Harvard Business School MOOC-based CORe program). Some liberal arts schools, such as Middlebury College, meanwhile offer such programs as options to current students. A number of independent boot camps, including those from Fullbridge and Business Boot Camp, are intended to provide skills that can work in any type of company. Others, like StartUp Institute, offer a boot camp specifically designed to help people get jobs in start-up organizations. While it does provide a core curriculum, it focuses on preparing individuals for specific positions, such as in product design, web development, technical marketing and sales, and account management.

Entrepreneurialism boot camps are especially popular among graduates directly out of school, corporate employees looking to launch their own business idea, or established professionals, such as doctors and lawyers, who are looking to transition from a larger firm to private practice. The Kaufman Institute, a nonprofit foundation dedicated to encouraging and facilitating entrepreneurship, is the largest player in this market. Its FastTrac programs, which are offered by a number of colleges across the country, are available in three different flavors: one for launching a new business; one for growing an existing small business; and one specifically targeted at the specialized needs of technology startups. As discussed in Chapter 8, a number of colleges and graduate schools already offer majors, minors, and specialized graduate degrees in entrepreneurship. A number of business schools, such as Babson and Syracuse University's Whitman School, also offer broad-based entrepreneurism boot camps. There are also a rapidly growing number of specialized programs. These include:

- Wisconsin Entrepreneurial Bootcamp is designed specifically for STEM majors;
- Social Enterprise Bootcamp is intended to help founders of for-profit and nonprofit businesses develop socially responsible businesses;
- Starter School combines coding and entrepreneurism boot camps into a program designed to prepare people to start their own software company; and
- Syracuse University's Whitman School and Purdue's Krannert School offer boot camps designed specifically for veterans with disabilities.

Speaking of specializations, Claremont Graduate University offers a boot camp specifically designed to help job hunters; General Assembly has one that focuses specifically on helping individuals optimize the business use of social media; and Northwest Michigan College has one to teach film production. Meanwhile, schools such as Hunter College and Northwest Michigan College offer programs focused on those looking to start software-as-a-service, bed-and-breakfast, and personal training businesses. John F. Kennedy University offers them in sports psychology and in exercise and sport performance.

Whatever set of skills you think you may need, there's probably a boot camp that will offer to help you develop them. And if there isn't one today, there probably will be tomorrow.

Credentials, Certifications, and Trust

High school degrees and college degrees are credentials. Unfortunately not all degrees are created equal. Some high school graduates may be unable to write (or in some cases, even read) a coherent sentence. Nor are all college educations equal. Even so, in order to receive and maintain certification, all schools must meet established minimum standards. Moreover, colleges are well enough established that you can often find some form of objective, third-party ratings not only for the school but also for specific departments. And, as discussed in Chapter 8, the Department of Education is also working on its own set of college ratings.

Although such ratings may or may not provide meaningful surrogates for the quality of education or the ability of an individual with a specific degree in a specific major to get a job and command a living salary, they do little to help employers determine whether a particular graduate has the type of real-world skills required to perform specific jobs.

And if it's this hard to measure the skills of a college graduate, how do you measure those of a "graduate" from less formal programs, such as apprenticeships, online courses, and boot camps? This is a huge gap that must be filled if employers are to accept these less formal programs as valid alternatives or supplements to college degrees.

A number of trades and professions do require state certifications that assure at least some base level of knowledge. This is true for professions from plumbing to real estate and insurance sales, to nursing, and law. However, many courses or programs offered in areas such as software development, web design, marketing, or business communication, much less for entrepreneurism, have objective standards.

Some large employers already assess individuals through their own proprietary tests, but if these less formal educational programs are to be viewed as serious alternatives to a formal education, there must be some form of standardized measurements or certification. This is especially true if individuals hope to demonstrate mastery from a combination of courses and hands-on learning experiences from different sources.

Although we have a long way to go, some progress is being made. Mozilla Open Badges, for example, is an open software standard that is intended to provide objective verification of the skills learned from and achievements made in different programs. More importantly, it allows students to combine multiple badges from different sources (such as colleges, professional bodies, community learning organizations, boot camps, and online initiatives) together into a single body of learning.

But testing for specific functional skills is one thing. Testing for much more abstract concepts such as critical thinking, creativity, and teamwork is altogether different. Although interviews, writing samples, and references can help address these needs, we need a more standardized, more objective means of comparison—especially when a potential employee has cobbled their own education from a broad range of traditional sources.

There are a number of attempts to do just this. The Lumina Foundation is offering a $10,000 award for ideas as to how to quantify the impact of certificates from a range of nontraditional sources. ACT's Career Readiness Certificate is trying to provide an objective measurement for certifying the combination of cognitive and soft skills required to predict workplace success. Educational Testing Service offers certificates for those who score well on proficiency profile tests designed to assess critical thinking, reading, writing, and math skills. Meanwhile, CAE's Performance Assessment Test, which is currently being used by more than 700 colleges, claims to measure critical thinking, problem solving, scientific and quantitative reasoning, writing, and the ability to critique and make arguments.

All of these tests can be taken by and certifications issued to anybody, regardless of how or where they learned their skills. Although there's still a long way to go before employers will begin to accept such certifications as measures of workplace success, progress is being made. Once one or more of these or other assessments begin to achieve critical mass, the still sharp distinctions between formal and informal learning programs will begin to fade. Until then, they can still provide some level of objective evidence that you have taken your learning seriously and that you value the type of skills that employers are looking for.

The Potential of Alternative Education Programs

There is no question, at least in my mind, that some form of college (two-year, four-year and for some, graduate degrees) will continue to be the primary and most popular path to the type of high-skill job that will maximize your chances of gaining control of your own career.

That being said, a formal college education is absolutely not the only path. For example:

- Community colleges play five incredibly valuable roles in providing postsecondary education. But given their low completion rates, they may be spread a bit too thin. They, however, face an even more immediate challenge—maintaining even current standards in the face of big state government funding cuts.
- Apprenticeships will continue to be an important semistructured alternative; not only for traditional trades but also increasingly for the type of mid-skill white-collar jobs that will provide many with an entry into occupations that would have not normally been open to nongraduates.
- Experiments such as Year Up, UnCollege, and Enstitute are certainly interesting and bear watching. If they are found to be effective and scalable, they have the potential of preparing people for, or serving as alternatives to, college. This being said, public–private approaches like P-TECH (again, if proven effective and scalable) have the potential of revolutionizing education and lifting thousands out of a life of poverty into secure jobs, higher education and quite possibly, into executive ranks or entrepreneurial careers.
- Self-directed learning programs like the Thiel Fellowships, and to a somewhat lesser extent, UnCollege are better suited to a smaller number of high-potential, self-directed high school

grads who either do not need college or who can benefit from experience before college.

- MOOCs and boot camps can provide entry-level or supplementary skills. MOOCs, in particular, have potential of being game-changers, totally transforming the education system—initially among tier-two and -three colleges, and potentially, even secondary-level school.

This all leads to the next question. Once you decide the type of career you are looking for and develop the skills and earn the credentials that are needed (however and wherever you develop them), just what type of job and what type of employer will be best suited as a launch pad for your career? If you follow the plan laid out in this book, chances are that you end up with at least one offer for a meaningful, career-track job. Ideally, you will find yourself in the enviable position of having to choose among offers. Which criteria should you use to plan you search, select your target employees and assess which job is best for you? These and a number of related issues are addressed in Chapter 10.

CHAPTER 10

Your First Job as Launchpad for a Lifelong Career

Steps 15 Through 20

70 percent of American workers are "not engaged" or "actively disen-
gaged" and are emotionally disconnected from their workplaces
—Gallup "2013 State of the American Workplace Report"

Key Points

- Think of your first job as a launch pad for your career.
- The best jobs will be those you make, not those you take.
- Learning opportunities and doing what you love should be your primary criteria for your first job—not salary.
- While internal advancement opportunities are certainly important, long-term marketability of your first job experiences is critical.
- Are you best suited to a large and mature, small and high-growth, or your own company?
- If you don't like your job or career path, change it—Fast.

This chapter is not a job search guide. You can find many good books, websites, workshops, college career service offices, and personal coaches who do this quite well. So, rather than examining what you have to do to sell yourself to the employer, this chapter focuses on what you should look for in your first real career-track job and in an employer.

This may sound like putting the cart before the proverbial horse. But, if you have followed the steps outlined in previous chapters, you will be well prepared for a formal search long before you are ready to actually begin to look for your first full-time, career-track job. You will have:

- Identified a number of potential career paths that build upon your skills, draw upon your interests, and ideally, allow you to pursue your passions;
- Evaluated the employment opportunities in these fields and understood the skills and traits employers are looking for in candidates to fill the positions you are targeting;
- Crafted and honed your own differentiated brand and triangulated it to match both your own interests and skills, and employer needs;
- Engaged in experiences and developed the skills required not only to prepare you for your first job but also for any career in which you may eventually find yourself;
- Begun to develop a network of advisors who can help you tune your resume, advise you on interview techniques, refer you to potential employers (since so many of the best jobs come from referrals), select the most promising opportunities, and serve as sounding boards throughout your career;
- Gained extensive experience in setting up and conducting the type of information interviews that are so critical in finding unposted jobs that are usually so much more interesting than publicly posted jobs, and in presenting yourself to people who may be in a position to create a job around your unique capabilities; and
- Gained hands-on experience in your field through part-time jobs, internships, or class projects (some of which have the potential of morphing into formal job offers).

Moreover, if you have followed this process and are now looking for the job of your dreams, you should already have a pretty good idea of which organizations are most likely to offer the types of jobs you have targeted. You may have already spoken or even interned with some of these firms.

This chapter identifies many of the critical issues you should consider in determining what to look for in your first job and employer. It discusses these issues in order of the priority that I—with the benefit of hindsight—would place on each in targeting a search and in selecting among offers. Then, for when you begin your job, it suggests how you can get the most out of your position and provide the most value to both your employer and yourself.

Although the following sections are generally aligned with the six steps (number 15 through 20) associated with getting and capitalizing on your first job, there are a number of discrepancies. The reasons: First, the sections are organized in order of importance, rather than when you should first consider them. Second, many of the factors are interrelated and, as with most of the 20 steps, must be evaluated in conjunction with each other.

Matching Your Needs with Your Employers (Steps 15 Through 17)

When you're finally ready to strike out on a search, exactly what should you look for in your first job, or in your first couple of jobs? Easy: you want your dream job in a world-renowned company, with a salary beyond your dreams, a generous bonus, your own assistant, a flexible work environment, "Google-like" perks, and a career path that will take you to a vice presidency in two years.

But what should you settle for when you discover that job isn't available? Would you be willing to accept any job, at any salary, as a means of getting your foot in the door, with the expectation that as you prove yourself you will shoot up through the ranks?

On one hand, you should definitely prepare for and work long and hard to get the job of your dreams. If you succeed, congratulations! Take the job, work hard, and create your dream life. But if you can't get this job, I strongly recommend against the opposite course of trying to get any job you can (at least unless you are out of all options). After all, employers don't want an employee—especially a high-skill, high-salary employee—that is desperate for a job and doesn't care where they work or what they do. They want someone who understands and is incredibly motivated to do the specific job that the employer is looking to fill.

Nor, at the other extreme, do they want somebody that is so locked into some idealized job or career path as to be inflexible. Employers, after all, aren't in the business of creating a dream job for entry-level employees. They're in the business of finding the specific individuals who are best suited to filling the job they have available (and that have the potential of delivering much greater value in the future). Not until AFTER you have proven yourself in your first job and have demonstrated the value you can deliver, should you even try to tailor this job, or request another job that is tailored to your needs. And even then, you have to position yourself as the ideal solution to an employer need—either a need that they already recognize or better yet, a need that you identify for them and have already demonstrated that you can address.

But I digress. When looking for your first job, you have to present yourself as someone who:

- Knows yourself, what you are good at, and what you are looking for in an initial job;
- Has a realistic understanding of your skills, how you can use them to deliver value to the specific employer and job, and also your limitations;
- Has demonstrated an ability to focus on and relentlessly pursue an objective (including the process of targeting and pursuing a job); but is also
- Sufficiently pragmatic and adaptable to recognize and fully capitalize on opportunities beyond your predefined visions.

Employers are looking for people who recognize that their first job isn't a reward for or capstone to their education, but an opportunity to begin an exciting new phase of their lives; an opportunity to learn new skills and to apply them in new ways; and a chance to use the first job as a foundation on which they can build a long-term career that will deliver real value to the company.

But exactly what should this job look like? What type of responsibilities and growth path should you look for? What salary and benefits? Just as importantly, where should you look for this job: in a large corporation, a small company, a start-up, or your own business? And speaking of where to look, do you want to live in or near your home town, or as I did, get as far away from your home town as possible? If the latter, what are you looking for in your new home? What size city? What leisure and cultural opportunities? What country?

A 2013 Accenture survey shows that 2012 and 2013 graduates already have pretty good ideas of what they are looking for from an initial employer. As shown in Figure 10.1, compensation and benefits are, by far, their primary goals.

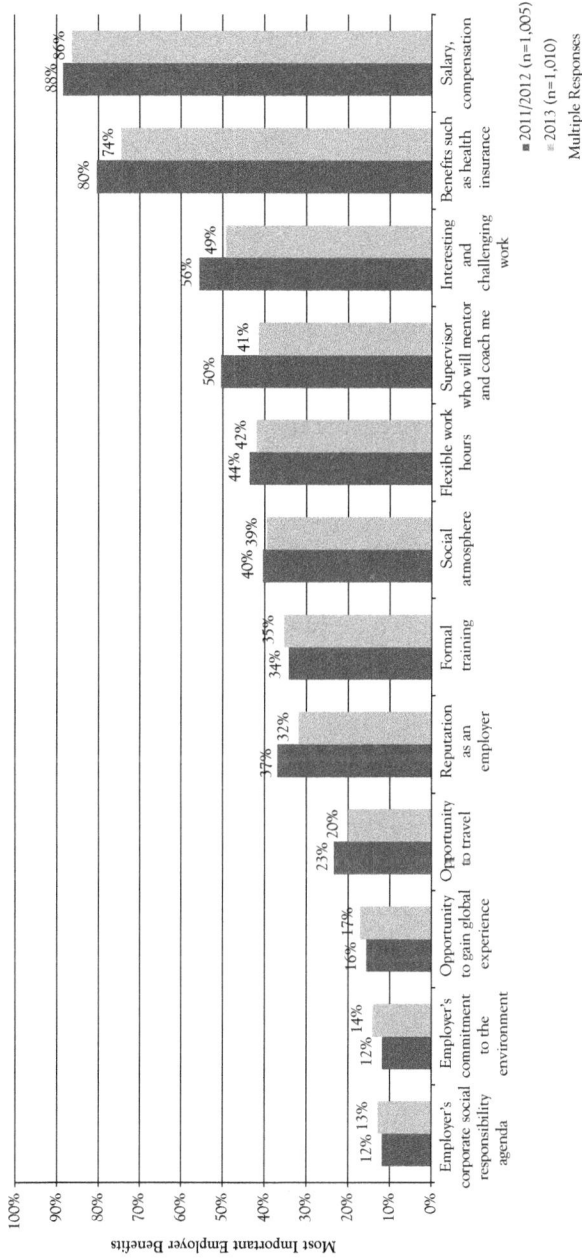

Figure 10.1 The most important benefits for an employer to offer

Source: "Accenture 2013 College Graduate Employment Survey: Key Findings" (2013), Slide 37.

This is certainly understandable given years of living on a student budget. Salary can also be a powerful validation of the value you believe you can bring to the world. But should these really be the most important criteria in evaluating a job that has the potential of being the foundation of a 40-year career?

Let me suggest a number of factors that you may want to consider above salary and benefits.

First Job as the Launchpad for Your Career—Whatever That Career May Be (Steps 15 and 16)

Given the changes in employers approaches to, and Millennials views of employment, you are likely to have many jobs over your working life. These jobs may include anything from part-time and summer jobs when you are in school to unpaid internships or fellowships, to jobs with a large corporation, to work in a business that you built around your own idea. Each of these jobs should help you learn something new about yourself (such as what you enjoy, what you're good at, and what additional skills you need to develop), the world of work (discipline, teamwork, adaptability, and so forth), and what you want and do not want in future jobs. Each of these positions, regardless of how unlikely it may initially seem, also has the potential of leading to a rewarding, full-time career.

Whatever combination of precollege or college jobs you may have had, you should look for more in your first real career-track job. This job, after all, will likely provide a critical foundation for your ultimate career; regardless of the field or company in which that career may be or the skills it will require.

Given this importance, just what should you look for in this job? Before you try to answer, consider an important factor. You should look for different things from a job during different stages of your career and depending on your unique life circumstances. For most young adults, your first job is likely to be your first real exposure to the real world of work—the first job in which you will hopefully support yourself, live on your own, and be responsible for managing your own lives.

Although your choices may be limited by student loans, family commitments, and other obligations, you should treat your first job as one of the greatest and most important learning opportunities of your life (certainly more so than any of your time in school). Although you certainly need to consider issues such as salary, job titles, and job security, you'll have plenty of time to improve upon these in later stages of your career.

Among the most important factors to assess in deciding on your first job are:

- What will I learn and how will I be challenged?
- What skills will I learn to apply and what new skills will I develop?
- Will I enjoy and get fully engaged in my work?
- What advancement opportunities will it provide?
- Will it improve my marketability?
- Which industry and company size will offer the best learning, growth, and long-term career opportunities?
- Will it allow me to expand, enhance, and especially deepen my network by developing deep professional relationships?
- Is the company's culture and image consistent with my needs and values?
- Are the salary and benefits appropriate and competitive?
- Where do I want to live?
- Although many of these factors are interrelated, let's look briefly at each.

Will I Enjoy My Work? (Step 16)

It's probably safe to assume that regardless of your job, you won't enjoy every task. No matter how much you may enjoy the core responsibilities of your job, every job has multiple components. You may be required to sit in endless meetings, submit meaningless administrative information, prepare and give presentations, or travel to locations in which you have no interest.

Still, in the end, you want to be able to go home with a sense of accomplishment from doing something you enjoy, and doing it well. Not only is this good for your psyche, it is also good for your long-term career growth. Enjoying what you do will incent you to work harder and learn more. On the other hand, continually engaging in meaningless or distasteful activities is likely to prompt you to disengage and become either complacent or rebellious. In addition to making you miserable, lazy, or both, it could get you fired or, at the very least, jeopardize your future job prospects. It will certainly make it less likely that you will be offered interesting assignments or promotions or get strong referrals or recommendations from colleagues or superiors.

Can you judge whether you are going to like a job before you accept? You should already know, from your own personal inventories and from evaluating your previous experiences, what you are and are not good at, and what you do and do not enjoy. Ask what the job will entail and what a typical day will look like. Then try to verify it. And what happens if, even after exercising due diligence, you find yourself in a job that is not challenging or that you do not enjoy? Speak with your supervisor or personnel department. Is there a possibility of modifying your job to better address your strengths? Can you volunteer to perform other tasks that need to be done and, after proving your value, gradually shed parts of your old job in favor of new ones? Can you qualify for other jobs in other groups within the company? If so, great: If not, you may need a plan to find another potential job.

After all, no matter how many opportunities you may find within your initial employer, the odds are that you will eventually change employers, not to speak of careers. Although reliable numbers are hard to find, a 2007 study by Princeton's Henry Farber found that men have an average of 11.4 jobs in their career (including different jobs in the same company) and an average tenure of 4.4 years: Women have an average10.7 jobs.[1]

This being said, younger workers, especially those in their 20s, change jobs most frequently, with turnover steadily reducing as they reach their 30s and beyond. These figures are broadly confirmed by the most recent iteration of a 30+-year longitudinal study by the Bureau of Labor Statistics. It found that younger Baby Boomers held an average of 11.3 jobs between ages 18 and 46. Nearly half of these jobs were held between ages 18 and 24, with 69 percent of these lasting less than a year and 93 percent lasting less than five years.[2]

Interesting, but what does it mean for you? Millennials are very different than even younger boomers. They have very different ideas of what they are looking for in jobs and the role that work should play in their lives. So, BLS launched a similar study that focused on Millennials, at least older Millennials born in the early 1980s. While results are necessarily cover shorter periods than the previous study, it is found that 57 percent of jobs held by workers between the ages of 21 and 26 lasted one year or less and another 14 percent lasted less than two years.[3] Although it is certainly too soon to draw long-term conclusions, it appears that Millenials are indeed on track for more, shorter duration jobs through their careers.

The good news is that, from hindsight, people do not typically regret the frequency of job changes—at least when they are voluntary. In fact, a failure to change jobs, change careers, or to leave a current job to start a new company is often cited as among the most common of all career regrets.[4] This can be especially true for those who feel locked into careers they no longer enjoy due to debt, family obligations, their investment in training, inertia, perceived risk, the fear of failure, and so forth.

> People do not typically regret the frequency of job changes—at least when they are voluntary. In fact, a failure to change jobs, change careers, or to leave a current job to start a new company is often cited as among the most common of all career regrets

No career is immune from these feelings. Multiple surveys, for example, have found that 40 to 50 percent of lawyers are generally dissatisfied with their careers. Even doctors have concerns.[5] Only about half of those represented in one 2012 survey would choose medicine as a career if they had to do it again: only 40 percent would choose the same specialty.[6] And remember, if you are dissatisfied with your career, it's much easier to change when you are young, than when you have a family, a mortgage, and college and retirement funding obligations.

What Will I Learn in My First Job? (Step 16)

Your first career-track job should, as discussed previously, be one of the biggest and most important learning experiences of your life. You will not only learn how to develop the skills needed in your chosen field but also get a chance to explore many others—possibly discovering areas that may interest you even more than your original field.

Ideally, this job will build upon your education, allowing you to apply and master skills you learned in college. Even more importantly, it will take you out of your comfort zone, forcing you to work in teams with all types of different people, with different skills across many functional areas, and from different backgrounds. This should help you develop not only a broad range of functional skills but also people skills and, even more importantly, perspective as to how different jobs and skill sets fit together.

The job should force—and help—you to develop a broad range of skills, beyond those you have previously developed: skills that will be valuable and transferable across whatever position you may hold in subsequent jobs, careers, and industries. It should provide responsibilities and challenges that will help you grow as a professional, as well as give you a sense of accomplishment. Ideally, it will give you a chance to actually work in different types of jobs, under and with people who are committed to helping you learn. And, it will ideally provide a lot of formal training.

> Your first career-track job should be one of the biggest and most important learning experiences of your life. It should allow you to apply and master skills you learned in college, take you out of your comfort zones, force you to work in diverse teams provide invaluable practical exposure to hwo companies operate.

Unfortunately, such jobs are few and far between. According to the previously referenced Accenture survey, although 77 percent of 2013 graduates expect their first job to provide formal training, only 48 percent of 2011/2012 graduates say they actually received this training in their first post-college job.[7] According to Wharton professor Peter Capelli, few companies are still willing to invest in training new employees.[8] They are looking for people who can fit right into an empty slot and deliver immediate value. Back in 1979, for example, companies gave new employees an average of 2½ weeks of training per year. By 1991, only 17 percent of employees reported getting *any training* during their first year. In 2010, only 21 percent of employees claimed to have received any training during the *previous five years*. The good news, found in a 2013 Accenture employer survey, shows that many companies acknowledge that they have not spent enough on training and that 51 percent plan to increase their budgets.[9]

A number of the leading—and most sought after—employers still provide training and opportunities to work across functions and departments. Their numbers, however, are limited. While start-ups and small companies seldom provide formal training, they, unlike many larger organizations, may not only allow but also actively encourage you to exercise many different types of skills in your job or to participate in a broad range of projects in other departments.

When interviewing for your first job, you should ask specifically about training programs and what they consist of and opportunities to work with other groups within the company. Then try to verify what the company is telling you. Search the web, ask your career services office, monitor social networks and job boards, and ask your continually expanding network of advisors and mentors. If the job and the company you want provides formal training, take full advantage of it. Generally, however, you should be prepared to train yourself and to create your own ongoing learning agenda.

What Advancement Opportunities Will It Provide? (Step 16)

Your first job (or at least one of your early jobs) must be a steppingstone, rather than a dead end. While you must understand the initial responsibilities of your first job and the primary factors on which your performance will be judged, you should be just as concerned with where the job will take you. This is much more than promotions and salary increases.

How, for example, can your current position evolve as you demonstrate an ability to accept greater responsibility? What are the likely career paths, both within your initial department and throughout the company? How will these career paths be determined? How personalized will they be? Will you have regular performance (as distinct from salary) reviews? How much flexibility will you have in moving into other functions within the organization (to broaden your perspective) and how will your position prepare you for these? Does the organization encourage lateral, as well as vertical moves?

Although any good recruiter can tell a good story about a company's advancement opportunities, ask for examples. What, for example, was the path taken by your initial manager? By her manager? Can they provide examples of how career paths have evolved as the individual's interests evolved and as they showed potential in other fields? More importantly, does the company provide mentorships to help newbies assess their options and plan their moves? Then, go to LinkedIn to trace the career paths of people in the company. You must, however, be judicious in your queries. After all, while every employer should be interested in your potential, they also expect you to focus on and excel in your current job. You don't want to appear so preoccupied with where you will go next as to appear disinterested or disengaged from today's work.

This gets back to the company's reputation. Do they have a reputation for training their employees, for proactive career planning, for exposing people to different types of jobs? Do other companies seek out the company's employees to fill their own managerial and executive slots?

You should also think well beyond your next position to your long-term career goals. You certainly don't want to lock yourself into a predetermined career path. Planned moves may be stymied or more interesting opportunities may arise. It is, however, never too early to begin planning for the type of skills that will be beneficial for your future. And while returning to school may be the last thing on your mind upon graduating from college and beginning your first job, it shouldn't be. According to the previously mentioned March 2013 Accenture survey, 57 percent of recent graduates believe they will need more training to get their desired jobs.[10] Forty-two percent of these expect this to require a graduate degree and 23 percent plan to take graduate-level or online courses that will not necessarily lead to degrees.[11]

What type of education? If you're in a rapidly changing field, such as technology, you must continually update your skills, or risk being relegated to legacy technologies. If you want to climb the management ladder, an MBA from a top-tier school will certainly help. If you plan to start your own business, Chapter 9 suggests all types of programs geared to aspiring entrepreneurs.

Given this need for continuing education, not to speak of the cost of obtaining it, you should at least ask about a company's tuition reimbursement policy and its flexibility in allowing you to balance work and school schedules. Even if you don't currently expect to use it, it will at least suggest that you are interested in continually learning and expanding your skills.

Will the Company and the Job Improve My Marketability? (Steps 16 and 20)

There used to be an implicit bond between employer and employee. The employee demonstrated competence and loyalty, and the employer reciprocated with job security, seniority-based raises, and moves up the career ladder. For better or worse, those days are gone. Employees must assume responsibility for managing their own career paths.

In an ideal world, you will respect the company in which you get your first job, the culture will be compatible with your own values, and it will offer opportunities for you to advance your career in a way that benefits both you and the company. If not, you should be in a position in which your first company (in addition to your first job in that company) provides a solid steppingstone into another job or organization. Consulting firms and law firms, for example, are built on this model. Few initial hires ever become partners. Other companies, however, covet the training, skills, the perspectives, and the connections that hiring lawyers or consultants from leading firms can bring to their own companies. And it often behooves the initial employer to encourage and even facilitate such a move since alumni often recommend or hire their previous employer to provide specialized help.

The primary factors underlying your marketability are intrinsic to yourself: the skills you possess, the results you have produced, the breadth and especially the depth of the network you have built, the strength of their references and recommendations, and so forth. You must, therefore, continually strive to enhance your own marketability. Of course, you should continually develop your core functional skills—specifically those required in your specific role—as well as those of the next position to which you aspire. Marketability, however, entails much more than developing specialized skills. As discussed, it also requires development of a range of complementary "transferrable skills," broad perspectives, good judgment, and deep and subtle "people skills"—not to speak of an ability to effectively market yourself and sell your capabilities and the type of value you can bring to an employer.

Another key marketability requirement is using your current job and the relationships you form to expand your network and to cultivate the type of relationships that can blossom into sponsorships, mentorships, recommendations, referrals, and even job offers. Although you certainly need for people to respect you, do they like working with you? Do they trust you? Do they want you to work with or for them? Are they willing to put their reputations on the line to recommend you to a friend or colleague?

You are, after all, at least partially known by the company you keep. You want to make sure that your first employer is respected (both in its own right in addition to the ways it trains and prepares its employees) by other potential employers, both within and beyond its industry. For example, two years in a company recognized to cultivate talent (such as Proctor & Gamble, Coca-Cola, Kraft, and IBM) could prove to be more valuable than five or more years in a company that is not known to develop their talent.

> Although advancement opportunities within your first company are important, it is even more important for that employment to improve your overall marketability. Two years in a company recognized to cultivate talent could prove to be more valuable than five in a company that is not known to do so.

Other types of reputation also matter. How well respected is your superior and your department, both within the organization and beyond? Is your department known as a source of talent, both within and beyond the company? Is your manager, and her superiors, respected throughout the organization and the industry? More importantly, have you earned the respect of your manager, your peers, and others throughout your company as well as in professional organizations to which you belong? Do they respect you and your skills? Do they see you as a team player? Perhaps most important of all, do they trust you and your integrity?

Although the reputation you develop in your job and that of the company for which you work will be critical in improving your marketability, your public identity and reputation outside your company is also important. This reputation, which can be based on your interests, your civic involvement, and your social activities, can help demonstrate your breadth as an individual—that you are much more than your job. It should reinforce your business identity around your competence, your judgment, your social and leadership skills, and your willingness and ability to pitch in and help, both individually and especially as part of a team. This reputation, and the connections you build around it, can also put you in contact with people and organizations that can help in your career or introduce you to totally new career opportunities, way beyond anything you may have imagined.

Which Industry and Company Size Will Offer the Best Learning and Growth Opportunities? (Step 15)

A tough question to which there is no easy answer. If you have a deep interest in a particular industry, that's probably a great place to begin your search. You should, however, look at your options pragmatically. Generally speaking, as shown in Step 8 (see Chapter 4), maturing industries with established industry structures and slower growth rates are more likely to be dominated by large companies, offer highly structured jobs and stable work environments, and predictable, albeit gradual promotions and salary bumps, along relatively well defined career paths.

Young industries with fast growth rates typically offer less structure, fewer training and mentorship programs and more risk than more established industries. These fast-moving, less structured environments, however, are often more open than mature industries to hiring people with nontraditional backgrounds and offer greater flexibility in job descriptions and career paths. Although they often offer less job security, they can provide more opportunities to experience different types of work and offer more long-term career opportunities and growth prospects.

They are almost inherently faster moving, higher risk, higher reward environments. Not all companies (or even entire industries) will succeed. But, even if a company fails, it should expand your growth prospects, at least if it provided a great learning experience and is well-regarded in its space. Many high-growth companies, after all, value the perspective of people who have "been through it all before." This is especially true if you use your time in your first company to build a strong reputation and network, develop high-demand skills and if the industry (even if not your specific company) continues to grow.

This is certainly more than can be said for industries that are at the other end of their lifecycles. Declining industries can combine the worse of both worlds—slow career and salary growth and a lack of job security. But even here, if you develop a good reputation, a strong network, and strong skills that are readily transferable to other industries, you should be able to find another job.

The questions about company size are often analogous to and inter-related with those of industry. Mature industries, for example, tend to be dominated by large and mid-size companies: New industries can be "cluttered" with a lot of start-ups. Generally speaking, the larger the company, the more structured the organization, the job and the career path, and the more formal the orientation and training programs. The smaller the company, the less structure, the less support (meaning that you have to do more for yourself) and the more likely you are also to get to wear many different hats.

> Generally speaking, the larger the company, the more structured the organization, the job and the career path, and the more formal the orientation and training programs. The smaller the company, the less structure, the less support (meaning that you have to do more for yourself) and the more likely you are also to get to wear many different hats. This having been said, a company's growth rate is even more important than its size.

A company's growth rate is even more important than its size. Apple is a very big company. And, while it does have much of the structure of big companies, its high growth rates and even higher margins allow it to attract some of the best talent in the industry, offer some of the best salaries, and provide virtually unlimited career growth opportunities. The same is generally true of Google. Smaller, well-capitalized technology companies, particularly in social networking and gaming, can offer generally similar opportunities, albeit typically with less structure, more opportunities for working in fields beyond your job title and with less job security. They are also more likely to offer lower salaries in return for greater upside potential, should the company succeed.

But with any start-up or young company, there is also the risk that the company may fail. Although any size and age company can fail, one recent study found that 50 percent of start-ups (including 63 percent of those in the information industry) fail within four years and 71 percent fail within 10.[12] Bloomberg considers even these figures to be wildly optimistic.[13] It estimates that 8 of 10 companies fail within their first four years. This is absolutely not to discourage you to take a flyer with a start-up, but if you do, think about how and where and how you may wish to land.

Which is better for you? It largely comes down to the type of environment and the type of structure that is best suited to the way you learn. After all, as discussed previously, your first job is all about learning!

Will It Allow Me to Expand, Enhance, and Especially Deepen My Network? (Steps 18 and 19)

Networking through relatives, friends, colleagues, former managers, and especially the guides and mentors you met through your career preparation interviews can be one of the best ways of finding a job. First, more than half of all jobs are thought to come from informal channels. More important than the number are the type of jobs that come from networks: these are often unadvertised jobs that can be tailored to the unique capabilities of an individual.

Once you get a job, networking takes on a very different flavor. Professional networking is not about collecting names and "likes" on Facebook. It is about forming deep, trusting, mutually beneficial relationships with colleagues, managers, and other professionals from whom you can learn, bounce ideas off, seek advice from, and when appropriate, get referrals and references. As discussed in previous chapters, every stage of your education and your career, not to speak of your social and extracurricular life, provides opportunities to meet and seek the counsel of others. This is particularly true inside your company.

Although your company network should include people from all parts and roles in the organization, two forms or relationships are particularly critical, especially for people at the early stages in their careers: those with mentors and sponsors. Some companies have formal mentoring programs, where established professionals volunteer or are assigned to mentor new hires. Sponsors are even more important than mentors. They provide not only advice, feedback, and referrals, but they also put their reputations on the line by using their influence with their peers and superiors to proactively advocate for you. They may promote your accomplishments, invite you to meetings that are typically above your station in the organization, and even take you with them as they move up the organization or to a new company. In return, you must live up to their expectations; delivering stellar performance and loyalty and making them look good.

Just where do you find such mentors and sponsors? Although they can come from anywhere, the most logical initial work mentor is your manager. In fact, your relationship with your manager should be one of the most critical determinants in deciding if a particular job is right for you. You want a manager who will treat you as an apprentice (and ideally a confidant) rather than as a worker. Someone who will take the time to explain what they are looking for, provide you with the tools and the guidance you will need to deliver, and then provide constructive feedback on your performance. You want someone who will care about your success in your job and the organization, will honestly advise you, and will help you find the right place and advance in the organization.

> Professional networking is not about collecting names and "likes" on Facebook. It is about forming deep, trusting, mutually beneficial relationships. In the end, the depth of your relationships will be more important than the breadth.

Although it's impossible to tell for sure in advance whether your prospective manager will provide such help, you can look for hints. What type of chemistry do you feel when you speak with her? What is the atmosphere in her department? What type of enthusiasm and camaraderie do you see? Look also beyond the walls of the company. What, if anything, can you learn about your prospective manager from your personal network? From LinkedIn and other social media sites? What is her record in retaining people, in getting them promoted? What do people who used to work for her say?

Your prospective peers—the people you are likely to work with, rather than report to—may well be among the best sources of information. Ideally, the company with whom you are interviewing will have you speak with such a person (ideally in a more casual setting, such as over lunch). If they don't, ask if you can speak with one of these people.

Professional networking should go beyond the company in which you work and include those in other companies who work in the same or complementary fields—people that you meet such as by:

- Attending professional events and volunteering to serve on professional organization committees and boards;
- Presenting to or working with your company's partners, clients, and customers; and of course by
- Continually expanding the size of your LinkedIn and other social networks.

Your network should also extend into complementary professions. This can include people with similar and complementary interests such as from clubs, sports teams, civic activities, or religious organizations. After all, people with totally different professions and backgrounds can provide you with different perspectives, different sources of advice, and can, as mentioned previously, introduce you to totally new career opportunities.

And don't forget online communities such as LinkedIn, Monster. com, and Jobvite. Not only are they important networking tools, they are also valuable recruitment and job search tools. LinkedIn, as discussed in a recent Bloomberg Businessweek article, is used as a recruiting tool of

97 percent of surveyed companies! Facebook, meanwhile, has introduced its own professional networking application, BeKnown, which is being integrated with Monster.com.[14]

Just as "true" networking entails much more than collecting virtual friends, the deeper the networking relationship, the deeper the commitment you make to each other. Keep people in your networks apprised of your progress, send them information that you believe may help them, and introduce them to people with whom they may share interests. And, of course, continually treat them with respect and integrity: showing them at least as much loyalty as they show you. True networking is, in other words, a two-way street.

Speaking of two-way streets, the further you advance in your education and your career, the greater your opportunity—and your obligation—to help others who are coming up behind you. In other words, be both a mentee and a mentor throughout your entire career. Being a mentee will, in fact, help you to become a better mentor.

Is the Company's Culture and Image Consistent with My Needs and Values? (Step 16)

No matter where you end up, you're probably going to spend at least 50 hours a week at work—even 80 hours in some jobs. For better or worse, a good part of your identity, at least to people you just meet (and increasingly to your own self-image) will be shaped by their image of the company at which you work. You should feel comfortable with the environment and the people with whom you work and with what the company stands for.

What type of feel do you get when you walk into the office? Is it very formal, structured, and fast-paced; or is it casual, relaxed, and collegial? Are the people you meet frazzled, curt, and strictly down-to-business; or are they more easy-going, conversational, and helpful? What type of vibe do you pick up from interactions among people who work there? Do the company and department appear to have a top-down, command-and-control structure or more of a collegial, peer-based culture? Does it appear that employees respect and proactively help each other, or is everybody competing with each other?

Does the company offer a flexible or structured work environment? Do people work in offices, cubicles, or open spaces? Do all offices and cubicles look the same, or does each reflect the occupant's individual taste? Are people all heads-down at work, or are people gathering around speaking and playing games? Does it have strict hours or does it allow employees to tailor their hours to their needs? Do they encourage or discourage remote work?

These questions don't have any right or wrong answers. It is all a question of the environment in which you are most comfortable and can best learn, in which you will do your best work, and what you are looking for at a particular stage in your life and your career. You may, for example, thrive in fast-pace, top-down, pressure-cooker environment, like Wall Street. Or you may prefer an equally hardworking, but much less formal, less hierarchical, and more laid-back, collegial environment, like Silicon Valley. Or perhaps, you are looking for more of a work–life balance of only working 40 hour weeks. You may be relatively laid back, but voluntarily choose to begin your career in a high-pressure environment as a means of maximizing your initial learning (and earnings) and creating a foundation for future, lower stress jobs.

But whatever you choose, you want to know what you're getting into before you accept a job. Your initial experiences with the company's recruiters and interviewers and in observing the office can give you an idea of what the organization is like. To really understand it, however, you need more direct, less structured view of life within the organization. The best opportunity to gain such an unvarnished view is to actually work there, perhaps as an intern or a part-time go-fer. If you can't work there first, what can you learn about the environment from articles written about the company, from chat boards and social media? Can you informally meet any of the people who work there, as through social media or going to a bar at which people from the company unwind?

And don't forget the company's image. As mentioned, you will be at least partially identified with where you work and it will gradually become part of your self-image. Is it an image with which you will be comfortable? Do you relate to the industry, to the company's image and practices? Is it an industry or company that you expect to be proud to work for, or may you come to resent or apologize for it?

All tough and very subjective questions. All important for such a big and important part of your life.

And Oh Yeah—What About the Salary and the Benefits? (Step 17)

I don't necessarily mean to imply that salary and benefits should be at the bottom of your list of what you look for in a job. After all, you probably have student loans to pay off and would prefer to live on your own or with friends, rather than being forced to live in your parents' basement. Besides, you've been scrimping for years living on an allowance or part-time wages and are ready to begin living. And let's not forget the self-image boost associated with making big bucks out of school. Plus, depending on your job, you will probably have to buy an entire new wardrobe.

But all this notwithstanding, you should not let initial salary and benefits play a major role in your choice of your first career-track job. There is simply too much at stake to sacrifice the foundation of a multidecade career for a few more dollars in your first job. You should be much more focused on developing the skills, the experience, the relationships, the networks, and the reputation that will establish you as a high-value professional for whom employers will pay a premium in future jobs.

Still, you want to be fairly paid. Compensation should be appropriate for your job and competitive with that offered by other employers in comparable locations and industries. But just what is fair and appropriate?

> Although you certainly want to be paid fairly, don't let initial salary and benefits play a major role in your choice of your first career-track job. You should be much more focused on developing the skills, the experience, the relationships, the networks, and the reputation—benefits that will result in much greater pay in future jobs.

The aforementioned Accenture College Graduate Survey suggests that most aspiring grads have overly optimistic views of what their skills will command in the real world—and with what their money will buy.[15] For example:

- Only 15 percent of pending 2013 grads expect to earn less than $25,000 a year, while one-third (32 percent) of 2011 and 2012 graduates who are employed report their current annual salary is $25,000 or less; and
- One-third (32 percent) of pending 2013 graduates plan to live at home after graduation, compared with 44 percent of 2011 and 2012 college grads who currently live at home.

You need to do some research to determine a fair salary for your skills and job. Take into account your major, your school, your ranking in your graduating class, the type of work experience you have had, your greatest accomplishments, in which industry and size company you plan to work, in what city or region of the country, and how do you come across in your interviews?

Luckily, you can find a number of guides to help with all of these variables. Your college may provide some salary information but you should probably view these data with a grain of salt, at least until standardized federal reporting guidelines are fully in place. Better yet are independent sources of salary information. The Bureau of Labor Statistics, for example, offers regular updates on salaries for a broad range of occupations, locations, and experience levels.[16] So do commercial companies such as Manpower and PayScale[17] (which also offer breakouts by college the employee attended). A number of industry-specific recruitment firms, like the Dice Holdings, provide hiring and salary reports for the technology, financial services, and oil and gas.[18]

The National Association of Colleges and Employers provides some of the most comprehensive information.[19] It surveys employers, not just on actual salaries, but also on job offers. It shows both by discipline and subdiscipline, and provides ranges, as well as averages, the salaries, and numbers of people hired by each industry. It provides data for graduate as well as undergraduate degrees and an online tool that allows applicants to drill down into the data, such as by industry, region of the country, gender, race, and years of experience.

You also need to add benefits such as insurance coverage, 401k contributions, and vacation policies into your compensation calculation. And, if you are looking at a leading Internet firm, benefits such as free prepared meals, dry cleaning, and concierge services can provide tremendous value and make it much easier to handle long hours. You also want to learn the criteria and the schedule on which your performance will be assessed, and how often your salary will be reviewed and bonuses paid.

Where Do I Want to Live? (Step 16)

While I place this criterion last on the list of what you should look for in a job, it is certainly not because it is the least important. It is that location is so subjective that only you can decide the value that a job location has to you.

Perhaps location is irrelevant to you. You would be just as happy in Podunk as in New York City or willing to move anywhere for the right job. Or, you may want or have to remain close to your family. Then there is the other extreme. My wife and I—from the time we finished grad school till now—first chose the cities in which we wanted to live (Chicago, Washington DC, Boston, and San Francisco) and then looked for jobs in that location. In Chicago and Boston, we each found rewarding jobs in the fields in which we wanted to work. While we were less success in DC (due to government hiring freeze), we chalked it up to a learning experience and moved to Boston where we were much more successful. Then after starting our own company, we made another lifestyle choice and moved to San Francisco. Location was extremely important to us for our lifestyle and was at the top of our job criteria list.

There are, however, a couple of big caveats for those who want to make a lifestyle choice of where to live. One of the most important is to determine, in advance, whether the city offers sufficient job opportunities for people with your skills and interests. Bio-tech engineers may have scant choice of jobs in Bismarck, North Dakota. Well-qualified nurses or software engineers with up-to-date skills, meanwhile, may have options in virtually any city or community. More generally, fast growing cities, like Austin or San Francisco, typically offer more opportunities than those that are shrinking, like Buffalo and Detroit.

You should objectively assess your qualifications and prospects for getting the type of job for which you are looking BEFORE you commit to moving to a new city in which you don't have some type of support network. In our case, we chose the city but did not permanently put down roots until we found jobs (which ended up being the prudent approach since we were unsuccessful in Washington DC). You may want to have an offer in hand before getting tied into a long-term lease or buying a house. But, if you do decide to move to a new city before you have a job, be sure that you have a financial cushion that will sustain you should you have trouble finding a job. Even better, having a working spouse or partner can provide not only financial support during this time but also the type of emotional support that can sustain you during a search.

What About Starting My Own Company?
(Steps 15 and 16)

There's always another option. Why subject your career to the whims of a manager or the fortunes of a large company when you can take charge of your career from the beginning? Or maybe you don't have a choice. After a prolonged search, what if you come up empty?

You can launch your own business anytime during your career. Peter Thiel, as discussed in Chapter 9, insists that it is best to do so at the beginning of your career—before even going to college. Although a decision as to when to go out on your own is a very individual decision, it may be a necessary one, such as if you have been laid off at 50, and have no job prospects.

There are two primary ways of building your own company: You can start big, with a big idea, third-party capital, and a staff. Or you can start small, as with an individual product, consulting, or freelance business and then either remain small or grow (either self-funded or with third-party loans or capital). In either case, anyone who is highly skilled in any field for which other people (even one or two, if they are willing to pay a sufficiently high price) are willing to pay has the potential of starting their own business.

The good news is that the combination of inexpensive computers, the Internet, outsourced and cloud-based services, offshore freelancers, 3D printing, and even crowdsourced funding has slashed the cost of starting your own business. The bad news is that becoming an entrepreneur requires a number of skills that not everyone may possess. For example, going back to the Partnership for 21st Century Skills Framework discussed in Chapter 3, you need the productivity and accountability skills to set and meet your own goals and to plan, prioritize, and manage your work without guidance. You must also have the information, media, and IT skills to make use of the tools that are available; the communication skills required to promote and sell yourself, and your value-add to customers or clients; and the initiative, self-direction, and accountability to do whatever is required for the timely delivery and quality of your work. And you must have the perseverance that will be required to put in months of work with the hope of future gratification and the flexibility and adaptability to rebound from inevitable setbacks.

Then of course, there are the business skills (basic accounting, finance, marketing, sales, IT support, etc.) required to run a business—skills that can often be learned from B-school, a few community college business classes, books, the Internet, or one of the rapidly growing number of entrepreneurship classes and workshops discussed in Chapters 8 and 9. But don't underestimate the amount of time you need to do simple things like troubleshooting a computer problem, invoicing, or even collecting money.

And speaking of money, don't forget the money you'll need to get the business off the ground. Even if you bootstrap everything, you still need to live until the business can sustain you over the inevitable lulls in your business. You also have to plan for the uncomfortable possibility that your business will not succeed[20,21] and will have to search for another job. Again, having a spouse or partner who has a steady paycheck and can fund your basic living expenses helps. If not, you need to put aside money for a rainy day—probably at least a year of minimal living expenses. This, of course, becomes much easier after you have spent some time working, saving money, and lining up a revenue stream from a client or two before you give up the security of a paycheck.

As you probably guessed, I am a huge fan of starting one's own business. After spending five years in a large company and another three in a small company, I decided it was time for a change. After weighing offers from a few companies, I decided to go out on my own. I personally found the experience, self-confidence, and the networks I built in my first two jobs to be extremely helpful in going out on my own. Moreover I loved the flexibility of being my own boss, of setting my own hours, and the rewards of building a company that was focused on my own vision and my own lifestyle.

Luckily I also had a trusted partner in this venture—my wife—who quit her consumer goods marketing job as my business really began to grow. She provided strong operational skills consisting of accounting, marketing, administrative, human resources, legal, and management services that I had neither the time nor desire to provide and—even more importantly—provided a valuable, trusted sounding board for big decisions. Although we both worked much harder and longer than we would have for any employer, we built a firm that allowed us to schedule our work hours to fit our desire to travel, to be in charge of our own destiny, and fund our retirements. Yes, we had many sleepless nights wondering how to meet our payroll, especially during economic downturns. But it was all worth it in the end.

Even if you don't have to or want to start your own business out of school, remember that the era of lifetime jobs is over. An economic slump, a disruption to the industry, or any number of other circumstances may force your employer to let you go. And a sad fact about layoffs is that they seldom occur in a strong economy when companies are hiring. Or maybe you just don't feel your company is the right fit for you or you have had it with your company and don't have another job to go to.

> Even if you never, ever plan to start your own business, you must ALWAYS be prepared to do so. In this era of uncertainty and reduced loyalty, you never know when you may have to do so.

No matter if starting your own firm is your own idea or is the only option open to you, just remember to always keep your options open, and keep your resume up to date, your network active, and your job search skills sharp. It will make it a lot easier to go out on your own. And, oh yes, work on developing the skills and the confidence required to start your own business, keep at least one year's minimum expenses in reserve, and have the self-confidence and communication skills required to market and sell yourself and your unique value add.

Avoiding Career Regrets

Your career can be a source of great fulfillment. It can, as suggested previously, also be a source of frustration. In the spirit of learning from the lessons of others, Daniel Gulati, author of "Passion & Purpose: Stories from the Best and Brightest Young Business Leaders," wrote a fascinating 2012 Harvard Business Review blog post titled "*The Top Five Career Regrets.*"[22] It is based on an admittedly unscientific sample of 30 interviews with business executives who, from the outside, most would judge to be very successful. They revealed some of the frustrations that can come from not following your passions and from becoming locked into a career. Their five greatest regrets, along with some of my own embellishments, were:

- *I wish I hadn't taken the job for the money*: This was, by far the biggest regret of those who ended up in high-paying but ultimately unsatisfying careers. As one investment banker said, "I dream of quitting every day, but I have too many commitments." A consultant said, "I'd love to leave the stress behind, but I don't think I'd be good at anything else."
- *I wish I had quit earlier*: Almost all those who had quit their jobs to pursue their passions wished they had done so earlier. While a 2013 Gallup survey (p. 12) found that 70 percent of American workers are "not engaged" in or are "actively disengaged" from their work, and are emotionally disconnected from their workplace.[23] A Deloitte survey, meanwhile, found only a miniscule 11 percent to be "passionate" about their work.[24] As one who eventually made the jump to a more rewarding job explained, "You can't ever get those years back."
- *I wish I had the confidence to start my own business*: According to a 2012 Edward Jones survey, only 15 percent of those who have not started their own businesses believe they "have what it takes" to be an entrepreneur.[25]
- *I wish I had used my time at school more productively*: Gulati's book research found that many of his interviewees wished they had thoughtfully parlayed their school years into a truly rewarding first job. After starting a family and signing up for a

mortgage, many were unable to carve out the space to return to school for advanced study to reset their careers.

- *I wish I had acted on my career hunches*: Several individuals he interviewed discussed regrets as to not taking "windows of opportunity" in their careers that they viewed as too risky at the time.

Speaking from the standpoint of one who did not use his time at school productively, but who did act on his hunches and made the jump relatively early in his own career (at least early in my second career), I agree full-heartedly with Gulati's rankings. However, I have absolutely no regrets about spending the time I did (five years and three years, respectively) at either of my two previous jobs as I learned much from each about myself, my interests, and what it is like to work in both large and small companies. Both provided invaluable experience and both helped me discover passions that I never imagined when I was in school.

Besides, I thoroughly enjoyed what I ended up doing in both of these jobs. Why? I subconsciously applied (before I ever heard) the maxim of Jim Spohrer, the IBM executive who encouraged me to write this book. That maxim: "the best jobs will be those that you make, not those that you take."

> The best jobs will be those that you make, not those that you take.

After beginning both my jobs in predefined roles—and demonstrating competence in each of the tasks I was assigned—I identified opportunities that I saw for the companies and persuaded my managers to allow me to run with them. In both cases, I was gradually allowed to reduce the time spent on parts of the original job that I did not enjoy (but had still performed diligently and well) and spent the vast majority of my time on projects (one in each job) that became two of the best learning experiences of my life, and two of my greatest passions. I ended up building my own company—and an incredibly fulfilling career—around one of these passions and never looked back.

Your first career-track job, as emphasized throughout this chapter, is a critical step in your long-term career. It will give you an opportunity to apply and hone the skills you have learned through your education to real-world needs. It will provide a unique opportunity to learn about yourself—what type of work you do—and do not—enjoy; what you are and are not good at and how to use your skills to deliver value in a differentiated way; what limitations you most need to address; and what type of groups and organizations you would most like to live in. Even more importantly—especially if you move to a new city—it will expand your horizons; expose you to new people, new learning activities, and cultural opportunities; and possibly even give you a new perspective on what you want to do with your life, not to speak of your career. Make sure that you take full advantage of this once-in-a-lifetime opportunity.

CHAPTER 11

You CAN Have It All, But You Will Have to Work for It

If something is important enough, you have to try, even if the most probable outcome is failure.

—Elon Musk
Founder of PayPal, Tesla, and SpaceX

The question is not whether *you can build a career around your passion or your major: The question is* how *you can best do it!*

—Tom Kucharvy

Key Points

- Although the current job market poses big challenges for most new graduates, it is producing unprecedented opportunities for others.
- "Average is Over; If you don't excel in your job, you're likely to find yourself out of a job."
- Any career worth dreaming about is worth fighting for— but every good plan also needs a safety career.
- Your dreams will change. Make sure you develop the skills and traits to allow you to evolve and transform your careers to match your new dreams.
- Maximize your career options by targeting high-growth fields in which you can highlight your unique skills—and always be ready to get a new job or go out on your own.
- Make sure that you can complement and extend the capabilities of, rather than compete with increasingly intelligent machines.
- If you don't take charge of your career, who will?

I began this book by asking a straightforward question: What do you want your life to be like when you're 25? 35? 55?

A vision of your future is a great place to begin your quest to achieve it. Imagining something, however, does not make it a reality. The bad news is that whatever your vision for your future career, it will take far more work to achieve it than was the case a generation ago. The good news is that those with the right preparation and the right skills will have far more options for not only building the career of their dreams, but also for managing that career around the lifestyle of their dreams.

That's where this book's 20-step plan fits in. But before summarizing the plan, how did we get here? Why, five years after the formal end of the 2007 recession, is growth still so anemic and jobs—much less good jobs—so hard to find? Most importantly, what will the job market look like when you are ready to graduate and what must you do now to give you the best chance of not just getting the job of your dreams, but of building the career of your dreams?

Planning a Career in the New Normal

Here we are, five years after the end of the so-called Great Recession. Economic growth rates remain far below those of previous post-recession recoveries and the United States still employs fewer workers than in 2007. Even those who have kept their jobs have not been spared pain. Real, after-inflation wages have fallen and then stagnated. Forget about 2007 wage rates. Today's inflation-adjusted wages are below those of 1999!

Welcome to the New Normal, an era of reduced economic growth and expectations. An era in which growth rates will continue to fall well below those of the boom years of the late 20th century, in which companies will limit the hiring of full-time employees as a means of keeping fixed costs down, and in which median wages will see slow—if any—real growth.

The recession and slow recovery has been particularly tough on those young adults who have had the misfortune of graduating since it began. As of the end of 2013, 10.9 percent of that year's graduates remained without jobs. Of those who did get jobs, 44 percent were "underemployed"—in jobs that did not require college degrees. And don't even begin to think about the number who could not get jobs within their major.

The good news is that the job market has improved significantly since the recession ended. The bad news is that nobody expects rapid improvement. Getting jobs—especially, good career-track jobs—will remain tough for years to come.

This said, today's job market, like the economy as a whole, is increasingly becoming a tale of two classes. High-skilled individuals in particular fields, such as healthcare and most STEM segments, will enjoy huge demand for their services and good, steadily growing salaries. Meanwhile, the traditionally huge base of mid-skill, mid-wage manufacturing, construction, and office jobs is being hollowed out by forces such as automation and offshoring. Many jobs are being eliminated and many others are being totally transformed. Most young adults entering the workforce will fall into one of two camps:

1. A large majority who will struggle to get any job that offers a reasonable salary, training, and long-term growth opportunities, much less a job that makes use of their education and skills or that allows them to pursue their passions; or
2. A small minority (perhaps 15 to 20 percent) who will receive multiple offers for challenging jobs within their field, generous salaries and benefits, and rapidly growing demand for their services.

> Today's job market is becoming a tale of two classes. High-skilled individuals in particular fields will enjoy huge demand (and high pay) for their services, Meanwhile, traditional mid-skill, mid-wage jobs are being decimated by forces such as automation and offshoring, pushing those with these skills into low-skill, low wage jobs.

The good news is that there have never been more opportunities for determined, high-skill individuals to chart and control their own career destinies, in virtually any field.

Since you have the good fortune of being born later than those who graduated between 2008 and 2012, you have a much better opportunity to prepare yourself to be among the big winners in this new market. You can position yourself to be among the winners in this new job market in three primary ways:

- The easiest and most straightforward approach is to gain a solid postsecondary education where you will major in, get good grades in, and land a pregraduation paid internship in one of the markets for which there is, and will continue to be great demand. These include a handful of high-skill trades (especially in advanced manufacturing or some construction fields); the vast majority of science, technology, engineering, and mathematics (STEM) fields; and most segments of healthcare (and especially those dealing with aging baby boomers).

- A more challenging, but potentially more psychically rewarding approach is to build an extraordinary resume (with a record of consistent achievement and demonstrable accomplishments) around your passion. Depending on your field, however, this approach may require more than passion and achievement. It may also require that you hedge your bets by simultaneously preparing for a complementary safety career in a field for which there is proven demand.

- Start your own business. Although this can be challenging for anyone, much less someone just out of school and without resources or a proven track record, it has seldom been easier or less costly to launch one's own businesses. Technologies including personal computers, cloud-based business services, and 3D printers have slashed the cost of starting a new business—provided new opportunities to create and launch totally new concepts (such as a new social media tool or small-volume, custom manufacturing) on the cheap and for even one-person companies to sell into a global market.

Identifying and Preparing for the Career
That's Right for You

No matter which route you choose, each has a relatively similar basic recipe for success that is embodied in Chapter 4's 20-step program. It begins by:

- Identifying your passions and your primary interests (Step 1);
- Identifying and objectively evaluating your skills and your limitations (Step 2);
- Determining ways you can apply different combinations of your skills to your passions (Step 3); and
- Prioritizing and developing deep understanding, skills, and recognition around a few of the passion/interest/skill combinations in which you have the greatest interest (Step 4).

Armed with this knowledge about yourself, you're ready to take your first cut at your lifetime effort of defining and continually honing and adapting your personal brand (Step 5), evaluating and validating potential career opportunities around your passion/interest/skills combinations and brand (Step 6), developing a network of advisors (Step 7) to help you identify career opportunities that may fit these combinations, and determining which offer the best and most flexible career options (Step 8).

You must then narrow these options down to a few complementary fields that can form the basis for the dream career, and just in case you can't get your dream job or it doesn't turn out to be as dreamy as you had anticipated, a safety career (Step 9).

Once you have identified primary and secondary career goals that best align with your passions, your skills, and market trends and realities, you're ready for the next steps of identifying the skills you must develop to prepare you not just to get your first job, but those you will need to succeed through your entire 40+-year career, regardless of the fields into which your ever changing passions, interests and skills (not to speak of market realities and serendipity) may take you (Step 10), and creating an education plan that will help you develop these skills (Step 11).

The New Skills Imperative

Many of the skills you will require will depend on the specific career options you have chosen. You must develop the domain knowledge—the key precepts, frameworks, methodologies, and knowledge that is required in your specific fields, along with demonstrable experience in working in these areas, documented accomplishments and references. That, of course, is a given.

More importantly, regardless of the specific career you target, you will need a number of foundational skills, differentiating value-added skills, and especially the personality traits that are required to succeed in virtually all high-skill jobs, as well as to manage your career (not to speak of your entire life) in an era of complexity and continual change. Among the more important of these foundational skills are communication and collaboration, information, media and information technology, statistics, entrepreneurship, and social and cross-cultural skills.

Although these skills will be important in all jobs, they are merely the ante: the stakes that are required just to get a seat at the table. A different set of higher level of skills will separate the real winners from the also-rans in the race to make it to the top level of virtually any high-skill profession. These include critical thinking, complex problem solving, creativity, innovation, and "complex communication" skills.

These high-level skills are necessary in propelling you to the top of your profession. Even they, however, aren't sufficient. You also need the personality traits that will give you the drive required to become the best, the grit required to keep going in the face of continual setbacks, the discretion to recognize the need to change course, and the flexibility to make these changes. These traits or attributes can be summarized as initiative and self-direction, flexibility and adaptability, self-restraint, and, since you will have to anticipate and adapt to continual change, an insatiable curiosity and passion for learning.

> Success in the 21st-century economy will require more and different skills and personality traits that were required in the 20th-century. And since few schools even attempt to teach them, you will have to develop many on your own.

There are many established vehicles for learning foundational skills such as IT, statistics, and communication. Unfortunately, this is not the case for higher order skills such as complex problem solving and creativity, much less personality traits including initiative, adaptability, and self-restraint. Even most colleges falter in these areas. A growing number of studies even suggest that most college graduates experience little or no increase in critical thinking and complex problem solving skills from the time they began their freshman years!

In other words, if you want to learn the skills that will be truly required for success in this new era, you have to take responsibility for your own learning and develop your own education plan (Step 12).

The Educational Dilemma

Some form of postsecondary education is critical in this new era. But just what type of education? College has certainly been the traditional route to a high-value job and continues to be the most favored route. In fact, a record 33.5 percent of Americans aged 25 to 29 now have at least a bachelor's degree and another five percent have an associate's degree. Although there are certainly exceptions (think Steve Jobs, Mark Zuckerberg, Ellen DeGeneres, Ted Turner), study after study shows that a college degree is one of the most effective—and cost-efficient—ways of getting a good job that pays a good wage. Those with college degrees, and especially graduate degrees, consistently earn more, are less likely to experience unemployment, will live in safer neighborhoods, and have children that are likely to out-earn those that do not graduate.

But how many families can even afford to send their children to colleges, with some costing more than $50,000 per year (for tuition, fees, room, and board). Besides, if a college education is so great, why are 10.9 percent of recent college graduates unemployed and 44 percent underemployed (in occupations that do not require a college degree)?

Sure, a college degree can be a bargain for one who graduates into an $80,000 per year engineering job or a $100,000 per year financial analyst position. But how about the average college graduate? How much better off is a barista with a college degree and $29,000 in college debt (the average for those who take out loans), or a humanities PhD with $150,000 in debt, than is someone who got the same job straight out of high school? Given the high cost of college, and the limited career and earning prospects for many graduates, it makes little sense to even begin college unless you know exactly what you plan to gain from your education, or if you aren't ready to take full advantage of the opportunity.

Some jobs absolutely require a bachelor's, or even a master's, professional, or doctorate degree. Many high-skill jobs, however, do not. And while many employers have come to favor or even require a college degree for jobs that do not really require that level of education, a growing number—including some of the premier employers in technology and finance industries—have come to recognize that college is not the only, or necessarily the best, means of developing the skills that are required for many of even the highest skill jobs.

So, while virtually all challenging, secure, and well-paying high-skill jobs require more than a high school education, there are a growing number of increasingly viable means of developing these skills. For example, community college associate degree, apprenticeship, and certification programs can prepare you for entry into high-demand trades that may well start at $30,000 to $50,000 per year and ultimately allow you to earn well into the six figures.

There are also a growing number of less formal education alternatives. These include self-directed career readiness and learning programs, informal office apprenticeships, boot camps, Massive Open Online Courses, or even self-directed independent learning and experience. Nor are such programs necessarily alternatives to a four-year college. They can be complements. Gap Year programs are generally intended to prepare participants to get more out of college, and community colleges can be great steppingstones into a four-year college program. Boot camps and MOOCs, meanwhile, are typically better suited as complements to, rather than substitutes for, college. Not only can they provide the hands-on skills that you do not often get in college, they may also allow you to get the type of certification that will demonstrate that a nongraduate can fill a specific job opening or that a college graduate with even the most obscure of majors (ancient African tribal arts?) can provide immediate value to a company in addition to offering long-term growth potential (Step 13).

> Although a four-year degree is the most common and most recognized background for high-skill jobs, many high-skill jobs don't require them. And a growing number of employers have begun to recognize and accept alternative qualifications.

In the end, almost everybody will need some form of postsecondary education to even get a shot at a good job. The type of education, however, depends on a combination of your own learning style, your objectives, the published and informal requirements of the specific job, your financial situation and your family, and other obligations. But whatever type of education you choose, it is up to you to ensure that you develop the life skills you will require for long-term career success, in addition to the practical skills you require for a specific job (Step 14). After all, as Harvard education expert Tony Wagner says, the world no longer cares how much you know; the world cares about what you can do with what you know." "To succeed in the 21st-century economy, students must learn to analyze and solve problems, collaborate, persevere, take calculated risks, and learn from failure."

Finding and Succeeding in Your Dream Job

Once you've decided what you want to do, and you have gotten the education, developed the skills, and earned the required certifications, you will be prepared to land your first job and begin making your mark on the world. But much has changed between the time you originally mapped out your career plans and the time you have completed your education. Before you begin your search you have to update your career and initial job expectations in light of market changes (Step 15), update your brand, and reengage and dramatically expand your career planning network. You must, for example, determine which specific positions will best utilize your skills and engage your passions, as well as what size and style company is best suited to you and your goals.

Since you will have thought so deeply about what you want to do, researched your options so thoroughly, designed your skills development and education programs so well, and built such as strong network, you will have dramatically improved your odds of finding your dream (or at least your safety) job. But before you jump at your first offer, remember: Your first career-track job will be one of your most important of, and the launch pad for your career.

You must, therefore, know exactly what you want to get out of that job and the potential for achieving your goals. Among the primary questions you want to answer before you accept an offer:

- Will I enjoy the job?
- What will I learn from it?
- What advancement opportunities will it provide?
- Will the company and the job improve my marketability?
- Will it allow me to expand, enhance, and especially deepen my network?
- Will it be consistent with my lifestyle goals?
- Is the company's culture and image consistent with my needs and values?
- Are the salary and benefits competitive?
- Would I be better off going out on my own or starting my own company?

The considerations are numerous. They are, however, eminently manageable. The best part is, the better you plan and the more thoroughly you assess your options, the more likely you are to end up in a job in which you will be able to excel and adapt to your own needs (Steps 16 and 17), and develop the type of work and life skills, network and the relationships (Steps 18 and 19) you will need through your career. And the more passionate about and the more you learn from and thrive in your work, the more likely you are to proactively search out the learning opportunities that will help you anticipate and stay ahead of the forces that will continually reshape your industry, your company, and your occupation (Step 20).

> There are many factors to assess in determining which job will the best in launching your career. Salary is one of the least important of these.

That's it: 20 "easy" steps to building, controlling, and thriving in a career you will love and that will enable the lifestyle you want for yourself and your family.

Twenty Principles for Building Your Dream Career

This book provides a 20-step process to help you identify, prepare for, and launch a career that is built around your passion and that will enable your chosen lifestyle. So it is probably fitting that it should end with another 20-item list—a list of 20 principles for guiding you along your entire career planning process.

As I've discussed throughout this book, there is nothing immutable about the process or the individual steps in my 20-step plan. Most steps must be repeated continually through your entire career and many merge into others. It is, however, at these intersections where the real lessons for planning and managing your career lie. Although these lessons, or guiding principles are discussed in detail in the book, I want to briefly highlight some of the most important. These include:

Dream, but Validate: I am a great believer in building a career around your passion and your interests. After all, it takes a lot of time, effort, and determination to build a meaningful high-skill, high-value career. It's much easier to motivate yourself to devote this effort to something you love, than it is to something that is "just a job." Identifying your passions and interests, however, is only the first step in building a career around them. You must also objectively determine how well suited your skills are to this passion, what job opportunities are likely to be available, what are the prospects of getting these jobs, and what you have to do (education, credentials, experience, etc.) to maximize your odds. You then have to put in the work not only to prepare yourself for your desired job but also to ensure that you are more qualified and prepared than are the thousands of others who are trying to get that same job. After all, nobody is going to hire you for your passion. They will only hire you for the value you can bring to them. Remember also that passions change. Even if you do get the job of your dreams, those who focus on preparing for a career around your passion without honing the broad skills required to succeed in multiple careers are mortgaging their futures.

Hedge your Dream Career with a Safety Career. Preparing for the career of your dreams is great. But there is something worse than not getting your dream job: it is not being able to get any job (or at least any meaningful job) at all. Unless your dream career has close to a 100 percent employment rate, and provides for lifetime employment, you need to also prepare for a safety career that takes into account your skills and interests in an area in which there are plenty of good jobs (nursing, accounting, sales, software development, etc.), and in a field for which you have a passion. Make your dream career your mission, but make your safety career your insurance policy or your parachute. It will multiply your prospects for getting a career-track job out of school and provide an alternative in case you don't get your dream job, or discover that it is not quite as dreamy as you once thought, or that it won't provide a lifetime of career satisfaction.

Experience Everything: You never know where you will find your next inspiration or your next passion. The more things you experience the more likely you are to discover something you love, are good at, and maybe even a new career idea. Read everything and sample all different types of classes and activities. When you find something you enjoy, dig in: learn about it, practice it. It may turn into your next dream or safety career option, or maybe just a hobby. Even if not, the experience will help you better hone in on what you do and do not enjoy, and what you are and are not good at. And you never know when some obscure type of knowledge or skill that you develop in a random activity may come in useful in the future. This being said, while you should spend your entire life searching for new experiences, you also have to know when to choose an area on which you do want to focus and dedicate the time and effort to "become an expert."

Know What You Want From Your PostSecondary Education. It is a waste of time and money to treat college as an extension of your adolescence. If you don't know what you want out of a college education or aren't ready to put in the effort required to learn, you're probably better off with finding an apprenticeship position, taking a detour through community college, or postponing school in favor of structured gap year program. Even Google, once obsessed with degrees, GPAs, and test scores, now acknowledges that these are not good predictors of success. In addition to coding ability, it now seeks employees with cognitive abilities (including the ability to learn and process information on the fly, pull together disparate bits of information, ask the right questions, and think predictively); emergent leadership capabilities (not in directing people, but the ability to work productively and effectively as a member of the team); intellectual humility (as in willingness to admit mistakes and embrace better ideas of others); willingness to own problems (regardless of their cause); adaptability; and the love of learning.

Don't Treat College as a Trade School: If you choose to go to a four-year college, you should certainly consider employment prospects as an important factor in deciding which college, major, and courses you should choose. You should, after all, approach potential employers with an actual practical skill, in addition to developable potential. That, however, does not mean that all of your coursework should focus on career preparation. Employers often contend that although many preprofessional programs do arm graduates with good knowledge of their specific discipline, they often lack the critical and creative thinking, writing, and complex communication skills and the interdisciplinary perspectives of those of liberal arts grads. True, liberal arts (and especially humanities) programs have been much maligned for producing graduates with lower employment prospects and lower salaries than for those with professional or preprofessional degree. Studies, however, show that these differences generally disappear by mid-career. They can also be mitigated with a professionally focused minor, boot camp certificate, or especially graduate degree. But even if you do choose a profession-specific program, integrating liberal arts into your major is likely to deliver greater career (not to speak of life) benefits than the next incremental professional course that you may add to a business or STEM major.

> To get the best jobs, you need to graduate with more than an education. You also need a skill

Consider Safe Career Bets: You can build a career in virtually any field in which you have a passion. This being said, your safest bets for finding a good job (either as your dream or safety career) lie in fields that offer the greatest growth prospects and face a shortage of workers with specific skills. While most such jobs require bachelor or, in the case of healthcare, advanced degrees, a number require less than a bachelor's degree (nursing has a minimum requirement of an associate's degree) or no degree at all. Coding and math skills can be learned anywhere and basic business skills can be learned by working in a business or by enrolling in a boot camp. High-skill manufacturing (especially those jobs involving the programming and operation of computer-controlled equipment) and construction (especially carpentry, plumbing and welding) jobs, meanwhile, typically require apprenticeships and possibly certificates.

Become an Expert: If you want to get and keep a job in a field, you have to be good at what you do. But if you want to build a high-value career that you can control, you have to be great at what you do. "Greatness" is a high bar. Not only does it require a lot of skill, education, and practice, you must also be better than others who have the same goal. Focusing on a specialty is one of the best ways of achieving mastery. This does not mean that you should strive to become a "microspecialist" in the narrowest, most obscure niche that you can find. You will find greater long-term opportunities and add more value to your company and your clients by being an interdisciplinary "macrospecialist" who combines deep (but not necessarily expert-level) knowledge and skills in two or three complementary fields that you can integrate in a way that allows you to come up with insights or approaches for exploring problems that others do not see.

Search for Breaking Waves: It is often easier for people (especially those with less traditional backgrounds) to get a job in a rapidly growing emerging field, than in a mature or shrinking field. First, emerging fields create more new job opportunities than do mature fields. Moreover, these employers are more open to employees with nontraditional backgrounds, and such fields generally offer more opportunities for advancement and a better chance for you to shape your job around your own particular interests and skills. The good news is that new fields are being created every day. Some of the most promising candidates include artificial intelligence, robotics, genomic medicine, Big Data analysis, wearable computers, mobile, digital medical devices, cloud computing, nanotechnology, 3D printing, and virtually any field which can find new uses for or better utilize the capabilities of ever cheaper and more powerful technologies.

Develop Skills over Content: Learning facts has always been overrated. This is becoming especially true now that virtually any fact or any type of information is now available at the click of a mouse. The real value, as explained by Harvard's Tony Wagner, is in "what you can do with what you know." But now that technology and offshoring increasingly perform many traditional cognitive jobs better and less expensively than U.S. workers, you have to look to even higher value skills to give you an edge. Although you still need core skills (reading, writing, IT, statistics, and so forth) your differentiation and value will come from higher level skills including critical thinking, problem identification and problem solving, creativity, conceptual synthesis, interdisciplinary analysis, and complex communication.

Master the Habits of Success: High-level skills are certainly critical for success. However, they are not sufficient. A number of personality traits may be even more important. These include flexibility, adaptability, initiative, self-direction, accountability, responsibility, integrity, the self-control required to defer gratification, and perhaps most importantly, persistence. It requires the ability to not only bounce back from inevitable failures but also to learn from these failures and to adapt your approach. It also requires a delicate, ever-changing balance between persistence and flexibility to allow you to recognize when it is best to redouble your focus and efforts, and when it may be best to pivot to Plan B, or as discussed later, possibly even to Plan Z.

Exceed Everybody's Expectations: When you get a job, don't just do the job, do a great job. You must certainly do everything your employer asks, but you must do it better and faster than she expects. Then show her how much more value you can provide by applying these same skills to other jobs that you identify. One of the best ways of exceeding expectations (beyond hard work) is by continually demonstrating a perspective that transcends that of your specific job or department: one that demonstrates that you have an understanding of the goals of your entire company, the dynamics of its industry (as well those that currently touch, or are likely to touch your industry), and hopefully, the broader social, economic, or political milieu in which your company operates.

Own Your Professional Brand: Whether you plan for it or not, you will be branded by how you are perceived. Although you can't control all aspects of your brand, the more you can define and shape it, the better your chances that your brand will help rather than hinder your career. Be proactive in creating a brand around your own aspirations, skills, and strengths—build a brand that not only shows what you have done in the past but also shows how the disparate, and perhaps random experiences that have shaped your life all work together to make you the ideal person for the job to which you aspire. Once you define your brand, continually evolve it, adding to it as you develop new skills and repositioning it as your visions of your next job and long-term career trajectory change.

Sell Thyself: Fame, especially in today's world of reality shows, social networking, and viral videos, can come from anywhere, at any time. But when it comes to building your career, you can't count on the market's whimsy. You have to continually promote yourself and your brand to potential employers, clients, and partners. No, don't blatantly hawk your brand like a two-bit barker at a county fair sideshow. You have to market yourself subtly and discretely. Leave behind a trail of good work; create a reputation as a good team member and leader; build a network of previous mentors, managers, co-workers, clients, and acquaintances, who have an interest in promoting you and the value you can bring to a job or an organization. Although this network must certainly include the broad business-focused social media networks (such as LinkedIn), the real power comes from the type of deep networks you build from former and current managers, references, mentors, and sponsors.

Plan, But Don't Over Plan: Just as you must find a delicate balance between persistence and flexibility, you must also find one between planning and spontaneity. On one hand, you have to always know where you want to go and the steps that you must take to get there. But you also have to understand when enough is enough. If, after repeated attempts and tweaks, Plan A just can't gain traction, it may be best to modify your approach to Plan B, and, just in case, have a worst-case fallback position—a Plan Z. Good planning, after all, is all about creating options for yourself. And the more options you create, the more likely you are to be presented with new opportunities of which you have never dreamed: An unanticipated call from a previous boss who just got a job at a new company or a friend of a friend of a friend who is starting a new company in a promising new field. Not that you should take every new opportunity that comes up, but you should certainly evaluate every option, regardless of how far from your original plan.

Become an Entrepreneur: Even if you don't have a burning desire to hang out your own shingle, you must always be prepared to do so. You may, after all, get laid off during a terrible job market or you may decide to leave a long-time employer after being passed over for a new position that should have gone to you. Or one day, you may come up with a business idea that is too promising to pass up. Whatever the reason, an estimated 40 percent of all U.S. workers are expected to be contingent workers within five years. You must keep your options open. And the more opportunities you have for creating new revenue streams, the more options you will have. This requires that you maintain a solid brand that can be leveraged into your own company or a freelance business; a network of potential references and clients; and a core set of sales, marketing, financial, and organizational skills. Even if you never use these entrepreneurial skills in your own business, they are likely to be helpful in just about any job you have, regardless of the size or nature of the organization.

Complement Machines: Don't Compete with Them: Computers are becoming small and inexpensive enough to be used everywhere and powerful enough to do virtually everything. Just as it has become impossible to out-power factory machines or to be more precise and reliable than a robot at certain jobs, it will become equally impossible to outthink computers at virtually anything they are programmed to do. It's a fool's errand to deny or to seek to compete with microprocessor-based computers and machines over the long term. You will have far more opportunities, and have far greater earning potential by doing something that machines can't do (as long as you are prepared for the day when they will be able to do even that), by using the machines to help you do your job better than that can be done by people alone, or by helping machines do their jobs more effectively. Better yet, you can design the machines that will be capable of doing new jobs or develop the programs that will allow them to master new skills.

Don't Fall into the Salary Trap: All too many college students consider salary to be the single most important criterion in assessing a potential job and employer. However, taking and remaining in a job for the money is one of the most frequently cited career regrets of accomplished mid-career professionals. Taking a job for the salary is particularly dangerous trap for your first job out of school, where you should be much more focused on factors including what you will learn, what you will enjoy, the opportunities for advancement, and for enhancing your long-term marketability.

Embrace and Learn from Failure: Failure is a necessary component of success. Every failure is—or at least should be—a learning experience. As Thomas Edison famously said, "I have not failed 1,000 times. I have successfully discovered 1,000 ways to NOT make a light bulb." So valuable are the lessons of failure that some venture capital firms are more inclined to invest in a founder that has failed than in one who has not. Failure tests—and is critical in—building resolve and resilience. The ability to learn from failure demonstrates adaptability. It is also an important marker of ambition. If you haven't failed at a significant undertaking, it suggests that you haven't really stretched yourself; that you are not comfortable in venturing outside your comfort zone.

Invent Your Own Jobs: This is one of the most important and inclusive themes in this book. It allows you to engage your skills around your interests and passions, extend your brand in directions in which you want to take it, and to further develop and promote your specialty—all while maximizing the value you deliver to employers and clients. True, you will be hard pressed to find an employer who will allow you to define your own job (especially in one of your first jobs out of school). However, once you have proven your capabilities and understand the needs of the organization, you may be in a position to identify a pressing company need that you are ideally suited to address. In addition to directly helping you and your employer, it will also demonstrate your enthusiasm and entrepreneurialism and provide a high-profile opportunity to prove yourself. And who knows, once you've honed your skills, achieved your objectives, and cataloged demonstrable achievements, you may even be able to sell your value proposition to a new employer or package it in a way that you can deliver it to multiple clients as a consultant or a packaged offering.

Continually Reinvent Yourself: In the not too distant past, you could learn to do your job once and keep doing the same thing, over and over again for your entire career. True, it may not be a very interesting existence and it wouldn't put you on a fast track for promotion, but it could allow you to keep your job and your paycheck. Today's world, of course, changes far too rapidly to tolerate such stasis. You must, at the very least, keep up with changes in your field and adapt to changing organizational requirements. More importantly, you must continually survey the landscape for any type of change, no matter how far from your core business, if you are to anticipate emerging competitive threats (such as the threat that online bookseller Amazon would come to pose to electronics and grocery stores), identify new business opportunities, or identify a new way of changing the rules against competitors. Continual learning is also required to keep your skills current, to develop new skills to qualify you for new positions, to forecast and prepare for changes in your own company and industry, and to identify new employment or business opportunities in emerging new fields.

Taking Charge of Your Life

Turning your dream career into reality requires a lot more than conceiving of dream and safety careers, coming up with an education and a career plan, and getting your first job. It also requires a lot of self-reflection, determination, initiative, and adaptability. And regardless of how much you put into it, there's no guarantee that your plan will work as you hope.

There is, however, one guarantee. If you diligently follow a logical set of steps in choosing your career and then work to develop the skills you will need for it, you will have a big advantage not only in getting a good career-track job out of school but also in building the foundation for a rewarding, high-value career doing what you love. The very process will be a journey of self-discovery through which you identify your real skills and interests, understand what does and does not motivate you, and discover what you really want out of your career and your life.

Just as importantly, the very process of planning and executing this plan will help you develop many of the skills and attributes that will be required in every stage of your education and career. It all comes down to creating a plan, doggedly working that plan, and continually adapting it on the basis of experience and new evidence (all while remaining open to the type of unanticipated, serendipitous opportunities that make it worthwhile to change even the best plans).

In case you missed it, each of the steps in this book's 20-step process has a common requirement: You!

Don't get me wrong. Nobody can create and build a career all by themselves. You need the help of others through every step of the process. For example, you need help in evaluating your skills, identifying weaknesses you should address, understanding and evaluating potential careers, and meeting people who can explain career opportunities in your chosen field or even offer you a job. You should look for professors who can guide your academic interests and suggest career opportunities, attract mentors and sponsors who can help open new career doors, and friends and acquaintances to keep you in mind if they hear of interesting opportunities in other departments and companies.

But no matter how much help you need, you can't count on other people or institutions to define and prepare you for, much less to manage your career for you. You certainly can't count on them to identify your dream!

Heck, most schools haven't yet fully agreed on the types of skills you will need to succeed in the new world, much less how to most effectively teach these skills. Even the most prescient of economists can't always predict forthcoming economic shifts or recessions or the most far-sighted of business executives anticipate challenges that have the potential of obsoleting their companies or their industries.

> In the end, you must take responsibility for defining your own dream; for identifying your own career objectives; for ensuring that you develop the skills and get the education required to achieve these objectives; and for managing your own career

So regardless of how much you look to institutions or individuals for help, in the end, you must take responsibility for defining your own dream; for identifying your own career objectives; for ensuring that you develop the skills and get the education required to achieve these objectives; and for managing your own career.

This is as it should be. After all, if you don't take responsibility for your dream, your career and your life, who will?

About the Author

Tom Kucharvy

Tom Kucharvy has had three very different careers—as a tax attorney; an IT industry market strategist and consultant; and, most recently, a blogger (TomKucharvy.com). Now, he is a book author exploring the future of the jobs market and how to build a rewarding career in this new market.

He has also begun to lay the foundation for his next career as a travel and life experience blogger (ActiveBoomerAdventures.com).

Throughout their many careers, Tom and his wife Joyce have lived their dreams, moving to and living in cities they most enjoyed, and continually traveling to and exploring every corner of the country and the world.

Notes

Introduction

1. Mourshed et al. (n.d.), p. 29.
2. "Accenture 2013 College Graduate Employment Survey" (2013).
3. Abel et al. (2014).
4. Abel et al. (2014).
5. Stone et al. (2012), p. 19.
6. "Accenture 2013 College Graduate Employment Survey" (2013).
7. Gallup (2013), p. 12.
8. McGeehan (2013).
9. http://www.thielfellowship.org/

Chapter 1

1. Autor (2014).
2. "Earnings and Unemployment Rates by Educational Attainment" (2014).
3. U.S. Bureau of Labor Statistics (2014).
4. Mourshed et al. (n.d.), Figure 2.
5. "Accenture 2013 Skills and Employment Trends Survey: Perspectives on Training" (2013).
6. "Accenture 2013 Skills and Employment Trends Survey: Perspectives on Training" (2013), p. 6.
7. "Accenture 2013 Skills and Employment Trends Survey: Perspectives on Training" (2013), p. 7.
8. "Accenture 2013 College Graduate Employment Survey" (2013), p. 38.
9. "Accenture 2013 College Graduate Employment Survey" (2013), p. 17.
10. Mourshed et al. (n.d.), p. 15.
11. Smith and LaVelle (2013), p. 2.
12. Smith and LaVelle (2013), p. 9.
13. Smith and LaVelle (2013), p. 23.
14. "Alternative Measures of Labor Underutilization" (2014).
15. Subramanian (2012).
16. Fogg and Harrington (2011).
17. "Failure to Launch: Structural Shift and the New Lost Generation" (2013).
18. http://www.ceri.msu.edu/
19. Stone et al. (2012).

20. Abel et al. (2014), p. 4.
21. Shierholz et al. (2013), Figure J.
22. Shierholz et al. (2013), Figure K.
23. Murray (2009).
24. Carnevale et al. (2013).
25. Chopra (2013).
26. Stone et al. (2012), p. 19.
27. "Change in U.S. Employment: Recoveries" (2014).
28. Brauer and Whalen (2014), p. 12.
29. Brynjolfsson and McAfee (2011).
30. Brynjolfsson and McAfee (2014).
31. Brynjolfsson and McAfee (2014), p. 133.
32. Cowen (2013).
33. Friedman (2012).

Chapter 2

1. Manyika et al. (2012).
2. Barker (2011), p. 1.
3. Davidson (2011).
4. Barker (2011).
5. Thompson (2012).
6. Nicholson (2012).
7. Ashkenas and Parlapiano (2014).
8. "Occupation Finder" (2014).
9. Autor (2010).
10. Rothwell (2014).
11. Gilliland et al. (2014).
12. Autor and Dorn (2013, August 23).
13. A. C. S. (2011).
14. Center on Education and the Workforce (2014).
15. Autor (2010).
16. Autor (2010).
17. Brynjolfsson and McAfee (2014), p. 133.
18. Kucharvy (2010a, 2010b).
19. Kucharvy (2010a, 2010b).
20. Brynjolfsson and McAfee (2014).
21. Beaudry et al. (2013).
22. Myers (2011).
23. Hyde (2011).
24. Szondy (2014).

25. https://nest.com/
26. http://canary.is/
27. Hertz et al. (2014).
28. Kucharvy (2011a, 2011b, 2011c).
29. "Memorial Sloan-Kettering Cancer Center" (2013).
30. http://www-03.ibm.com/innovation/us/watson/watson_in_finance. shtml?csr=caus_watsonfinance-20130626&cm=k&cr=google&ct= USBRB301&S_TACT=USBRB301&ck=watson_banking&cmp= USBRB&mkwid=sB0lMREt0-dc_35175050257_432t5q28552
31. "Moore's Law" (2014).
32. "IBM Forms News Watson Group to Meet Growing Demand for Cognitive Innovations" (2014).
33. Frey and Osborne (2013), p. 38.
34. Manyika et al. (2013).
35. Andreessen (2011).
36. Cowen (2013), p. 226.
37. Cowen (2013), p. 77.
38. Brynjolfsson and McAfee (2014), p. 189.
39. Manyika et al. (2011), p. 13.
40. Davenport and Patil (2012).
41. Cowen (2013), p. 20.
42. Autor (2014).
43. Perry (2008).
44. Brynjolfsson and McAfee (2014), p. 47.

Chapter 3

1. Autor et al. (2003).
2. Autor et al. (2003).
3. Autor et al. (2003).
4. Autor (2010).
5. Brynjolfsson and McAfee (2014).
6. Kucharvy (2011a, 2011b, 2011c).
7. Kucharvy (2011a, 2011b, 2011c).
8. Wladawsky-Berger (2013).
9. "Framework for 21st Century Skills" (n.d.).
10. "Read the Standards" (2014).
11. "Intuit 2020 Report: Twenty Trends that Will Shape the Next Decade" (2010).
12. Friedman (2013).
13. Wladawsky-Berger (2012).

14. Florida (2012).

15. Friedman (2009).

16. Hoffman and Casnocha (2012), p. 21.

17. Chua and Rubenfeld (2014).

18. Pink (2005).

19. Friedman and Mandelbaum (2011).

20. http://howardgardner.com/books/

21. Wagner (2008).

22. Wagner (2008).

23. Hart Research Associates (2013).

24. Adams (2013), p. 109.

25. Wagner (2012).

Chapter 4

1. Newport (2014).

2. Adams (2013), p. 13.

3. Gladwell (2008).

4. Newport (2012).

5. Dobson (2010).

6. http://www.oecd.org/pisa/

7. http://gradschool.about.com/od/admissionstests/

8. The President and Fellows of Harvard College (2014).

9. Sofferet (2010).

10. Keirsey (1998).

11. "Hiring an MBTI Consultant" (n.d.).

Chapter 6

1. Halvorson (2011).

2. "Big data" (2014).

3. Hoffman and Casnocha (2012), p. 57.

4. Levitz and Belkin (2013).

5. Simon and Barry (2013).

6. Weiss (2013).

7. "World-of-Work Map" (2013).

8. "ACT College Search for iPhone and iPod Touch" (2014).

9. "Choosing Your College Major (2014).

10. http://www.onetonline.org/

11. U.S. Department of Education (n.d.).

12. United States Department of Labor (2014).
13. http://www.bls.gov/k12/students.htm
14. Bureau of Labor Statistics (2014).
15. Bureau of Labor Statistics (2011).

Chapter 7

1. Bureau of Labor Statistics (2013).
2. "Occupation Finder" (2014).
3. Rattner (2012).
4. Supiano (2011).
5. Acemoglu and Autor (2010).
6. "Wealthy by Degrees: The Returns to Investing in a University Education Vary Enormously" (2014), p. 66.
7. Rampell (2013a).
8. Carnevale, Strohl, and Melton (2011).
9. "2013 College Education ROI Rankings: Does a Degree Always Pay Off?" (2013).
10. Looney and Greenstone (2012).
11. Jantti et al. (2006), p. 27.
12. "Pursuing the American Dream" (2012), p. 23.
13. Rampell (2013b).
14. Smith and LaVelle (2013), p. 2.
15. U.S. Bureau of Labor Statistics (2012), p. 1.
16. "Fastest Growing Occupations" (2014).
17. U.S. Bureau of Labor Statistics (2010), p. 4.
18. Mourshed et al. (n.d.), p. 16.
19. Arum and Roksa (2011).
20. Arum and Roksa (2011), p. 121.
21. Goldin and Katz (2008).
22. Caplan (not yet published).
23. Brooks (2014), p. A23.
24. Delbanco (2012).
25. Christensen et al. (2011).
26. www.thielfellowship.org
27. http://www.uncollege.org/
28. U.S. Department of Education (2013).
29. "Accenture 2013 College Graduate Employment Survey: Key Findings" (2013), Slide 15.
30. U.S. Department of Education (2013).
31. Torpey (2013), p. 2.

32. "Gallup-Purdue Index Inaugural National Report" (2014).
33. Gehlhaus (2008).
34. Light (2011).
35. United States Department of Labor. (2014).
36. "Fastest Growing Occupations" (2014).
37. Salcito (n.d.).

Chapter 8

1. Berger (2013).
2. Rampell (2013a, 2013b).
3. Carnevale et al. (2010), p. 13.
4. Sheehy (2013).
5. http://colleges.usnews.rankingsandreviews.com/best-colleges
6. Fleming (2014).
7. "Annual Programs" (2012).
8. Peralta (2012).
9. "Most New Jobs" (2014).
10. "Occupation Finder" (2014).
11. Carnevale et al. (2011a), p. 4.
12. "Accenture 2013 College Graduate Employment Survey: Key Findings" (2013), p. 4.
13. Stone et al. (2012), p. 21.
14. Carnevale et al. (2011b).
15. "From College Major to Career" (2014).
16. Carnevale et al. (2011b).
17. Carnevale et al. (2011c), p. 40.
18. Carnevale et al. (2011c), p. 22.
19. Carnevale et al. (2011c), p. 22.
20. "2013-2014 PayScale College Salary Report" (2014).
21. "Majors That Pay You Back" (2014).
22. Carnevale et al. (2011c), p. 41.
23. Carnevale et al. (2011c), p. 35.
24. Carnevale et al. (2011c), p. 36.
25. Carnevale et al. (2011c), p. 32.
26. Ante (2012).
27. Bildner (2013).
28. Kucharvy (2011c).
29. Jue (2012).
30. "The Most Popular U.S. College Majors" (2012).
31. Colby et al. (2011).

32. Torpey (2014).
33. "Healthcare Occupations" (2014).
34. "Occupations matching 'Healthcare'" (n.d.).
35. "Explore Majors in Medical & Health Sciences" (n.d.).
36. Hart Research Associates (2013).
37. "Overview of Joint Degree and Cooperative Programs" (2014).
38. Olsen (2014).
39. "Class of 2013: Paid Interns Outpace Unpaid Peers in Job Offers, Salaries" (2013).
40. Rankin (2013).
41. "Top 10 College Majors" (2014).
42. Persing (2014).
43. Korn (2012).
44. Rudesill (2013).
45. Paulson and Faust (n.d.).
46. "At Olin the Culture is the Curriculum" (n.d.).
47. "Centers & Institutes" (2012).
48. "Cooperative Education" (2014).
49. U.S. Department of Education (2013a, 2013b, 2013c).
50. Clark (2012).
51. "State by State Data" (2013), p. 1.
52. Arum and Roksa (2011).
53. "Cooperative Education" (2014).
54. Baum and Ma (2013), p. 11.
55. Baum and Ma (2013), p. 22.
56. "Enrollment Rates of 18–24-year-olds in Degree-Granting Institutions" (2011).
57. Martin (2013).
58. Mis (2008).
59. Administration of Barack H. Obama (2012).
60. Symonds et al. (2011).
61. The Subprime Opportunity (n.d.), p. 3, Table 1.
62. Lynch et al. (2010), p. 3.
63. Carnevale et al. (2011a, 2011c).
64. "College Navigator" (n.d.).
65. Driscoll (2011).
66. http://www.unigo.com/
67. http://ready.ccr.mcgraw-hill.com/
68. "College Personality Quiz" (2008).
69. Zmirak (2014).
70. "Find the Best Colleges for You: Focus on the Information that Matters" (2011).

71. "Major and Career Search" (2014).
72. "Major and Career Search" (2014).
73. http://www.dice.com/
74. Carnevale et al. (2011a, 2011c).
75. "Recruiting Trends 2012-2013 Supporters: Thank You" (2013).
76. Staklis and Skomsvold (2014).
77. College Board (2012).
78. Andrews (2006).
79. Nadler (2006).
80. Baum and Ma (2013).
81. Carnevale et al. (2011a, 2011c).
82. U.S. Department of Education (2011).
83. Administration of Barack H. Obama (2012).
84. Caplan (2012).
85. Beck (2013).
86. Blackman (2012).
87. Graduate Management Admission Council (2013), p. 9.
88. Korn (2012).
89. Kucharvy (2010a, 2010b, 2010c).
90. Korn (2013).
91. Kucharvy (2010a, 2010b, 2010c).
92. Friedman (2014).
93. Jaschik (2013).
94. Zlomek (2014).
95. Mitchell (2014), p. A2.

Chapter 9

1. "Skills for America's Future Community College Facts" (2014).
2. Bailey (2008), p. 2.
3. "Accenture 2013 College Graduate Employment Survey: Key Findings" (2013), Slide 5.
4. "Most New Jobs" (2014).
5. Kucharvy (2010a, 2010b, 2010c).
6. "Average Published Undergraduate Charges by Sector, 2013-14" (2014).
7. Greenstone and Looney (2011).
8. "The Center" (n.d.).
9. "2012 Bay Area Workforce Funding Collaborative Grantees" (2012).
10. "Workforce Partnerships" (2014).
11. Schneider (2013).

12. "First Year Earnings of Recent College Graduates in Colorado Vary Widely, Depending Upon Their School and Their Degree, New Report Finds" (2013).
13. U.S. Department of Education (2013).
14. "Enrollment, Staff, and Degrees/Certificates Conferred in Postsecondary Institutions" (2011).
15. Torpey (2013a, 2013b).
16. Carnevale et al. (2010).
17. Carnevale et al. (2010), p. 4.
18. Carnevale et al. (2010), p. 18.
19. Carnevale et al. (2010), p. 23.
20. "Glossary" (2014).
21. Carrns (2014).
22. Phillips (2014).
23. Morrison et al. (2011), p. 8.
24. Phillips (2014).
25. Downs (2014).
26. Lerman (n.d.), p. 2.
27. Phillips (2014).
28. Phillips (2014).
29. "Model of Success: Pathways in Technology Early College High School (P-TECH)" (2014).
30. Foroohar (2014), p. 22.
31. "STEM Pathways to College and Careers Schools: A Development Guide" (2012).
32. "About the Fellowship" (2011).
33. Wadhwa (2013).
34. "Financial Aid" (2012).
35. Stephens (2013).
36. "Gap Year" (2013).
37. "Financial Aid" (2012).
38. "Intro to Artificial Intelligence" (2014).
39. "A is for Algorithm" (2014).
40. Manning (2013).
41. https://www.balloon.com/
42. Porter (2014), p. B1.
43. "Entrepreneurship" (2013).
44. "Earn an XSeries Certificate from One of the Top Institutions in the World" (2014).
45. Jargon and Belkin (2014), p. B3.

46. "Online Master of Science in Computer Science: Offered in Collaboration with Udacity and AT&T" (2013).
47. "The Digital Degree" (2014), p. 22.
48. http://openbadges.org/
49. "Do MOOCs Upend Traditional Business Education?" (2014).
50. "HBC CORe: The Language of Business" (2014).
51. Korn and Weber (2014).

Chapter 10

1. Farber (2007), p. 27.
2. Bureau of Labor Statistics (2012).
3. Bureau of Labor Statistics (2014).
4. Gulati (2012).
5. Jerome (2011).
6. Tanne (2012).
7. "Accenture 2013 College Graduate Employment Survey: Key Findings" (2013), Slide 14.
8. "Why Good People Can't Get Jobs: Chasing After the 'Purple Squirrel'" (2012).
9. Smith et al. (2013).
10. "Accenture 2013 College Graduate Employment Survey: Key Findings" (2013), Slide 13.
11. "Accenture 2013 College Graduate Employment Survey: Key Findings" (2013), Slide 15.
12. "Startup Business Failure Rate by Industry" (2014).
13. Wagner (2013).
14. Farrell (2012).
15. "Accenture 2013 College Graduate Employment Survey: Key Findings" (2013), Slide 27.
16. "Overview of BLS Wage Data by Area and Occupation" (2013).
17. "List of Salaries For Popular Careers" (2014).
18. "Marketplace Trends" (n.d.).
19. Koc et al. (2013).
20. Startup Business Failure Rate by Industry" (2014).
21. Wagner (2013).
22. Gulati (2012).
23. Gallup (2013), p. 12.
24. Hagel et al. (2013), p. 12.
25. Mielach (2012).

References

2012 Bay Area Workforce Funding Collaborative Grantees. [Data Table]. 2012. The San Francisco Foundation: http://www.sff.org/about-tsff/about-our-work/annual-reports/2012-online-annual-report/2012-bay-area-workforce-funding-collaborative-grantees/ (accessed May 3, 2014).

2013-2014 PayScale College Salary Report. [Data Table]. 2014. PayScale: http://www.payscale.com/college-salary-report-2014/full-list-of-schools (accessed May 2, 2014).

A is for Algorithm. 2014. The Economist: http://www.economist.com/news/international/21601250-global-push-more-computer-science-classrooms-starting-bear-fruit (accessed May 3, 2014).

Abel, J.R, R. Deitz, and Y. Su. 2014. *Current Issues in Economics and Finance* (Vol. 20). New York, NY: Federal Reserve Bank of New York. http://www.newyorkfed.org/research/current_issues/ci20-1.pdf (accessed April 20, 2014).

About the Fellowship. 2011. Thiel Fellowship: http://www.thielfellowship.org/become-a-fellow/about-the-program/ (accessed May 3, 2014).

Accenture 2013 College Graduate Employment Survey: Key Findings: Accenture. 2013. http://www.accenture.com/SiteCollectionDocuments/PDF/Accenture-2013-College-Graduate-Employment-Survey.pdf (accessed April 20, 2014).

Accenture 2013 Skills and Employment Trends Survey: Perspectives on Training: Accenture. 2013. http://www.accenture.com/us-en/Pages/insight-accenture-2013-skills-employment-trends-survey-perspectives-on-training.aspx?c=mc_prposts_10000055&n=otc_1013 (accessed April 20, 2014).

Acemoglu, D., and D. Autor. 2010. *Skills, Tasks and Technologies: Implications for Employment and Earnings.* Cambridge, MA: National Bureau of Economic Research.

ACT College Search for iPhone and iPod Touch. n.d. The ACT: http://www.act.org/mobileapps/collegesearch/ (accessed April 30, 2014).

Adams, S. 2013. *How to Fail at Almost Everything and Still Win Big: Kind of the Story of My Life.* New York, NY: Penguin Group.

Administration of Barack H. Obama. 2012. *Jobs and Income: Today and Tomorrow.* Washington, DC: Economic Report of the President. http://www.gpo.gov/fdsys/pkg/ERP-2012/html/ERP-2012-chapter6.htm (accessed May 1, 2014).

Alternative Measures of Labor Underutilization. [Data Table]. 2014. http://www.bls.gov/news.release/empsit.t15.htm (accessed April 20, 2014).

Andreessen, M. August 20, 2011. "Why Software is Eating the World." *The Wall Street Journal.* http://online.wsj.com/news/articles/SB10001424053111903480904576512250915629460 (accessed April 24, 2014).

Andrews, L.L. 2006. *How to Choose a College Major.* The McGraw-Hill Companies.

Annual Programs. 2012. The University of Chicago: https://careeradvancement. uchicago.edu/about/annual-programs (accessed May 1, 2014).

Ante, S.E. May 31, 2012. "Revenge of the Nerds: Tech Firms Scour College Campuses for Talent." *The Wall Street Journal.* http://online.wsj.com/news/ articles/SB10001424052702303360504577408431211035166?mg=reno64-wsj&url=http%3A%2F%2Fonline.wsj.com%2Farticle%2FSB1000 1424052702303360504577408431211035166.html (accessed May 2, 2014).

Arum, R., and J. Roksa. 2011. *Academically Adrift: Limited Learning on College Campuses.* Chicago, IL: The University of Chicago Press.

Ashkenas, J. & Parlapiano, A. 2014. "How the Recession Reshaped the Economy, in 255 Charts." *The New York Times*: http://www.nytimes.com/ interactive/2014/06/05/upshot/how-the-recession-reshaped-the-economy-in-255-charts.html?_r=1 (accessed July 11, 2014).

At Olin the Culture is the Curriculum. n.d. Olin College of Engineering: http:// www.olin.edu/academics/curriculum/ (accessed May 4, 2014).

Autor, D. 2010. *The Polarization of Job Opportunities in the U.S. Labor Market: Implications for Employment and Earnings.* Washington, DC: Center for American Progress & The Hamilton Project.

Autor, D. May 23, 2014. "Skills, Education, and the Rise of Earnings Inequality Among the 'Other 99 Percent.'" *Science Mag*: http://www.sciencemag.org/ content/344/6186/843.abstract (accessed July 11, 2014).

Autor, D., and D. Dorn. 2013. "The Growth of Low Skill Service Jobs and the Polarization of Job Opportunities in the U.S. Market." *American Economic Review* 103, no. 5, pp. 1553–1597.

Autor, D.H., and D. Dorn. August 24, 2013. "How Technology Wrecks the Middle Class." *The New York Times.*

Autor, D.H., F. Levy, and R.J. Murnane. 2003. *The Skill Content of Recent Technological Change: An Empirical Exploration.* Boston, MA: Massachusetts Institute of Technology and National Bureau of Economic Research & Harvard University and National Bureau of Economic Research. http:// economics.mit.edu/files/569 (accessed April 24, 2014).

Average Published Undergraduate Charges by Sector, 2013-14. [Data Table]. 2014. CollegeBoard: http://trends.collegeboard.org/college-pricing/figures-tables/ average-published-undergraduate-charges-sector-2013-14 (accessed May 4, 2014).

Bailey, T. 2008. *Challenge and Opportunity: Rethinking the Role and Function of Developmental Education in Community College.* New York, NY: Community College Research Center, Teachers College, Columbia University. http:// ccrc.tc.columbia.edu/media/k2/attachments/challenge-and-opportunity.pdf (accessed May 4, 2014).

Barker, M.M. 2011. *Manufacturing Employment Hard Hit During the 2007–09 Recession*: Washington, DC: Bureau of Labor Statistics.

Baum, S., and J. Ma. 2013. *Trends in College Pricing 2013*. CollegeBoard: https://trends.collegeboard.org/sites/default/files/college-pricing-2013-full-report.pdf (accessed May 1, 2014).

Beaudry, P., D.A. Green, and B.M. Sand. 2013. *The Great Reversal in the Demand for Skill and Cognitive Tasks*. Cambridge, MA: National Bureau of Economic Research. http://www.nber.org/papers/w18901 (accessed April 24, 2014).

Beck, M. March 14, 2013. "Squeeze Looms for Doctors." *The Wall Street Journal*. http://online.wsj.com/news/articles/SB10001424127887324096404578356544137516914?mg=reno64-wsj&url=http%3A%2F%2Fonline.wsj.com%2Farticle%2FSB100014241278873240964045783565441377516914.html (accessed May 3, 2013).

Berger, B. May 9, 2013. "Why a College Degree May Not Be Worth It." *U.S. News*. http://www.usnews.com/opinion/articles/2013/05/09/why-a-college-degree-no-longer-guarantees-success (accessed May 1, 2014).

Big data. 2014. Wikipedia: http://en.wikipedia.org/wiki/Big_data (accessed April 28, 2014).

Bildner, M. March 27, 2013. "17-Year-Old British Teen's Start-Up Aquired by Yahoo." *Daily Deal Media*. http://www.dailydealmedia.com/639-17-year-old-british-teens-start-up-acquired-by-yahoo/ (accessed May 2, 2014).

Blackman, S. June 1, 2012. "The Future Looks Bright for B-School Grads." *U.S. News*. http://www.usnews.com/education/blogs/mba-admissions-strictly-business/2012/06/01/the-future-looks-bright-for-b-school-grads (accessed May 3, 2014).

Brauer, D., and C. Whalen. 2014. *The Slow Recovery of the Labor Market*. Congress of the United States Congressional Budget Office. http://www.cbo.gov/sites/default/files/cbofiles/attachments/45011-LaborMarketReview.pdf (accessed April 21, 2014).

Brynjolfsson, E., and A. McAfee. 2011. *Race Against the Machine: How the Digital Revolution is Accelerating Innovation, Driving Productivity, and Irreversibly Transforming Employment and the Economy*. Lexington, MA: Digital Frontier Press.

Brynjolfsson, E., and A. McAfee. 2014. *The Second Machine Age: Work, Progress, and Prosperity in a Time of Brilliant Technologies*. New York, NY: W.W. Norton & Company, Inc.

Bureau of Labor Statistics. 2011. *Career Guide to Industries, 2010-11*. United States Department of Labor: http://www.bls.gov/search/cgi.htm (accessed April 30, 2014).

Bureau of Labor Statistics. 2012. *Number of Jobs Held, Labor Market Activity, and Earnings Growth Among the Youngest Baby Boomers: Results from a Longitudinal Survey*. Washington, DC: U.S Department of Labor. http://www.bls.gov/news.release/pdf/nlsoy.pdf (accessed May 4, 2014).

Bureau of Labor Statistics. 2013. *Education and Training Assignments by Detailed Occupation, 2012.* United States Department of Labor: http://www.bls.gov/emp/ep_table_112.htm (accessed April 30, 2014).

Bureau of Labor Statistics. 2014. *Occupational Injuries and Illnesses: Counts, Rates, and Characteristics, 2004.* United States Department of Labor: http://www.bls.gov/iif/oshbulletin2004.htm (accessed April 30, 2014).

C. S. 2011. *The Return of Artisanal Employment.* The Economist: http://www.economist.com/blogs/freeexchange/2011/10/labour-markets (accessed April 24, 2014).

Caplan, L. July 14, 2012. "An Existential Crisis for Law Schools." *The New York Times.* http://www.nytimes.com/2012/07/15/opinion/sunday/an-existential-crisis-for-law-schools.html?_r=1& (accessed May 3, 2014).

Carnevale, A.P., A.R. Hanson, and A. Gulish. 2013. *Failure to Launch: Structural Shift and the New Lost Generation.* Washington, DC: Georgetown University. https://georgetown.app.box.com/s/8tchnjo0wq9meamwwn5f (accessed April 20, 2014).

Carnevale, A.P., J. Strohl, and M. Melton. 2011c. *What's It Worth?: The Economic Value of College Majors.* Washington, DC: Center on Education and the Workforce. http://cew.georgetown.edu/whatsitworth (accessed May 1, 2014).

Carnevale, A.P., N. Smith, and J. Strohl. 2010. *Help Wanted: Projections of Jobs and Education Requirements Through 2018.* Washington, DC: Georgetown University Center on Education and the Workforce. http://www.thecb.state.tx.us/reports/PDF/2644.PDF?CFID=32886006&CFTOKEN=42032985 (accessed May 4, 2014).

Carnevale, A.P., N. Smith, and M. Melton. 2011b. *STEM: Science Technology Engineering Mathematics.* Washington, DC: Georgetown University Center on Education and the Workforce. https://georgetown.app.box.com/s/cyrrqbjyirjy64uw91f6 (accessed May 2, 2014).

Carnevale, A.P., S.J. Rose, and B. Cheah. 2011a. *The College Payoff: Education, Occupations, Lifetime Earnings.* Washington, DC: Georgetown University. http://cew.georgetown.edu/collegepayoff/ (accessed May 1, 2014).

Carrns, A. March 24, 2014. "Sweet Smell of Money for Plumbers." *The New York Times.* http://www.nytimes.com/2014/03/25/your-money/sweet-smell-of-money-for-plumbers.html?_r=1 (accessed May 3, 2014).

Center on Education and the Workforce. June 2013. *Recovery: Job Growth and Education Requirements Through 2020.* Washington, D.C.: Georgetown University. http://cew.georgetown.edu/recovery2020 (accessed July 11, 2014).

Centers & Institutes. 2012. Northeastern University Research: http://www.northeastern.edu/research/about/centers-institutes/ (accessed May 1, 2014).

Change in U.S. Employment: Recoveries. [Data Table]. 2014. https://www.minneapolisfed.org/publications_papers/studies/recession_perspective/index.cfm (accessed April 21, 2014).

Choosing Your College Major. 2014. The ACT: http://www.actstudent.org/career/majors.html (accessed April 30, 2014).

Chopra, R. July 17, 2013. "Student Debt Swells, Federal Loans Now Top a Trillion." *Consumer Financial Protection Bureau.* http://www.consumerfinance.gov/newsroom/student-debt-swells-federal-loans-now-top-a-trillion/ (accessed April 20, 2014).

Christensen, C.M., M.B. Horn, L. Soares, and L. Caldera. 2011. *Disrupting College: How Disruptive Innovation Can Deliver Quality and Affordability to Postsecondary Education.* Center for American Progress: http://www.americanprogress.org/issues/labor/report/2011/02/08/9034/disrupting-college/ (accessed April 30, 2014).

Chua, A., and J. Rubenfeld. 2014. *The Triple Package: How Three Unlikely Traits Explain the Rise and Fall of Cultural Groups in America.* New York, NY: The Penguin Press.

Clark, K. 2012. *Tuition at Public Colleges Rises 4.8%.* CNN Money: http://money.cnn.com/2012/10/24/pf/college/public-college-tuition/index.html (accessed May 1, 2014).

Class of 2013: Paid Interns Outpace Unpaid Peers in Job Offers, Salaries. 2013. National Association of Colleges and Employers: http://www.naceweb.org/s05292013/paid-unpaid-interns-job-offer.aspx (accessed May 1, 2014).

Colby, A., T. Ehrlich, W.M. Sullivan, and J.R. Dolle. 2011. *Rethinking Undergraduate Business Education: Liberal Learning for the Profession.* San Francisco, CA: The Carnegie Foundation for the Advancement of Teaching.

College Navigator. n.d. National Center for Education Statistics: http://nces.ed.gov/collegenavigator/ (accessed May 1, 2014).

College Personality Quiz. 2008. U.S. News: http://www.usnews.com/education/best-colleges/right-school/choices/articles/2008/08/21/college-personality-quiz (accessed May 1, 2014).

CollegeBoard. 2012. *Book of Majors 2013.* 7th ed. New York, NY: CollegeBoard.

Cooperative Education. 2014. Northeastern University Experiential Learning: http://www.northeastern.edu/experiential-learning/cooperative-education/ (accessed May 1, 2014).

Cowen, T. 2013. *Average is Over: Powering America Beyond the Age of the Great Stagnation.* New York, NY: Penguin Books Ltd.

Davenport, T.H., and D.J. Patil. 2012. *Data Scientists: The Sexiest Job of the 21st Century.* Harvard Business Review: http://hbr.org/2012/10/data-scientist-the-sexiest-job-of-the-21st-century/ar/1 (accessed April 24, 2014).

Davidson, A. December, 2011. *Making It in America: The Atlantic.* http://www.theatlantic.com/magazine/archive/2012/01/making-it-in-america/308844/ (accessed April 24, 2014).

Delbanco, A. 2012. *College: What It Was, Is, and Should Be.* Princeton, NJ: Princeton University Press.

Dobson, T. 2010. *Exams by State*. High School Exit Exams: https://sites.google. com/site/highschoolexits/home/examsbystate (accessed April 28, 2014).

Domhoff, G.W. 2013. *Wealth, Income, and Power.* http://www2.ucsc.edu/ whorulesamerica/power/wealth.html (accessed April 22, 2014).

Downs, P. January 6, 2014. "Can't Find Skilled Workers? Start an Apprentice Program." *The Wall Street Journal.* http://online.wsj.com/news/articles/SB10 001424052702304617404579304913308674896 (accessed May 3, 2014).

Driscoll, E. 2011. *Thinking of Hiring a College Consultant? Here's What to Expect.* Fox Business: http://www.foxbusiness.com/personal-finance/2011/05/13/ college-consultants/ (accessed May 1, 2014).

Earn an XSeries Certificate from One of the Top Institutions in the World. 2014. edX: https://www.edx.org/xseries (accessed May 3, 2014).

Earnings and Unemployment Rates by Educational Attainment. [Data Table]. 2014. http://www.bls.gov/emp/ep_chart_001.htm (accessed April 20, 2014).

Economic Report of the President. 2012. Washington, D.C.: United States Government. http://www.whitehouse.gov/sites/default/files/docs/erp_2012_ complete.pdf (accessed April 21, 2014).

Employment by Major Industry Sector. [Data Table]. 2013. Bureau of Labor Statistics: http://www.bls.gov/emp/ep_table_201.htm (accessed April 24, 2014).

Enrollment Rates of 18-24-year-olds in Degree-Granting Institutions. 2011. National Center for Education Statistics: http://nces.ed.gov/programs/digest/d11/ tables/dt11_213.asp (accessed May 1, 2014).

Enrollment, Staff, and Degrees/Certificates Conferred in Postsecondary Institutions. [Data Table]. 2011. National Center for Education Statistics: http://nces. ed.gov/programs/digest/d11/tables/dt11_196.asp (accessed May 3, 2014).

Entrepreneurship. 2013. UnCollege: http://www.uncollege.org/entrepreneurship/ (accessed May 3, 2014).

Explore Majors in Medical & Health Sciences. n.d. WorldWideLearn: http://www. worldwidelearn.com/online-education-guide/health-medical/index.html (accessed May 2, 2014).

Failure to Launch: Structural Shift and the New Lost Generation. 2013. Washington, D. C.: Georgetown University. https://cew.georgetown.edu/ (accessed April 20, 2014).

Farber, H.S. 2007. *Is the Company Man an Anachronism? Trends in Long Term Employment in the U.S., 1973–2006.* Princeton, NJ: Princeton University Industrial Relations Section. http://dataspace.princeton.edu/jspui/ bitstream/88435/dsp01ft848q61h/1/518.pdf (accessed May 4, 2014).

Farrell, C. June 14, 2012. "College Graduates' Best Job Bet: Word of Mouth." *BloombergBusinessweek.* http://www.businessweek.com/articles/2012-06-14/ college-graduates-best-job-bet-word-of-mouth (accessed May 4, 2014).

Fastest Growing Occupations. [Data Table]. 2014. U.S. Bureau of Labor Statistics: http://www.bls.gov/ooh/fastest-growing.htm (accessed April 30, 2014).

Financial Aid. 2012. American Gap Association: http://www.americangap.org/financial-aid.php (accessed May 4, 2014).

Find the Best Colleges for You: Focus on the Information that Matters. 2011. Consumer Reports: http://www.consumerreports.org/cro/resources/streaming/college-choices/final/college-choices.htm (accessed May 1, 2014).

First Year Earnings of Recent College Graduates in Colorado Vary Widely, Depending Upon Their School and Their Degree, New Report Finds. 2013. American Institutes for Research: http://www.air.org/news/press-release/first-year-earnings-recent-college-graduates-colorado-vary-widely-depending-upon (accessed May 3, 2014).

Fleming, B. 2014. *The Elusive National Online Opportunity*. Eduventures: http://www.eduventures.com/tag/market-data/ (accessed May 1, 2014).

Florida, R. 2012. *The Rise of the Creative Class Revisited*. New York, NY: Basic Books.

Fogg, N.P., and P.E. Harrington. 2011. *Rising Mal-Employment and the Great Recession: The Growing Disconnection between Recent College Graduates and the College Labor Market*. Philadelphia, PA: Drexel University. http://www.drexel.edu/provost/clmp/docs/CLMP_RisingMal-EmploymentandtheGreatRecession.pdf (accessed April 20, 2014).

Framework for 21st Century Learning. n.d. Partnership for 21st Century Skills: http://www.p21.org/our-work/p21-framework (accessed April 24, 2014).

Frey, C.B., and M.A. Osborne. 2013. *The Future of Employment: How Susceptible Are Jobs to Computerisation?* Oxford, UK: Oxford University. http://www.oxfordmartin.ox.ac.uk/downloads/academic/The_Future_of_Employment.pdf (accessed April 24, 2014).

Friedman, T.L. 2009. *The New Untouchables*. Blogspot: http://roymitsuoka.blogspot.com/2009/10/new-untouchables-by-thomas-l-friedman.html (accessed April 24, 2014).

Friedman, T.L. January 24, 2012. "Average is Over." *The New York Times*. http://www.nytimes.com/2012/01/25/opinion/friedman-average-is-over.html?_r=1& (accessed April 22, 2014).

Friedman, T.L. March 30, 2013. "Need a Job? Invent It." *The New York Times*. http://www.nytimes.com/2013/03/31/opinion/sunday/friedman-need-a-job-invent-it.html?_r=0 (accessed April 24, 2014).

Friedman, T.L., and M. Mandelbaum. 2011. *That Used to Be Us: How America Fell Behind in the World It Invented and How We Can Come Back*. New York, NY: Picador.

From College Major to Career. [Data Table]. 2014. The Wall Street Journal: http://graphicsweb.wsj.com/documents/NILF1111/#term= (accessed May 2, 2014).

Gallup. 2013. *State of the American Workplace: Employee Engagement Insights for U.S. Business Leaders: Gallup, Inc.* http://www.gallup.com/strategicconsulting/163007/state-american-workplace.aspx (accessed April 20, 2014).

Gap Year. 2013. UnCollege: http://www.uncollege.org/program/ (accessed May 3, 2014).

Gehlhaus, D. 2008. *What Can I Do With My Liberal Arts Degree?* Washington, DC: Bureau of Labor Statistics. Occupational Outlook Quarterly: http://www.bls.gov/opub/ooq/2007/winter/art01.pdf (accessed April 30, 2014).

Gilliland, G., R. Varadarajan & R. Devesh. May 27, 2014. "Code Wars: The All-Industry Competition for Software Talent." *The Boston Consulting Group*: https://www.bcgperspectives.com/content/articles/hardware_software_human_resources_code_wars_all_industry_competition_software_talent/ (accessed July 11, 2014).

Gladwell, M. 2008. *Outliers: The Story of Success.* New York, NY: Little, Brown and Company.

Goldin, C., and L.F. Katz. 2008. *The Race Between Education and Technology.* Cambridge, MA: The Presidents and Fellows of Harvard College.

Graduate Management Admission Council. 2013. *2013 Corporate Recruiters Survey: Hiring Report. Graduate Management Admission Council.* http://www.gmac.com/~/media/Files/gmac/Research/Employment%20Outlook/crs-2013-hiring-report-01.pdf (accessed May 4, 2014).

Graduation. n.d. Washington, DC: U.S. Department of Education. http://nces.ed.gov/pubs2014/2014003.pdf (accessed May 1, 2014).

Greenstone, M., and A. Looney. 2011. *Where is the Best Place to Invest $102,000—In Stocks, Bonds, or a College Degree?* Brookings: http://www.brookings.edu/research/papers/2011/06/25-education-greenstone-looney (accessed May 4, 2014).

Gulati, D. 2012. *The Top Five Career Regrets.* Harvard Business Review: http://blogs.hbr.org/2012/12/the-top-five-career-regrets/#comment-736026656 (accessed May 4, 2014).

Hagel, J., S.S. Brown, and T. Samoylova. 2013. Unlocking the Passion of the Explorer: Report 1 of the 2013 Shift Index Series. Deloitte University Press. http://d2mtr37y39tpbu.cloudfront.net/wp-content/uploads/2013/09/DUP402_Worker-Passion_vFINAL3.pdf (accessed May 4, 2014).

Halvorson, H.G. 2011. *Why Keeping Your Options Open is a Really, Really Bad Idea.* http://www.fastcompany.com/1755546/why-keeping-your-options-open-really-really-bad-idea

Hart Research Associates. 2013. *It Takes More Than A Major: Employer Priorities for College Learning and Student Success.* Washington, DC: The Association of American Colleges and Universities.

Healthcare Occupations. [Data Table]. 2014. Bureau of Labor Statistics: http:// www.bls.gov/ooh/healthcare/home.htm (accessed May 2, 2014).

Hertz, N., D. Barton, M. Murko & S. Andes, R. Plant, & C. Mainardi. July 3, 2014. "What Jobs Will Robots Have in the Future?" *The Wall Street Journal*: http://online.wsj.com/articles/robots-how-will-they-be-employed-in-the-future-1404390617 (accessed July 11, 2014).

Hiring an MBTI Consultant. The Myers & Briggs Foundation: http://www. myersbriggs.org/my-mbti-personality-type/hiring-an-mbti-consultant/ (accessed April 28, 2014).

Hoffman, R., and B. Casnocha. 2012. *The Start-Up of You: Adapt to the Future, Invest in Yourself, and Transform Your Career*. New York, NY: Crown Publishing Group.

How Much Protection Does a College Degree Afford? The Impact of the Recession on Recent College Graduates. 2013. Washington, D.C.: The Pew Charitable Trusts.   http://www.pewstates.org/uploadedFiles/PCS_Assets/2013/Pew_college_grads_recession_report.pdf

http://econlog.econlib.org/archives/2012/03/table_of_conten.html **

http://gradschool.about.com/od/admissionstests/**

http://howardgardner.com/books/

http://www.bls.gov/k12/students.htm **

http://www.ceri.msu.edu/ **

http://www.oecd.org/pisa/ **

http://www.onetonline.org/ **

http://www.uncollege.org/

Hyde, J. 2011. *This Is Google's First Self-Driving Car Crash*. Jalopnik: http:// jalopnik.com/5828101/this-is-googles-first-self-driving-car-crash   (accessed April 24, 2014).

IBM Forms New Watson Group to Meet Growing Demand for Cognitive Innovations. 2014. Armonk, NY: IBM News Room. http://www-03.ibm.com/press/us/en/pressrelease/42867.wss (accessed April 24, 2014).

Intro to Artificial Intelligence. 2014. Udacity: https://www.udacity.com/course/cs271 (accessed May 3, 2014).

Jantti, M., K. Roed, R. Naylor, A. Bjorklund, B. Bernt, R. Oddbjorn...T. Eriksson. 2006. *American Exceptionalism in a New Light: A Comparison of Intergenerational Earnings Mobility in the Nordic Countries, the United Kingdom and the Unites States*. Bonn, Germany: IZA. http://ftp.iza.org/dp1938.pdf (accessed April 30, 2014).

Jaschik, S. 2013. *Tenure Tracks Alt-Ac*. Inside HigherEd: http://www.insidehighered.com/news/2013/02/19/research-aaas-meeting-notes-difficult-job-market-academic-science#sthash.uZgL6Nwj.dpbs   (accessed   May   4, 2014).

Jerome, O.M. 2011. *What Do We Know About the Satisfaction/Dissatisfaction of Lawyers? A Meta-Analysis of Research on Lawyer Satisfaction and Well-Being.* Vol. 8. Is. 2. Art. 7. University of St. Thomas Law Journal. http://ir.stthomas.edu/cgi/viewcontent.cgi?article=1252&context=ustlj (accessed May 4, 2014).

Jue, K. July 19, 2012. "Computer Science Becomes Stanford's Most Popular Major." *The Stanford Daily.* http://www.stanforddaily.com/2012/07/19/computer-science-becomes-stanfords-most-popular-major/ (accessed May 2, 2014).

Keirsey, D. 1998. *Please Understand Me II: Temperament, Character, Intelligence.* Del Mar, CA: Prometheus Nemesis Book Company.

Koc, E., A. Koncz, and A. Longenberger. 2013. *NACE Salary Survey: Starting Salaries for New College Graduates, Data Reported by Employers, January 2013 Executive Summary.* Bethlehem, PA: National Association of Colleges and Employers. http://www.naceweb.org/uploadedFiles/NACEWeb/Research/Salary_Survey/Reports/SS_Jan2013_ExecSummary.pdf (accessed May 4, 2014).

Korn, M. April 3, 2014. "Chinese Deluge U.S. Master's Programs." *The Wall Street Journal.* http://online.wsj.com/news/articles/SB1000142412 78873248836045783988318476211160?KEYWORDS=Chinese+Deluge+US+Master%27s&mg=reno64-wsj&url=http%3A%2F%2Fonline. wsj.com%2Farticle%2FSB100014241278873248836045783988318 47621160.html%3FKEYWORDS%3DChinese%2BDeluge%2BUS%2B Master%2527s (accessed May 4, 2014).

Korn, M. May 3, 2012. "Real Work for Future M.B.A.s." *The Wall Street Journal.* http://online.wsj.com/news/articles/SB10001424052702303990604577368321102243392?mg=reno64-wsj&url=http%3A%2F%2Fonline. wsj.com%2Farticle%2FSB1000142405270230399060457736832 1102243392.html (accessed May 1, 2014).

Korn, M. September 17, 2012. "B-School Applicants Decline for Four Years." *The Wall Street Journal.* http://online.wsj.com/news/articles/SB1000087239 6390444433504577651962999932518?mg=reno64-wsj&url=http%3A% 2F%2Fonline.wsj.com%2Farticle%2FSB10000872396390444433504577651962999932518.html (accessed May 4, 2014).

Kucharvy, T. 2010a. *The Community College Contribution.* The Future of U.S. Knowledge Work in a Global Economy: http://www.tomkucharvy.com/growing-importance-of-community-colleges.html (accessed May 4, 2014).

Kucharvy, T. 2010b. *The Draws of Specialized MBAs and Business Masters Programs.* The Future of U.S. Knowledge Work in a Global Economy: http://www.tomkucharvy.com/specialized-mbas-and-business-masters-programs.html (accessed May 4, 2014).

Kucharvy, T. 2010c. *The Globalization of Cisco: Emergence of a Corporate Co-Headquarters.* The Future of U.S. Knowledge Work in a Global Economy:

http://www.tomkucharvy.com/the-globalization-of-cisco-emergence-of-a-corporate-co-headquarters.html (accessed April 30, 2014).

Kucharvy, T. 2011a. *Core Skills for Knowledge Workers in a Global Economy.* The Future of U.S. Knowledge Work in a Global Economy: http://www.tomkucharvy.com/core-skills-for-knowledge-workers-in-a-global-economy.html (accessed April 30, 2014).

Kucharvy, T. 2011b. *Elementary, My Dear Watson?.* The Future of U.S. Knowledge Work in a Global Economy: http://www.tomkucharvy.com/future-impact-of-ibms-watson-technology.html (accessed April 30, 2014).

Kucharvy, T. 2011c. *Expanding the Ranks of STEM Professionals.* The Future of U.S. Knowledge Work in a Global Economy: http://www.tomkucharvy.com/expanding-the-ranks-of-stem-professionals.html (accessed May 2, 2014).

Kucharvy, T. 2011d. *Tomorrow's Jobs Require Tomorrow's Skills.* The Future of U.S. Knowledge Work in a Global Economy: http://www.tomkucharvy.com/tomorrows-jobs-require-tomorrows-skills.html (accessed April 30, 2014).

Lerman, R. n.d. *Expanding Apprenticeship—A Way to Enhance Skills and Careers.* Urban Institute: http://www2.ed.gov/PDFDocs/college-completion/03-expanding-apprenticeship.pdf (accessed May 3, 2014).

Levitz, J., and D. Belkin. June 6, 2013. "Humanities Fall from Favor: Far Fewer Students Express Interest in Field with Weak Job Prospects." *The Wall Street Journal.* http://online.wsj.com/news/articles/SB10001424127887324069104578527642373232184?mg=reno64wsj&url=http%3A%2F%2Fonline.wsj.com%2Farticle%2FSB100014241278873240691045785276423732322184.html (accessed April 28, 2014).

Levy, F, THE NEW DIVISION OF LABOR © 2004 BY Russell Sage Foundation. Published by Princeton University Press. Reprinted by permission of Princeton University Press.http://www.slideshare.net/cristobalcobo/preparing-students-to-thrive-in-21st-century-america-the-role-for-afterschool Slide 6

Library of Economics and Libetry site (n.d.) "Table of Contents for The Case Against Education." http://econlog.econlib.org/archives/2012/03/table_of_conten.html.

Light, J. October 6, 2011. "Business Majors, but With a Twist." *The Wall Street Journal.* http://online.wsj.com/news/articles/SB10001424053111903285704576556553753330210?mg=reno64-wsj&url=http%3A%2F%2Fonline.wsj.com%2Farticle%2FSB100014240531119032857045765565553753330210.html (accessed April 30, 2014).

List of Salaries For Popular Careers. 2014. PayScale: http://www.payscale.com/salaries-by-occupation (accessed May 4, 2014).

Looney, A., and M. Greenstone. 2012. *Regardless of Cost, College Still Matters.* Washington, DC: The Hamilton Project. http://www.hamiltonproject.org/papers/regardless_of_the_cost_college_still_matters/ (accessed April 30, 2014).

Lynch, M., J. Engle, and J.L. Cruz. 2010. *Subprime Opportunity: The Unfulfilled Promise of For-Profit Colleges and Universities.* Washington, DC: The Education Trust. http://www.edtrust.org/sites/edtrust.org/files/publications/files/Subprime_report.pdf (accessed May 1, 2014).

Major and Career Search. 2014. bigfuture by CollegeBoard: https://bigfuture.collegeboard.org/majors-careers (accessed May 3, 2014).

Majors That Pay You Back. [Data Table]. 2014. PayScale: http://www.payscale.com/college-salary-report-2014/majors-that-pay-you-back# (accessed May 2, 2014).

Manning, M. 2013. *Coding.* UnCollege: http://www.uncollege.org/resources/coding/ (accessed May 3, 2014).

Manyika, J., J. Sinclair, R. Dobbs, G. Strube, L. Rassey, J. Mischke,…S. Ramaswamy. 2012. *Manufacturing the Future: The Next Era of Global Growth and Innovation.* McKinsey&Company: http://www.mckinsey.com/insights/manufacturing/the_future_of_manufacturing (accessed April 24, 2014).

Manyika, J., M. Chui, B. Brown, J. Bughin, R. Dobbs, C. Roxburgh, and A.H. Byers. 2011. *Big Data: The Next Frontier for Innovation, Competition, and Productivity.* McKinsey & Company.

Manyika, J., M. Chui, J. Bughin, R. Dobbs, P. Bisson, & A. Marrs. May 2013. *Disruptive Technologies: Advances that will Transform Life, Business, and the Global Economy.* McKinsey & Company. http://www.mckinsey.com/insights/business_technology/disruptive_technologies (accessed July 11, 2014).

Marketplace Trends. n.d. Dice Holdings, Inc.: http://www.diceholdingsinc.com/phoenix.zhtml?c=211152&p=irol-dicereport (accessed May 4, 2014).

Martin, A. January 10, 2013. "Downturn Still Squeezes Colleges and Universities." *The New York Times.* http://www.nytimes.com/2013/01/11/business/colleges-expect-lower-enrollment.html (accessed May 1, 2014).

McGeehan, P. April 1, 2014. "Half of New York's Tech Workers Lack College Degrees, Report Says." *The New York Times.* http://www.nytimes.com/2014/04/02/nyregion/half-of-new-yorks-tech-workers-lack-college-degrees-report-says.html?_r=0 (accessed April 20, 2014).

Memorial Sloan-Kettering Cancer Center. 2013. Somers, NY: IBM Corporation. http://www-03.ibm.com/innovation/us/watson/pdf/MSK_Case_Study_IMC14794.pdf (accessed April 24, 2014).

Mielach, D. 2012. *Workers Have Entrepreneurial Bug but Lack Confidence.* Business News Daily: http://www.businessnewsdaily.com/3070-entrepreneurial-experience-work.html (accessed May 4, 2014).

Mis, P. 2008. *Elite University Scholarships.* Scholarships.com: https://www.scholarships.com/blog/college-savings-accounts/elite-university-scholarships/206/ (accessed May 1, 2014).

Mitchell, J. March 25, 2014. "Grad Students Driving the Growing Debt Burden." *The Wall Street Journal.* http://online.wsj.com/news/articles/SB1000142

4052702303949704579459803223202602?mg=reno64-wsj&url= http%3A%2F%2Fonline.wsj.com%2Farticle%2FSB100014240 5270230394970457945980322320602.html (accessed May 4, 2014).

Model of Success: Pathways in Technology Early College High School (P-TECH). 2014. The Aspen Institute: http://www.aspeninstitute.org/policy-work/ economic-opportunities/skills-americas-future/models-success/ibm (accessed May 3, 2014).

Moore's law. 2014. Wikipedia: http://en.wikipedia.org/wiki/Moore%27s_law (accessed April 24, 2014).

Morrison, T., B. Maciejewski, C. Giffi, E.S. DeRocco, J. McNelly, and G. Carrick. 2011. *Boiling Point? The Skills Gap in U.S. Manufacturing. Deloitte.* The Manufacturing Institute http://www.themanufacturinginstitute.org/~/ media/A07730B2A798437D98501E798C2E13AA.ashx (accessed May 3, 2014).

Most New Jobs. [Data Table]. 2014. Bureau of Labor Statistics: http://www.bls. gov/ooh/most-new-jobs.htm (accessed May 1, 2014).

Mourshed, M., D. Farrell, and D. Barton. *Education to Employment: Designing a System that Works.* McKinsey&Company. http://mckinseyonsociety.com/ downloads/reports/Education/Education-to-Employment_FINAL.pdf (accessed April 20, 2014).

Murnane, R., and F. Levy. 2004. *Preparing Students to Thrive in 21st Century America: The Role for After-School.* Slideshare: http://www.slideshare.net/ cristobalcobo/preparing-students-to-thrive-in-21st-century-america-the-role-for-afterschool (slide 6) (accessed April 24, 2014).

Murnane, R.J. February 29, 2008. *Preparing to Thrive in 21st Century America. Presentation to the Mobile Area Education Foundation.* www.maef.net/LinkClick. aspx?fileticket=dtU7L3RtUNo%3D&tabid=708&&mid=1497 (slide 25)

Murray, S. May 9, 2009. "The of the Class of 2009: For College Grads Lucky Enough to Get Work This Year, Low Wages are Likely to Haunt Them for a Decade of More." *The Wall Street Journal.* http://online.wsj.com/news/ articles/SB124181970915002009 (accessed April 20, 2014).

Myers, A. 2011. *Stanford Team Trains Computer to Evaluate Breast Cancer.* Sanford School of Medicine: http://med.stanford.edu/ism/2011/november/ computer.html (accessed April 24, 2014).

Nadler, B J. 2006. *The Everything College Major Test Book: 10 Tests to Help You Choose the Major that is Right for You.* Avon, MA: Adams Media.

Newport, C. 2012. *So Good They Can't Ignore You: Why Skills Trump Passion in the Quest for Work You Love.* New York, NY: Hachette Book Group.

Newport, C. 2014. *Richard Feynman Didn't Win a Nobel by Responding Promptly to E-mails.* Study Hacks Blog: Decoding Patterns of Success: http://calnewport. com/blog/ (accessed April 28, 2014).

Nicholson, S. 2012. *LinkedIn Industry Trends: Winners and Losers During the Great Recession.* LinkedIn Official Blog: http://blog.linkedin.com/2012/03/08/economic-report/ (accessed April 24, 2014).

Occupation Finder. [Interactive Entry]. 2014. Bureau of Labor Statistics: http://www.bls.gov/ooh/occupation-finder.htm (accessed April 24, 2014).

Occupations matching "Healthcare." [Data Table]. n.d. O*NET OnLine: http://www.onetonline.org/find/result?s=healthcare&a=1 (accessed May 2, 2014).

Olsen, E. March 17, 2014. "A Degree Where Techie Meets Business Smarts." *The New York Times.* http://www.nytimes.com/2014/03/18/education/a-degree-where-techie-meets-business-smarts.html?_r=1 (accessed May 1, 2014).

Online Master of Science in Computer Science: Offered in Collaboration with Udacity and AT&T. 2013. Georgia Tech College of Computing: http://www.omscs.gatech.edu (accessed May 3, 2014).

Overview of BLS Wage Data by Area and Occupation. 2013. Bureau of Labor Statistics: http://www.bls.gov/bls/blswage.htm (accessed May 4, 2014).

Overview of Joint Degree and Cooperative Programs. 2014. Stanford Law School: http://www.law.stanford.edu/degrees/joint (accessed May 2, 2014).

Paulson, D.R., and J.L. Faust. n.d. *Active Learning For the College Classroom.* Los Angeles, CA: California State University. http://web.calstatela.edu/dept/chem/chem2/Active/ (accessed May 1, 2014).

Peralta, E. April 23, 2012. "AP Analysis: Half of Recent College Grads Are Jobless or Underemployed." *NPR.* http://www.npr.org/blogs/thetwo-way/2012/04/23/151217630/ap-analysis-half-of-recent-college-grads-are-jobless-or-underemployed (accessed May 1, 2014).

Percent Change in Nonfarm Payroll Employment. [Data Table]. 2014. http://www.cbpp.org/cms/index.cfm?fa=view&id=3252 (accessed April 21, 2014).

Perry, M.J. 2008. *Google Chief Economist Hal Varian on Data Analysis.* Carpe Diem: Professor Mark J. Perry's Blog for Economics and Finance: http://mjperry.blogspot.com/2008/02/googles-chief-economist-varian-on-data.html (accessed April 24, 20140.

Persing, T.E. 2014. *The Role of Apprenticeship Programs.* New Haven, CT: Yale-New Haven Teachers Institute. http://www.yale.edu/ynhti/pubs/A16/persing.html (accessed May 1, 2014).

Phillips, M. March 20, 2014. "Welders, America Needs You." *Bloomberg Businessweek.* http://www.businessweek.com/articles/2014-03-20/skilled-welder-shortage-looms-in-u-dot-s-dot-with-many-near-retirement (accessed May 3, 2014).

Pink, D.H. 2005. *A Whole New Mind: Why Right-Brainers Will Rule the Future.* New York, NY: Penguin Group.

Pursuing the American Dream: Economic Mobility Across Generations. 2012. Washington, D.C.: The Pew Charitable Trusts: http://www.pewstates.org/

uploadedFiles/PCS_Assets/2012/Pursuing_American_Dream.pdf (accessed April 30, 2014).

Rampell, C. June 12, 2013b. "Data Reveals a Rise in College Degrees Among Americans." *The New York Times*. http://www.nytimes.com/2013 /06/13/education/a-sharp-rise-in-americans-with-college-degrees.html? pagewanted=all&_r=0 (accessed April 30, 2014).

Rampell, C. May 3, 2013a. "College Graduates Fare Well in Jobs Market, Even Through Recession." *The New York Times*. http://www.nytimes. com/2013/05/04/business/college-graduates-fare-well-in-jobs-market-even-through-recession.html?pagewanted=all&_r=2& (accessed April 30, 2014).

Rankin, J. May 30, 2013. "Goldman Sachs Receives 17,000 Applications for Internship Programme." *The Guardian*. http://www.theguardian.com/business /2013/may/30/goldman-sachs-internship-applications (accessed May 1, 2014).

Rattner, S. March 25, 2012. "The Rich Get Even Richer." *The New York Times*. http://www.nytimes.com/2012/03/26/opinion/the-rich-get-even-richer. html?scp=1&sq=The%20Rich%20Get%20Even%20Richer&st=cse&_r=0 (accessed April 30, 2014).

Read the Standards. 2014. Common Core State Standards Initiative: http://www. corestandards.org/read-the-standards/ (accessed April 24, 2014).

Recruiting Trends 2012-2013 Supporters: Thank You. 2013. Michigan State University: http://www.ceri.msu.edu/recruiting-trends/recruiting-trends-2012-2013-supporters/ (accessed May 3, 2014).

Rothwell, J. July 1, 2014. "Still Searching: Job Vacancies and STEM Skills." *Brookings*: http://www.brookings.edu/research/interactives/2014/job-vacanc-ies-and-stem-skills?utm_campaign=Brookings+Brief&utm_source=hs_ email&utm_medium=email&utm_content=13346638&_hsenc=p2ANqtz--zCmA9mh5j0OtpSHx-ZHBbv5Ey-miVGVBQfazIDiDmYQXRTpUfDb BK2TyWnlG_O16tgX8nFF74w-r5KgePViP0tz1rsw&_hsmi=13346638#/ M10420 (accessed July 11, 2014).

Rudesill, D.S. February 18, 2013. "Starting Out: The Lawyer's Apprentice." *The New York Times*. http://www.nytimes.com/2013/02/25/opinion/starting-out-the-lawyers-apprentice.html?_r=0 (accessed May 1, 2014).

Salcito, A. n.d. *Tony Wagner: Innovation Education Fellow, Technology & Entrepreneurship Center, Harvard*. daily edventures: http://dailyedventures. com/index.php/2012/05/30/tony-wagner-usa/ (accessed April 30, 2014).

Schneider, M. 2013. *Two-Year Technical Degree Grads in Texas have Higher First-Year Median Earnings then Bachelor Grads*. CollegeMeasures: http:// collegemeasures.org/post/2013/05/The-Initial-Earnings-of-Graduates-of-Texas-Public-Colleges-and-Universities.aspx (accessed May 3, 2014).

Sheehy, K. October 8, 2013. "Explore the World's Top Universities." *U.S. News*. http:// www.usnews.com/education/top-world-universities/articles/2013/10/08/ explore-the-worlds-top-universities (accessed May 4, 2014).

Shierholz, H., N. Sabadish, and N. Finio. 2013. *Unemployment Rate of Workers Under Age 25 and All Workers* [Fig A]. http://www.epi.org/publication/class-of-2013-graduates-job-prospects/ (accessed April 20, 2014).

Shierholz, H., N.Sabadish, and N. Finio. 2013. *Young Graduates Still Face Dim Job Prospects*. Washington, DC: Economic Policy Institute. http://www.epi.org/publication/class-of-2013-graduates-job-prospects/ (accessed April 20, 2014).

Simon, R., and R. Barry. February 18, 2013. "A Degree Drawn in Red Ink: Graduates of Arts-Focused Schools Are Shown to Rack Up the Most Student Debt." The Wall Street Journal. http://online.wsj.com/news/articles/SB10001424127887324432004578306610055834952?mg=reno64wsj&url=http%3A%2F%2Fonline.wsj.com%2Farticle%2FSB10001424127887324432004578306610055834952.html (accessed April 28, 2014).

Skills for America's Future Community College Facts. 2014. http://www.aspeninstitute.org/policy-work/economic-opportunities/skills-americas-future/what-we-do/community-college-facts (accessed May 4, 2014).

Smith, D., and K. LaVelle. 2013. *The New Skills Imperative: Reconnecting Work with the Workforce*: Accenture. http://www.accenture.com/us-en/outlook/Pages/outlook-online-2013-new-skills-imperative-reconnecting-work-with-workforce.aspx (accessed April 20, 2014).

Smith, D., K. LaVelle, B. Marshall, and S. Cantrell. 2013. *Outlook Point of View Talent & Organization: Do You Have the Skills to Compete?* Accenture: http://www.accenture.com/us-en/outlook/Pages/outlook-online-2013-do-you-have-the-skills-to-compete.aspx (accessed May 4, 2014).

Sofferet, A. 2010. *5 Best Career Aptitude Tests to Help You Find the Perfect Job*. Yahoo! Voices: http://voices.yahoo.com/5-best-career-aptitude-tests-help-find-the-5870110.html (accessed April 28, 2014).

Staklis, S., and P. Skomsvold. 2014. *New College Graduates at Work: Employment Among 1992-93, 1999–2000, and 2007–08 Bachelor's Degree Recipients 1 Year After.*

Startup Business Failure Rate By Industry. 2014. [Data Table]. Entrepreneur Weekly, Small Business Development Center, Bradley Univ, University of Tennessee Research. Statistic Brain: http://www.statisticbrain.com/startup-failure-by-industry/ (accessed May 4, 2014).

State by State Data. 2013. [Interactive Entry]. The Project on Student Debt: http://projectonstudentdebt.org/state_by_state-data.php (accessed May 1, 2014).

STEM Pathways to College and Careers Schools: A Development Guide. 2012. New York, NY: IBM. http://citizenibm.com/wp-content/uploads/STEM-Pathways-Playbook_Feb-2012.pdf (accessed May 3, 2014).

Stephens, D.J. 2013. *Hacking Your Education: Ditch the Lectures, Save Tens of Thousands, and Learn More Than Your Peers Ever Will*. New York, NY: Penguin Group.

Stone, C., C. Van Horn, and C. Zukin. 2012. *Chasing the American Dream: Recent College Graduates and the Great Recession*. New Brunswick, NJ: Rutgers University. http://www.heldrich.rutgers.edu/sites/default/files/content/Chasing_American_Dream_Report.pdf (accessed April 20, 2014).

Subramanian, C. April, 2012. "Half of New College Grads Jobless or Underemployed." *Time*. http://newsfeed.time.com/2012/04/23/half-of-new-college-grads-jobless-or-underemployed/ (accessed April 20, 2014).

Supiano, B. August 4, 2011. "When it Comes to Earnings, Higher Education Isn't the Whole Story." *The Chronicle of Higher Education*. http://chronicle.com/article/Education-Pays-but-So-Does/128526/ (accessed April 30, 2014).

Symonds, W.C., R.B. Schwartz, and R. Ferguson. 2011. *Pathways to Prosperity: Meeting the Challenge of Preparing Young Americans for the 21st Century*. Boston, MA: Harvard Graduate School of Education. http://www.gse.harvard.edu/news_events/features/2011/Pathways_to_Prosperity_Feb2011.pdf (accessed May 4, 2014).

Szondy, D. July 6, 2014. "Daimler Future Truck 2025 Completes First Autonomous Highway Run." *Gizmag*. http://www.gizmag.com/future-truck-2025-daimler-mercedes-self-driving/32811/ (accessed July 11, 2014).

Tanne, J.H. 2012. *Income and Job Satisfaction Fall Among US Doctors*. BMJ Careers: http://careers.bmj.com/careers/advice/view-article.html?id=20007204 (accessed May 4, 2014).

The Center. n.d. Bluegrass Community & Technical College: http://bluegrass.kctcs.edu/en/About/Our_Campuses/Georgetown/Georgetown_Advanced_Manufacturing_Center.aspx (accessed May 4, 2014).

The Low-Wage Recovery and Growing Inequality. 2012. National Employment Law Project: http://www.nelp.org/page/-/Job_Creation/LowWageRecovery2012.pdf?nocdn=1 (accessed April 21, 2014).

The Most Popular U.S. College Majors. [Graphic]. 2012. visual.ly: http://visual.ly/most-popular-college-majors-2012 (accessed May 2, 2014).

The President and Fellows of Harvard College. 2014. *What Job is Right for You?*. Office of Career Services Harvard University, Faculty of Arts and Sciences: http://www.ocs.fas.harvard.edu/students/undecided/selfassessment.htm (accessed May 4, 2014).

Thompson, D. January, 2012. *Where Did All the Workers Go? 60 Years of Economic Change in 1 Graph: The Atlantic*. http://www.theatlantic.com/business/archive/2012/01/where-did-all-the-workers-go-60-years-of-economic-change-in-1-graph/252018/ (accessed April 24, 2014).

Top 10 College Majors. 2014. The Princeton Review: http://www.princetonreview.com/college/top-ten-majors.aspx (accessed May 1, 2014).

Torpey, E. 2013a. *Certificates: A Fast Track to Careers*. Washington, DC: Bureau of Labor Statistics. http://www.bls.gov/ooq/2012/winter/art01.pdf (accessed May 3, 2014).

Torpey, E. 2013b. *College to Career: Projected Job Openings in Occupations That Typically Require a Bachelor's Degree.* Washington, DC: National Center for Education Statistics. http://www.bls.gov/ooq/2013/summer/art03.pdf (accessed April 30, 2014).

Torpey, E. 2014. *Healthcare: Millions of Jobs Now and in the Future.* Washington, DC: U.S. Bureau of Labor Statistics. http://www.bls.gov/ooq/art03.pdf (accessed May 2, 2014).

Glossary. 2014. Bureau of Labor Statistics: http://www.bls.gov/ooh/about/mobile/glossary.htm (accessed May 3, 2014).

U.S. Bureau of Labor Statistics. 2012. *Education and Training Outlook for Occupations, 2012-22.* Division of Occupational Employment Projections: http://www.bls.gov/emp/ep_edtrain_outlook.pdf (accessed April 30, 2014).

U.S. Department of Education, National Center for Education Statistics. 2013a. *The Condition of Education 2013* (NCES 2013-037), Institutional Retention and Graduation Rates for Undergraduate Students.

U.S. Department of Education, National Center for Education Statistics. 2013b. *Digest of Education Statistics, 2012* (NCES 2014-015), Chapter 3. http://nces.ed.gov/fastfacts/display.asp?id=98 (accessed April 30, 2014).

U.S. Department of Education, National Center for Education Statistics, Integrated Postsecondary Education Data System (IPEDS). 2011. *Institutional Characteristics component and Spring 2012, Student Financial Aid component.* http://collegecost.ed.gov/catc/ (accessed May 3, 2014).

U.S. Department of Education, National Center for Education Statistics. 2013c. *The Condition of Education 2013* (NCES 2013-037), Institutional Retention and Graduation Rates for Undergraduate Students.

U.S. Department of Education. n.d. *College Scorecard.* College Affordability and Transparency Center: http://collegecost.ed.gov/scorecard/index.aspx (accessed April 30, 2014).

United States Department of Labor. 2014. *Occupational Outlook Handbook.* Bureau of Labor Statistics: http://www.bls.gov/ooh/ (accessed April 30, 2014).

Wadhwa, V. 2013. *The Pernicious Myth that You Don't Need College to Be an Entrepreneur.* PBS Newshour: http://www.pbs.org/newshour/making-sense/the-pernicious-myth-that-you-d/ (accessed May 3, 2014).

Wagner, E.T. September 12, 2013. "Five Reasons 8 Out Of 10 Businesses Fail." *Forbes.* http://www.forbes.com/sites/ericwagner/2013/09/12/five-reasons-8-out-of-10-businesses-fail/ (accessed May 4, 2014).

Wagner, T. 2008. *Global Achievement Gap: Why Even Our Best Schools Don't Teach the New Survival Skills Our Children Need and What We Can Do About It.* New York, NY: Basic Books.

Wagner, T. 2012. *Creating Innovators: The Making of Young People Who Will Change the World.* New York, NY: Scribner.

Weiss, D.C. June 20, 2013. "Only 64% of Law Grads Land Jobs Requiring Bar Passage, Even as BigLaw Jobs Rise 27% in Two Years." *ABA Journal.* http://www.abajournal.com/news/article/biglaw_jobs_for_grads_rise_27_percent_in_two_years_even_as_overall_employme/ (accessed April 28, 2014).

Why Good People Can't Get Jobs: Chasing After the 'Purple Squirrel'. 2012. Wharton University of Pennsylvania: http://knowledge.wharton.upenn.edu/article/why-good-people-cant-get-jobs-chasing-after-the-purple-squirrel/ (accessed May 4, 2014).

Wladawsky-Berger, I. 2012. *Design Principles for Complex, Unpredictable, People Oriented Systems.* http://blog.irvingwb.com/blog/2012/04/design-principles-for-complex-unpredictable-people-oriented-systems.html (accessed April 24, 2014).

Wladawsky-Berger, I. 2013. *The Era of Cognitive Computing.* http://blog.irvingwb.com/blog/2013/07/the-dawn-of-a-new-era-in-computing.html (accessed April 24, 2014).

Workforce Partnerships. 2014. SkillWorks: http://www.skill-works.org/workforce-partnerships.php (accessed May 3, 2014).

World-of-Work Map. 2013. The ACT: http://www.act.org/world/world.html (accessed April 30, 2014).

www.thielfellowship.org

Zlomek, E. May 1, 2014. "Watch Out, MBAs! Ph.Ds Are After Your Jobs." *BlombergBusinessweek.* http://www.businessweek.com/articles/2014-05-01/more-doctoral-grads-compete-with-mbas-for-jobs (accessed May 4, 2014).

Zmirak, J. 2014. *Choosing the Right College.* Wilmington, DE: ISI Books.

.

Index

OTHER TITLES IN THE HUMAN RESOURCE MANAGEMENT AND ORGANIZATIONAL BEHAVIOR COLLECTION

Jean Phillips and Stan Gully, Rutgers University, Editors

- *Manage Your Career: 10 Keys to Survival and Success When Interviewing and On The Job* by Vijay Sathe
- *Culturally Intelligent Leadership: Leading Through Intercultural Interactions* by Mai Moua
- *Letting People Go: The People-Centered Approach to Firing and Laying Off Employees* by Matt Shlosberg
- *The Five Golden Rules of Negotiation* by Philippe Korda
- *Cross-Cultural Management* by Veronica Velo
- *Conversations About Job Performance: A Communication Perspective on the Appraisal Process* by Michael E. Gordon and Vernon Miller
- *How to Coach Individuals, Teams, and Organizations to Master Transformational Change Surfing Tsunamis* by Stephen K. Hacker
- *Managing Employee Turnover: Dispelling Myths and Fostering Evidence-Based Retention Strategies* by David Allen and Phil Bryant
- *Effective Interviewing and Information Gathering: Proven Tactics to Improve Your Questioning Skills* by Thomas Diamante
- *Essential Concepts of Cross-Cultural Management: Building on What We All Share* by Lawrence Beer
- *Growing Your Business: Making Human Resources Work for You* by Robert Baron
- *Developing Employee Talent to Perform: People Power* by Kim Warren
- *Fostering Creativity in Self and the Organization: Your Professional Edge* by Eric W. Stein
- *Designing Creative High Power Teams and Organizations: Beyond Leadership* by Eric W. Stein

Announcing the Business Expert Press Digital Library

Concise E-books Business Students Need
for Classroom and Research

This book can also be purchased in an e-book collection by your library as
- a one-time purchase,
- that is owned forever,
- allows for simultaneous readers,
- has no restrictions on printing, and
- can be downloaded as PDFs from within the library community.

Our digital library collections are a great solution to beat the rising cost of textbooks. E-books can be loaded into their course management systems or onto students' e-book readers.

The **Business Expert Press** digital libraries are very affordable, with no obligation to buy in future years. For more information, please visit **www.businessexpertpress.com/librarians**. To set up a trial in the United States, please email **sales@businessexpertpress.com**.

www.ingramcontent.com/pod-product-compliance
Lightning Source LLC
Chambersburg PA
CBHW060320200326
41519CB00011BA/1790